Hiking Tennessee

HELP US KEEP THIS GUIDE UP TO DATE

Every effort has been made by the authors and editors to make this guide as accurate and useful as possible. However, many things can change after a guide is published—trails are rerouted, regulations change, techniques evolve, facilities come under new management, etc.

We would appreciate hearing from you concerning your experiences with this guide and how you feel it could be improved and kept up to date. While we may not be able to respond to all comments and suggestions, we'll take them to heart, and we'll also make certain to share them with the authors. Please send your comments and suggestions to the following address:

Globe Pequot
Reader Response/Editorial Department
246 Goose Lane
Guilford, CT 06437

Or you may e-mail us at:
editorial@falcon.com
Thanks for your input, and happy trails!

Hiking Tennessee

A Guide to the State's Greatest Hiking Adventures

Second Edition

Kelley Roark and Stuart Carroll

FALCONGUIDES

GUILFORD, CONNECTICUT
HELENA, MONTANA

An imprint of Rowman & Littlefield
Falcon, FalconGuides, and Outfit Your Mind are registered trademarks of Rowman & Littlefield.

Distributed by NATIONAL BOOK NETWORK

Copyright © 2016 Rowman & Littlefield

Unless otherwise indicated, all interior photos are by the authors.

British Library Cataloguing in Publication Information Available
Library of Congress Cataloging-in-Publication Data

Roark, Kelley, 1957-
  Hiking Tennessee : [a guide to the state's greatest hiking adventures] / Kelley Roark and Stuart Carroll.
—Second Edition.
      pages cm.—(A Falcon guide)
  "Distributed by NATIONAL BOOK NETWORK"—T.p. verso.
   ISBN 978-1-4930-0656-4 (paperback)—ISBN 978-1-4930-2393-6 (ebook) 1. Hiking—Tennessee—
Guidebooks. 2. Natural resources—Tennessee—Guidebooks. 3. Tennessee—Guidebooks. I. Title.
  GV199.42.T2R63 2015
  796.5109768—dc23
                            2015025421

∞™ The paper used in this publication meets the minimum requirements of American National Standard for Information Sciences—Permanence of Paper for Printed Library Materials, ANSI/NISO Z39.48-1992.

Contents

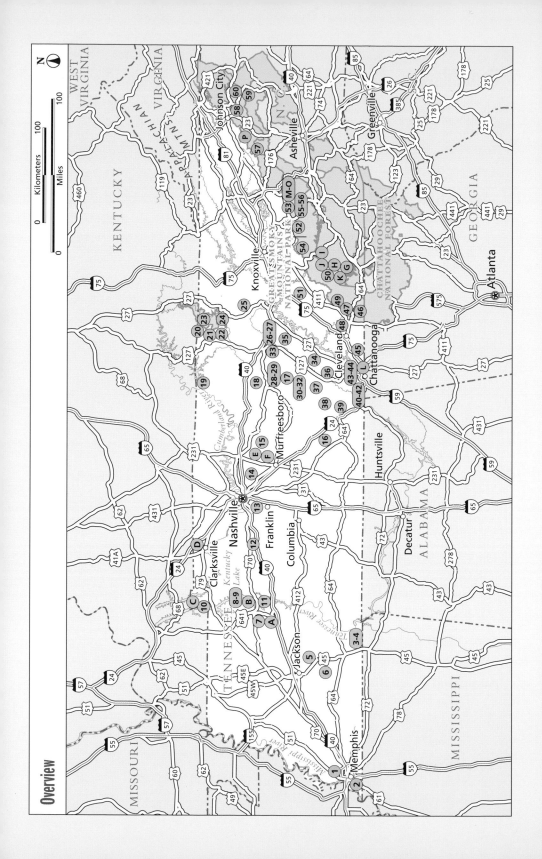

The South Cumberlands

Chattanooga and the Southeast

Additional Great Hikes

The Smokies and the Northeast

Additional Great Hikes

Acknowledgments

The first edition of *Hiking Tennessee* was produced with the assistance of many Tennesseans, and the second edition benefits from their contributions as well. While this edition draws on much of the original material, there have been some very substantial changes, particularly for hikes in the Cumberland region. For the second edition, Stuart Carroll, Park Manager at Virgin Falls and Lost Creek State Natural Areas, has graciously agreed to come onboard as a co-author, drawing upon his thirty-two years of experience within the Tennessee parks system and his overall knowledge as one of Tennessee's native born. I am particularly honored to have him onboard because his remarkable writing skills, encyclopedic knowledge of the region, dedication and love for its natural assets, unshakable good humor, and dedication have made him a pleasure to work with.

While it is not possible to thank individually everyone who helped in both editions, I would like to thank the dedicated rangers and staff of the entire Tennessee park system, together with the equally dedicated rangers and staff of our beautiful federal lands in Great Smoky Mountains National Park, Cherokee National Forest, and the other federally managed parks. Without them and their expertise, this book would literally not be possible. And a further thank-you to the many volunteer organizations whose efforts keep the trails open for us to enjoy. These include but are not limited to: Friends of the Cumberland Trail, Tennessee Eastman Hiking Club, Friends of the Smokies, Southern Appalachian Back Country Horsemen, and the many other "Friends of" groups that organize themselves around favorite parks. I have seen firsthand the dedication and hard work of these volunteers in removing trees, adding footing, building bridges . . . and they do it all with a smile.

Thanks to all of you!

And finally, a special thanks to my own father, Richard Roark, who has now passed on to greater places, for instilling in me my love for mountains and taste for adventure, and for traveling throughout the state with me from campground to campground in the preparation of the first edition. And thank you to my daughter, Gabriela, in whom I hope to instill the same love for mountains and adventure, for traveling throughout the state with me in the preparation of the second edition!

—Kelley Roark

Introduction

This book is an introduction to the trails found across the diverse topography that we call Tennessee. And it can be only an introduction, because it would be impossible to detail all of the beautiful trails found across such a varied landscape. From the Chickasaw Bluffs above Memphis to the Roan Balds some 550 miles away, from 178 feet above sea level at Meeman-Shelby to over 6,643 feet above sea level at Clingmans Dome, the described hikes are slices of the diverse natural and cultural landscapes that define Tennessee.

The trails featured in this book often have a variety of themes. For instance, the Wall Trail at Old Stone Fort is a discovery hike into a 2,000-year-old Native American structure that explores the way it was built and conjectures about its use. But drop down on joining trails to the forks of the Duck and Little Duck Rivers, and you might encounter a family of armadillos working trailside, looking for grubs, or a large doe, standing with ears erect and alert, scoping you out before letting out an indignant snort and bounding off. And all this within the city limits of Manchester. We could go trail to trail and illustrate the diversity found in the parks and natural areas. The hike at Shiloh is a solemn but beautiful testament to the tragedy of the Civil War, situated as it is along the bluffs of the Tennessee. But right in the middle of the area are the mounds constructed by people who called this area home millennia before the armies of blue and gray charged back and forth across the landscape.

Recurrent themes are there: the amazing biodiversity of the state, and the topography—in some places subtle, in some places jaw dropping—that give rise to this biodiversity. The Native American imprint on the landscape is shown at Pinson, Shiloh, and Old Stone Fort . . . or even in the name of the state itself: "Tanasi." The history of the "Civilized Tribes," as they were called, can be explored at Red Clay, the last formal meeting place of the Cherokee before the Trail of Tears, in the southeast, or the richness of the culture of the Choctaw found at Chucalissa in Memphis. The Civil War left its scars across Tennessee, explored at Shiloh, Johnsonville, and two hikes related to the battle at Chattanooga.

While this book may be an introduction, let's consider it more of an enticement to peel back a few pages of Tennessee's diverse history. Or marvel at the changing pageant that is nature. Or to simply entice you to dust off the old walking shoes or boots and venture out to where the pavement ends and the journey of discovery begins.

Tips for Safe Hiking

We go into the backcountry areas for the wilderness experience. As the parking lot disappears behind us, we head in not only to experience the beauty of pristine nature but also to challenge ourselves. And that challenge involves a certain amount of risk, implicit in the experience we are seeking. However, there are ways that we can minimize this risk and reduce the chances of getting injured or lost.

"Know thyself" might be tweaked for hiking into "Know thy ability." While there are trails across Tennessee for every level of hiking ability, from paved trails with no grade and wheelchair accessibility to "billy goat" trails that involve steep grades, cables for safety, and the need to use both feet and hands. Find the right trails for your ability. But also, increase your ability.

It would be a mistake to pick up this book and, after years of sitting, decide you were going to hike all the way into Virgin Falls, for instance. You should build up to these more strenuous hikes. And that can start with walks around the neighborhood, or the weekend walks with church groups or other "meet-up"–type groups, perhaps on more relaxed trails in local parks. If you have a preexisting medical condition, consult your doctor first. But most health-care providers will be ecstatic that you have put on your hiking boots, turned off the TV or computer, and headed out the door.

Gearing up for a more extensive hike might involve the local outdoor shop. But it might just involve rummaging around in the closet. Choice of clothing will, of course, depend on the season and the situations you might be encountering. Rule of thumb: During the months of the year when nighttime temperatures fall into the thirties, better to leave the cotton clothing at home and go with wool or a polyester blend if you can. A day that starts out in the sixties can wind up in the thirties, and if you get lost or injured and wet and are in cotton clothing, it will not dry. Seasoned hikers know the wisdom of this oft-repeated rule.

Here's a list of essentials to bring on your hike:

1. Extra clothes. Among hiking folks, there is a lot of talk about packing the "Ten Essentials," and while the list itself may vary some, the concept doesn't. One of those essentials is extra clothing. When packing your daypack, look at the forecast, and pack a few extra layers, as if you might have to spend the night. An extra windbreaker, rain jacket, fleece vest, or other items can be lifesavers. And at the end of the day, if your undershirt has become wet, you can get comfortable again with something dry. Even if you don't need the extra layers, someone in your party might.

2. Water. A second essential is water. Always carry your own water and never drink out of any surface creeks in Tennessee—ever—without first treating, filtering, or boiling the water. Serious hikers often make a water filter part of the "Essentials" pack.

3. Snacks. Extra carbs are also a must. Throw some hiking bars into your pack in addition to your planned meals. Even though you might not need it, again, your fellow hikers might.

4. Cell phone. Many of us are trying to escape from the busyness and noise of the paved world, and cell phones are emblematic of this treadmill. If you are looking to escape your cell phone, you can turn it off and bury it in your backpack. But

do carry it with you. If someone in your party gets injured, it can be a lifesaver. And most cell phone providers have it set up so that a 911 call will work off any tower. Another safety aspect of cell phones is that when a person is lost and he or she calls out, the signal can be "pinged," giving a general location. (And some cell phones have GPS tracking devices in them too!)

5. Flashlight. If you take longer than expected on a hike and run out of daylight, a good flashlight can carry you safely back to your car. Not having a flashlight might mean you have to sit and spend the night. Or have a ranger come looking for you. Most experienced hikers, with the advent of the new, lightweight LED lights, carry several lights. There are as many "lost" people in parks that simply run out of daylight because of wrong turns or misjudging distances as there are truly lost people. And a light can be your lifeline in those situations.

Other extras: You can make up your own list of "Ten Essentials," or eight or twelve for that matter. But other useful items include a lighter, a first-aid kit, a knife, and some string, which comes in handy in a variety of situations. If you do a lot of back-country hiking, think about just leaving these items in your pack when you come home. You can freshen the water in the bottle if you need to, but the bottle will be there.

Guides such as this one are great places to start when planning a trip to a trail you have never been on. Several of the trails described in this book can be just downright hard to find, and a little bit of prep work can save a lot of driving and ensure you reach your destination on the trail.

Most of the rangers and other staff at these areas are very helpful, and most of these hikes have phone numbers to call if there are questions. But this guide is a general one, and conditions can change. Use common sense when coming to swollen creeks, or crossing blowdowns, and looking for trails that have almost disappeared. Things can change, and quickly. Sometimes the managing ranger will not know of a large blowdown that might have blocked and even obscured a trail. Make a note of the location of the problem—and let the park know so they can both advise other hikers and fix the problem.

The Weather

There is an old saying in Tennessee: "If you don't like the weather, wait a day or so." That is true in some respects, and for the most part the weather of Tennessee, a "mid-South" state, possesses the extremes of the heat of the Gulf Coast and the cold of the states north of the Ohio River.

The state does have four distinct seasons, with each one offering something different on the trails. From the lowlands to the highlands, there is a sequence of spring blooms. The spring wildflowers can be breathtaking and generally begin in mid-March, but the timing can vary trail to trail. The first wildflowers will open first in the lowlands or on warm, south-facing slopes and will often continue until early May. Yet

BE AWARE OF BEARS!

The following is provided by the National Park Service to guide hikers who encounter bears in eastern Tennessee:

"Bears inhabit all elevations of the park. Though populations are variable, biologists estimate that roughly 1,500 bears live in the park. This equals a population density of approximately two bears per square mile.

Bears in the park are wild and their behavior is sometimes unpredictable. Although extremely rare, attacks on humans have occurred, inflicting serious injuries and death. Treat bear encounters with extreme caution and follow these guidelines:

Bears are most active during early morning and late evening hours in spring and summer.

If you see a bear remain watchful. Do not approach it. If your presence causes the bear to change its behavior (stops feeding, changes its travel direction, watches you, etc.)—you're too close. Being too close may promote aggressive behavior from the bear such as running toward you, making loud noises, or swatting the ground. The bear is demanding more space. Don't run, but slowly back away, watching the bear. Try to increase the distance between you and the bear. The bear will probably do the same.

If a bear persistently follows or approaches you, without vocalizing, or paw swatting, change your direction. If the bear continues to follow you, stand your ground. If the bear gets closer, talk loudly or shout at it. Act aggressively to intimidate the bear. Act together as a group if you have companions. Make yourselves look as large as possible (for example, move to higher ground). Throw non-food objects such as rocks at the bear. Use a deterrent such as a stout stick. Don't run and don't turn away from the bear. Don't leave food for the bear; this encourages further problems.

From nps.gov/grsm/naturescience/black-bears.htm#CP_JUMP_95932

on Roan Mountain, the famous Rhododendron Festival is in June. And as the trees leaf out across the hillsides, this is colorful too, albeit more subtle than the fullness of the fall colors.

Backcountry hiking in summer is a completely different experience. The hottest month in Tennessee is July, with August a close second. Average daytime highs are around 90°F in those months, though they vary several degrees—from hot Gulf of

Mexico weather in Memphis to the cooler weather of Bristol, 500 miles away. But it isn't the temperatures that can make the summers unpleasant as much as the humidity and the bugs. (Ticks can be a real problem.) The summers call for a change in strategies: Many hikers head for the cooler Cumberlands, or for the Appalachians in the east. Other folks put their hiking boots away and drag out their bikes. And cycling provides the added benefit that it normally strengthens your muscles and joints, preparing you for more hiking in the fall. Swimming provides some of the same benefits.

The heat and humidity start breaking by mid-September, and the nights get cooler. Expect the first frosts toward the middle of October, and the fall colors are in full riot by the third or fourth week of October. Not only do those frosts set the hillsides ablaze with colors, but colder temperatures also send a lot of the annoying bugs, such as ticks, mosquitoes, and yellow jackets, into cover. And with the first hard freezes, these bugs will go into dormancy and you can hike for at least a few months free of these pests.

Winters can be cold, and those "polar vortex" events can drop down from Canada, making the hike to the woodstove about as far as you want to go. But those events are uncommon, and the average daytime high in January, the coldest month, is 49°F—not a bad temperature for hiking. Added benefits of winter hiking are that with the leaves off the trees, you get a totally different perspective on the landscape. And with ticks and yellow jackets dormant, you can head down valleys and across hillsides without fear of being bitten or stung, and enjoy some cross-country hiking.

On higher-elevation trails in the Smokies and in Cherokee National Forest (CNF), snow and ice will often block access to the parking lots and trailheads during the middle of winter. And often higher-elevation trails can be much tougher going because you'll be walking through snow or across ice. Check with the local ranger station for the latest trail conditions. The depth of snow on the upper-elevation trails varies a lot from one winter to another, or even from week to week. But there are almost always lower-elevation trails to hike in the Smokies or CNF—delightful trails that follow along the creeks and rivers, filled with boulders and cascades, and wreathed with mountain laurel and rhododendron. In this state there is a hike for every season.

Park and Forest Rules and Regulations

A number of different agencies manage the trails in this book, with varying degrees of regulation. In general, activities are more regulated in state parks and national parks than in national or state forests, possibly reflecting the fact that forest management and fire control are more their mandate than monitoring recreational activities. However, you can check with either a park or forest unit to find out trail conditions or any regulations that might impact you as a hiker.

In the parks, both national and state, backcountry camping is in designated sites only. And both agencies require some sort of registration, although at most state parks you can do it at the trailhead. In the different areas managed by the Cumberland Trail, you will need to call, or go to the Friends of the Cumberland Trail website (friends ofthecumberlandtrail.org) to register. (If you are registering online, don't wait until you get to the trailhead, because you might not have a phone signal.) Neither the national forest nor the Appalachian Trail require registration. Although at this point there is no charge for backcountry camping, that may change in the future. Pick up a list of park rules to find out where they don't want you to pitch your tent. And wherever you camp, always minimize your impact (apply the "Leave No Trace" rule).

In almost all state parks, you can have dogs on the trails. But they must stay on-leash. That leash law is widely disregarded, and unfortunately, an off-leash dog can present a variety of problems. Expect to see that regulation enforced in the future, and please keep your dog on a leash. In the Smokies dogs are not allowed on hiking trails and are only allowed on a few of the walking trails around Sugarlands and Oconaluftee Visitor Centers, or in campgrounds, on a 6-foot leash. However, at Big South Fork, which is run by the National Park Service, dogs are allowed on trails, with the leash no longer than 6 feet long.

Most public land managers want you off the trails by dark. In some areas they say "sunset," and that can be 45 minutes to an hour before dark. (Stuart was locked in at Laurel Snow, along with two other cars, thinking the closing time was dark, instead of sunset!) Pay attention to the signage as you enter the parking area. It will usually specify sunset or dark, and sometimes the actual time will be posted (since sunset changes daily). If you have questions about the rules and regulations that cover the trail you are heading for, refer to the hike contact information in this book and call for clarification.

How to Use this Guide

This guidebook contains detailed descriptions of sixty hikes located in Tennessee, and descriptions of sixteen "Additional Great Hikes," which are found at the end of the chapters. Each description contains a trail map, directions to the trailhead, and what you are likely to find along the way. The Trail Finder chart following this introduction will help you locate hikes with specific features.

Most importantly, this guide does more than focus on the natural aspects of the region and where to find the next turn in each trail. It also provides historic and cultural insights into the state and its residents. These are interwoven into the hike descriptions, along with personal observations about hikers' experiences along the trails.

The people of Tennessee have always been very close to the land, often barely scraping a living from its harsh but beautiful hills and mountains. Until the New Deal reclamation programs of the 1930s, the state was ravaged, eroded, and nearly lost to poor land-management practices. Now it has been restored to its former richness of vegetation, with the larger-than-life presence of huge dams and waterworks projects now dotting the landscape and controlling Tennessee's former runaway flooding problems. It seems fitting to recognize this beneficial interaction and integration of man with nature in this state, perhaps above all others in the country.

So this revised and updated second edition of *Hiking Tennessee* tells you a little bit of everything. Where to find hand-loomed goods and steamboat life, what creatures live in Tennessee's 100-foot waterfalls, and which falls you might swim in. It also tells you where you are likely to find old moonshine stills along your hiking path, who used to live here 3,000 years ago, and who won the Battle of Shiloh and at the cost of how many lives.

You'll also learn the story of the charge up Lookout Mountain, where you are likely to find good birding, where you might find a dozen deer in less than an hour's time along a quiet path, and where you can take a private wooded walk in the middle of town, and then catch some catfish for dinner along the lakeshore on your way out.

Tennessee is good for stories, and we are happy to pass them along to you, in keeping with the good ol' Tennessee tradition!

Trail Finder

Hikes for Backpackers

Hike 11: Eagle Point Overnight Trail at Mousetail Landing State Park

Hike 12: Overnight Trail at Montgomery Bell State Park

Hike 20: Natural Bridge–Hazard Cave Combination Loop at Pickett CCC Memorial State Park

Hike 23: Twin Arches Loop with Charit Creek Lodge at Big South Fork National River and Recreation Area

Hike 25: South Old Mac–Lookout Tower–North Old Mac–Panther Creek Combination Trail at Frozen Head State Park

Hike 26: Brady Mountain Trail

Hike 27: Black Mountain Trail

Hike 28: Virgin Falls Trail at Virgin Falls State Natural Area

Hike 32: Lower Loop of the Cane Creek Overnight Trail at Fall Creek Falls State Park

Hike 34: Laurel Creek Overlook Trail at Laurel Snow State Natural Area

Hike 35: Piney River Trail with Twin Rocks

Hike 36: North Chickamauga Creek Trail at North Chickamauga State Natural Area

Hike 37: Savage Day Loop at Savage Gulf State Natural Area

Hike 38: Stone Door, Big Creek Rim, and Laurel Combination Trail at Savage Gulf State Natural Area

Hike 39: Grundy Forest Day and Sycamore Falls Combination Loop at Grundy Forest State Natural Area

Hike 41: West Rim Trail at Franklin State Forest

Hike 42: Climber's Loop at Foster Falls Small Wild Area

Hike 43: Trail from Signal Point to Edwards Point at Prentice Cooper State Forest

Hike 46: Big Frog Trail to Low Gap (CNF Trail No. 64) at Cherokee National Forest, Ocoee District

Hike 49: John Muir Trail (CNF Trail No. 152, Benton MacKaye Trail No. 2) at Cherokee National Forest, Ocoee

Hike 50: Bald River Falls (CNF Trail No. 88) at Cherokee National Forest, Tellico District

Hike 56: Appalachian Trail: Newfound Gap to Icewater Shelter

Hike 58: Appalachian Trail: Dennis Cove to Laurel Fork Creek Trailhead (CNF Trail No. 1) at Cherokee National Forest, Watauga Ranger District

Hike 59: Appalachian Trail: Section from Carvers Gap to Roan High Bluff, Highlands of Roan at Cherokee National Forest

Hike 60: Appalachian Trail: Section from Carvers Gap to US 19E (CNF Trail No.1)

Hikes for Children

Hike 2: Chucalissa Indian Town Trail at T.O. Fuller State Park

Hike 4: Riverside and Indian Mounds Loop Trail at Shiloh National Military Park

Hike 6: Lakeshore Trail at Chickasaw State Park

Hike 7: Fairview Gullies Loop at Natchez Trace State Park

Hike 11: Eagle Point Overnight Trail at Mousetail Landing State Park

Hike 13: Ganier Ridge–Lake Trail Combination at Radnor Lake State Park

Hike 14: Couchville Lake Trail at Long Hunter State Park

Hike 15: Hidden Springs Trail at Cedars of Lebanon State Park and Forest

Hike 16: The Enclosure Wall Trail at Old Stone Fort State Archaeological Park

Hike 44: Bluff Trail at Chickamauga and Chattanooga National Military Park

Hike 45: Council House and Council of Trees Loop Combination Trail at Red Clay State Historic Park

Hike 47: Benton Falls (CNF Trail No. 131) at Cherokee National Forest, Ocoee District

Hike 49: John Muir Trail (CNF Trail No. 152, Benton MacKaye Trail No. 2) at Cherokee National Forest, Ocoee District

Hike 51: Meadow-Ridgetop Combination Loop at Fort Loudoun State Park

Hike 52: Laurel Falls–Cove Mountain at Great Smoky Mountains National Park

Hike 53: Grotto Falls Trail at Great Smoky Mountains National Park

Hike 54: Abrams Falls Trail at Great Smoky Mountains National Park

Hike 56: Appalachian Trail: Newfound Gap to Icewater Shelter

Hike 57: Margarette Falls (CNF Trail No. 189) at Cherokee National Forest, Nolichucky District

Hike 59: Appalachian Trail: Section from Carvers Gap to Roan High Bluff, Highlands of Roan at Cherokee National Forest

Hikes for History Lovers

Hike 2: Chucalissa Indian Town Trail at T.O. Fuller State Park

Hike 3: Shiloh Monuments Hike at Shiloh National Military Park

Hike 4: Riverside and Indian Mounds Loop Trail at Shiloh National Military Park

Hike 7: Fairview Gullies Loop at Natchez Trace State Park

Hike 8: Combination Trail at Nathan Bedford Forrest State Park

Hike 9: Johnsonville Redoubts Trail at Johnsonville State Historic Park

Hike 10: Telegraph and North–South Connector Combination Trail at Land Between the Lakes

Hike 16: The Enclosure Wall Trail at Old Stone Fort State Archaeological Park

Hike 17: The Downstream and Upstream Trails at Rock Island State Park

Hike 18: River and Ridge Combination Trail at Burgess Falls State Park

Hike 19: Lake Trail at Standing Stone State Park

Hike 20: Natural Bridge–Hazard Cave Combination Loop at Pickett CCC Memorial State Park

Hikes for Waterfall Lovers

Hikes with Great Views

Hikes for Dogs

Hikes with Canyons

Hike with Nature Trails

Map Legend

Municipal

═24═	Interstate Highway
═127═	US Highway
═156═	State Road
═154═	Local/County Road
═FS 221═	Forest Service Road
= = =:	Gravel Road
= = =:	Unpaved Road
┣━━━┫	Railroad
─ ─ · ─	State Boundary
●─·─●─	Power Line

Trails

- - - - - -	**Trails**
- - - - - -	Featured Trail
────────	Trail
	Paved Trail

Water Features

⬭	**Water Features**
≈	Body of Water
∿	Marsh
⌒	River/Creek
≋	Intermittent Stream
⟳	Waterfall
	Spring

Symbols

▦	Bench
⦵	Bridge
▲	Backcountry Campground
▥	Boardwalk/Steps
⛵	Boat Launch
■	Building/Point of Interest
⛺	Campground
∩	Cave
▬	Dam
⛓	Gate
🛏	Lodging
🅿	Parking
⧓	Pass
▲	Peak
🎪	Picnic Area
🏛	Ranger Station/Park Office
🍴	Restaurant
🚻	Restroom
👁	Scenic View
🗼	Tower
○	Town
①	Trailhead
❓	Visitor/Information Center

Land Management

▣	National Park/Forest
▢	National Wilderness/Recreation Area
▢	State Park/Forest, County Park
⬚	State Natural Area

Memphis and the West

The westernmost of Tennessee's three Grand Divisions contains approximately 25 percent of the state's land area and 25 percent of its population, sandwiched between the Mississippi River to the west and the Tennessee River to the east. These "divisions" are both political and geographic, with no more than two of the State's Supreme Court justices permitted to be selected from each division. This division is distinct from the rest of the state for several reasons. Though the area was included when Tennessee was made a state in 1796, previously it was recognized as Chickasaw territory, which was later ceded by treaty to the United States. Historically, West Tennessee shares its roots more with the Deep South than the rest of the Tennessee, and sided with the South for the most part during the Civil War, whereas the rest of the state was split in its loyalties. Also, nearly 60 percent of the state's black population is found in this region, strongly influencing the musical traditions of jazz, soul, and rock 'n' roll centered in Memphis, the cultural center of West Tennessee and the home of many notable musicians, including Elvis Presley, the "King" of rock 'n' roll.

Geographically, it is part of the Gulf Coastal Plain and is flatter than the areas to the east. This flatness is broken by the Chickasaw Bluffs, however, which run roughly north–south along the Mississippi River, rising 50 to 200 feet above the floodplain, and by the bluffs that border the Tennessee River in the east. The hills tend to be forested, while the plains are in farmland. This seemingly stable region is actually part of the New Madrid Seismic Zone, with a fairly high earthquake risk. In fact, in 1811 and 1812 the area suffered three of the largest earthquakes in US history, even briefly reversing the flow of the Mississippi. Reelfoot Lake, a 20-square-mile water body that is part bayou and part lake, was created by one of these quakes.

The hiking in this part of the state includes trails on the hilly bluffs on the Mississippi River to the west and on the Tennessee River to the east, as well as trails throughout the flatlands, from the southern Mississippi border to the northern Kentucky state line.

1 Pioneer Springs–Chickasaw Bluff Combination Trail at Meeman-Shelby Forest State Park

This trail begins at the well-marked trailhead at Poplar Tree Lake and heads north along Chickasaw Bluff No. 3, hugging the edge of marshy bottomland that is rich in wildlife (including mosquitoes!). The trail passes the Pioneer Springs, connecting briefly with the Woodland Trail and the Bicycle Trail near the Woodland Shelter, and continues along the bluff paralleling Riddick Road. There you might see raccoons and beaver, in addition to the usual squirrels, frogs, and toads. The trail then turns in to end at the Piersol Lake access loop roads. (You can also hike the reverse, from north to south, but the trailhead is harder to find at the north end.)

Start: Pioneer Springs Trailhead sign by the Poplar Tree Lake parking lot
Distance: 7.6 miles out and back (3.8 miles with shuttle)
Hiking time: About 5 hours
Difficulty: Moderate
Trail surface: Dirt
Best seasons: Fall and winter (many mosquitoes on the swampy bottomlands in summer)

Other trail users: None
Canine compatibility: Leashed dogs permitted
Fees and permits: None
Schedule: 7 a.m. to 10 p.m. daily
Map: USGS quad 403SE, Locke
Trail contact: Meeman-Shelby Park Headquarters, 910 Riddick Rd., Millington, TN 38053. Visitor center: (901) 876-5215.

Finding the trailhead: Take US 51 north from Memphis and exit at North Watkins Street (Route 388). Go north until it ends at Lock-Cuba and turn left (CITGO gas station on left). Go 0.7 mile to a four-way stop at the country store and take a right onto Bluff Road. Take the next left into the park entrance. The visitor center is on the immediate right. Turn left after the visitor center and continue until you T-end, and turn right onto Grassy Lake Road (the road will make a sharp left after you pass the pool). Park in the Poplar Tree Lake parking lot and walk back out the entrance to the trailhead. If you decide to do this hike with a shuttle, you can continue straight behind the visitor center, and park in the Piersol Lake Group Camp parking area. **GPS:** N35 18.476' / W90 04.089'
Special considerations: The park facilities are bordered on the west by the Shelby Forest Wildlife Management Area, which contains areas of swamp with names such as "Barnishe Bayou" and "Cypress Slough." Because of this swamp, there is no direct improved trail access to the Mississippi. The wildlife management area also has hunting permitted in season, so be careful before you venture from established trails.

The Hike

Meeman–Shelby Forest State Park is located on Chickasaw Bluff No. 3, along the Mississippi River, 13 miles north of Memphis. Its 13,476 acres include 20 miles of improved hiking trails, a 5-mile bicycle trail, an 8.5-mile horse trail, an Olympic-size

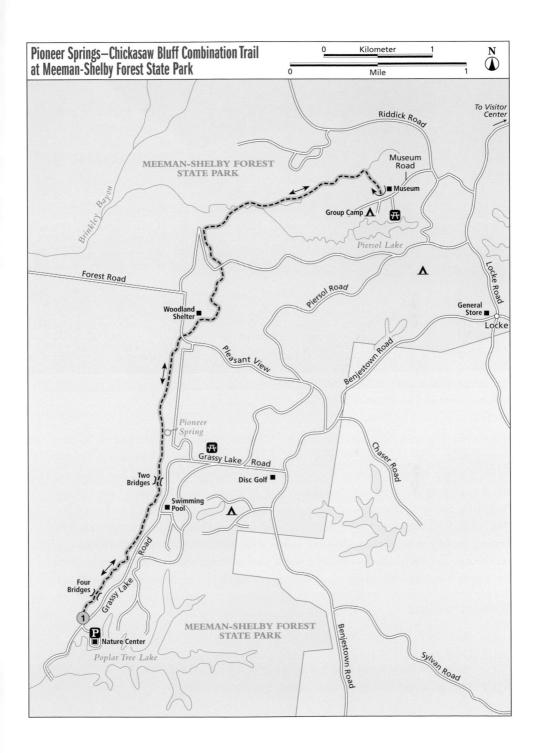

Pioneer Springs–Chickasaw Bluff Combination Trail at Meeman-Shelby Forest State Park

0   Kilometer   1

0   Mile   1

N

Riddick Road

To Visitor Center

MEEMAN-SHELBY FOREST STATE PARK

Brinkley Bayou

Museum Road

■ Museum

Group Camp

Piersol Lake

Forest Road

Woodland Shelter

Piersol Road

General Store ■

Locke ■

Locke Road

Pleasant View

Benjestown Road

Pioneer Spring

Grassy Lake Road

Chaser Road

Disc Golf ■

Two Bridges

Swimming ■ Pool

Four Bridges

Grassy Lake Road

①

P

■ Nature Center

Poplar Tree Lake

MEEMAN-SHELBY FOREST STATE PARK

Benjestown Road

Sylvan Road

The uniquely green water at Poplar Tree Lake, near the trailhead. The lake is enjoyed by fisher-men, picnickers, and a community of geese.

swimming pool, and fishing and boating on 125-acre Poplar Tree Lake and on 25-acre Piersol Lake. A 36-hole disc (Frisbee) golf course is also popular. The park is heavily utilized in the summer months because of its proximity to Memphis, but it still has some private spots to be found and enjoyed. The park has a variety of hardwoods, including ten state champion trees and two national champion trees, and over 200 species of birds have been spotted on its hardwood bluffs or river bottomlands. The Nature Center at Poplar Tree Lake is worth a look, if only because its profusion of taxidermic and other displays make it seem almost "over-the-top" in its enthusiasm for nature. You can walk along the riverbank to watch the riverboats go by at sunset.

Miles and Directions

0.0 Start from trailhead near Poplar Tree Lake at the entrance to the parking area.

0.2 Climb down stone steps to the bottom, where you will encounter some mushy ground for a good part of the year, and cross four small bridges within a tenth of a mile.

0.6 Enjoy Mississippi River bottomland, teeming with life and mystery.

THE TRAGEDY OF THE SULTANA

If you had been standing on the Chickasaw Bluffs, near where Meeman-Shelby is today, in the early morning hours of April 27, 1865, you might have been witness to what some have called the worst maritime disaster in US history. The loss of life with the explosion and burning of the SS *Sultana* on the Mississippi River far exceeds the death toll of the sinking of the *Titanic,* and yet many people have never even heard of this tragedy.

The *Sultana* was heading up the Mississippi, carrying mostly newly freed Civil War POWs, many of whom were already weak or sick. The *Sultana* was designed for 400 passengers but was carrying more than 2,400 when a boiler exploded, throwing passengers into the air and into the cold Mississippi current, which was swollen with spring rain. More than 1,800 perished, and bodies continued to be discovered for weeks afterward as the death toll grew. (The *Titanic,* by comparison, had a death toll of 1,150.)

Why has the tragedy of the *Sultana* been all but forgotten? Was it because at the time, the news was overshadowed by the assassination of Abraham Lincoln, which took place twelve days earlier? Or did it fail to capture the imagination of the public because the *Sultana* was loaded with emaciated POWs as opposed to the likes of millionaire John Jacob Astor? Or was it simply that no one had ever boasted that the *Sultana* was unsinkable, as they had done with the *Titanic*? Or was it because the nation was just too weary after the preceding four years, having seen the loss of over 600,000 of its sons to combat? One thing is certain: The sinking of the *Sultana* was a monumental tragedy in an era of monumental tragedies.

1.2 Cross two more bridges before reaching the Pioneer Springs and shelter. Don't expect a refreshing splash—the water is a bit murky. There is a small shelter, however, if you run into some weather.

1.4 Junction with Bicycle Trail. You have the option of looping right onto the tail end of the paved Bicycle Trail and returning to your car on the paved Grassy Lake Road.

1.9 As you continue, meet pavement and Bicycle Trail again. Cross over and head left to continue in the same direction to the Woodland Shelter, where you have another opportunity to jump off the trail onto the Woodland Trail. Follow around the shelter and right to continue northeast. Head downhill for a portion of the trail that parallels a gravel road along the base of the bluff, then up and down again.

2.6 Leave the road and ascend, and cross Riddick Creek. You might encounter some wildlife, including snakes, so keep an eye out! Follow the river ravine.

3.5 Ascend and descend again as you make your way to Piersol Lake Group Camp.

3.8 End of hike at Piersol Lake Group Camp. (**Note:** Some literature says that the Chickasaw Bluff Trail is 8.0 miles long, but this may be because of confusion on where the north end of the trail ends. If you continue to Mississippi Group Camp, you will add an extra couple of miles to your journey, though trail markings are unclear, coming from the south.) Turn around and return back the way you came. (If you would like to make this a one-way shuttle hike, there is plenty of parking at the Piersol Lake Group Camp.)

7.6 Arrive back at the trailhead and parking lot.

Hike Information

Local Events/Attractions

Alex Haley Museum: The childhood home of Alex Haley, the author of *Roots,* the bestselling novel that was made into a TV miniseries in the 1970s. The series chronicles the lives of generations of a black family that came originally from Africa, headed by Kunta Kinte, and takes them through pre–Civil War years, addressing racial issues of the time. Haley based his novel on the true stories told to him by his grandmother and aunt right on the front porch of this Haley home. Alex Haley died in 1992, and his gravesite is on the front lawn. The museum located in the house is dedicated as a "Tribute to Kunta Kinte's worldwide family." Alex Haley Museum and Interpretive Center, 200 S. Church St., Henning, TN 38041; (731) 738-2240; alexhaleymuseum .org.

Lodging

Meeman–Shelby has forty-nine camping spaces available by permit and six two-bedroom cabins for a fee. Reserve at tnstateparks.itinio.com/meemanshelbyforest.

Hike Tours

From Memorial Day to Labor Day, guided nature hikes every Saturday, pontoon boat trips on Poplar Tree Lake Friday through Sunday, and guided swamp canoe trips weekends. Inquire at visitor center.

Organizations

Friends of the Forest, shelbyfriends.org.

2 Chucalissa Indian Town Trail at T.O. Fuller State Park

The Indian Town Trail is a segment of the 4-mile Discovery Trail, which takes you from the campground, past the picnic shelter, and to the Indian village grounds and museum. A prehistoric Chucalissa Indian village once thrived on this site, which has a sense of internal organization and a peaceful air that is characteristic of many Native American sites in Tennessee.

Start: Fuller State Park campground
Distance: 1.9-mile lollipop loop
Hiking time: About 1.25 hours
Difficulty: Easy
Best season: Any time of year
Trail surface: dirt and paved
Canine compatibility: Leashed dogs permitted

Other trail users: Hikers only
Fees and permits: None
Schedule: Sunrise to sunset, 7 days a week
Map: USGS quad Southwest Memphis
Trail contact: T.O. Fuller State Park Headquarters, 1500 Mitchell Rd., Memphis, TN 38109; (901) 543-7581

Finding the trailhead: Take I-55 south from Memphis and merge onto South US 61/TN 14. Continue 1.8 miles on US 61/TN 14 and turn right onto East Mitchell Road. After 3.4 miles Mitchell Road will make a slight right and lead you into the park entrance and past the visitor center. Make the first left onto Plant Road, with a quick second left onto Boxtown Road. Just before the ranger's office, turn right, then turn left at the T and drive into the campground. You can park at the showers parking lot and enter the woods behind a campsite across the street and to the right. (If you have trouble finding the trail, the very friendly Campground Host is ever-present and will be glad to assist you.) **GPS:** N35 03.462' / W90 07.693'
Special considerations: It would be good to speak to the Campground Host on the way in to let him know you are leaving your car to do the hike.

The Hike

T.O. Fuller State Park, located within the southern limits of the city of Memphis, was the first state park open to African Americans east of the Mississippi River, and the second in the nation. Its 1,138 acres contain more than 8 miles of hiking trails, including the Discovery Trail, a 4-mile loop, and 4 miles of walking trails in the day-use area. Its namesake, Dr. Thomas O. Fuller, spent his life empowering and educating African Americans. In excavations to build the park in 1940, Civilian Conservation Corps (CCC) camp number 1464-SP-10, comprised entirely of African Americans, unearthed evidence of a prehistoric Chucalissa Indian village, and the site has since been developed into an archaeological site and museum. The Indian Town Trail passes through the site. The park also contains an Olympic-size pool, other sports facilities, forty-five campsites, and picnic areas throughout.

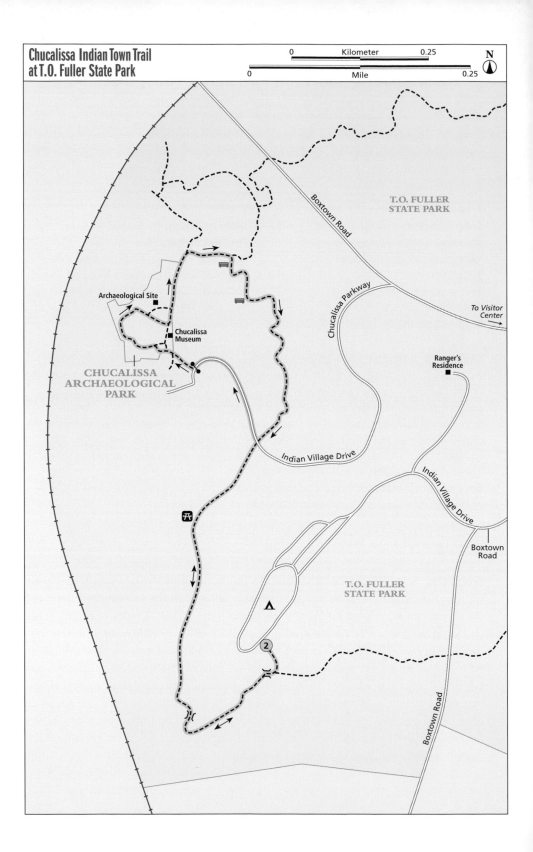

Chucalissa Indian Town Trail
at T.O. Fuller State Park

Kilometer
0   0.25
0   0.25
Mile

N

Boxtown Road

T.O. FULLER
STATE PARK

Chucalissa Parkway

To Visitor
Center

Archaeological Site

Chucalissa
Museum

Ranger's
Residence

CHUCALISSA
ARCHAEOLOGICAL
PARK

Indian Village Drive

Indian Village Drive

Boxtown
Road

T.O. FULLER
STATE PARK

2

Boxtown Road

Visitors to T.O. Fuller are treated to a parade of flowers on their way to the various sports and recreation facilities the park offers in addition to traditional camping and hiking offerings.

Miles and Directions

0.0 Start from the campground, across from the shower parking area. At 100 feet the trail turns to the right. Immediately after leaving the campsite, you will be plunged into forest and feel that you are alone with nature. The trail is surprisingly pleasant for such an urban location. It winds down and turns to the right, continuing down and then up to follow a ridgetop.

0.3 Follow a ridge through a beautiful stand of trees that has nice filtered light in the afternoons.

0.4 Reach a small meadow and enter behind a large wooden shelter that does not appear to be well attended. Reenter the woods at the other end of the meadow to continue.

0.6 Reach a gate that opens onto the road to Chucalissa Indian Village Museum, which you will see on your left. Turn left to continue on the hike.

0.8 Reach entrance to museum by following the paved road. If the museum is open, you can enter through it and enjoy the exhibits. If it is closed, it is possible to get to the site by walking behind some outbuildings to the left side of the museum.

1.0 The Indian village is easily the most fascinating part of the hike, with very clear and geometric mounds making one wonder at the supposedly "primitive" civilizations that predated European settlers by a thousand years or more. Informative plaques guide you through a circular path. Enjoy the site, and finish walking through the archaeological site and enter woods again behind the largest mound, which appears to be ceremonial, with wide steps up the front.

1.1 The trail passes through a nice glade and turns right after a bench. Shortly after, you will again choose the right fork (If you choose to go left here, you will end up on the 4-mile Discovery Loop trail) to return to the park's museum road.

1.4 You arrive at the same gate you passed through on your way to the museum.

1.9 Retrace your steps along the ridge and down to the campground and the trail's end.

Hike Information

Local Events/Attractions

In the park: Memphis in May Festival, annually in May; FullerFest, first Sat in Aug; Fall Festival, Oct 31.

In Memphis: National Civil Rights Museum, 450 Mulberry St., Memphis; (901) 521-9699. Admission charged.

Graceland, 3765 Elvis Presley Blvd., Memphis; (901) 332-3322. Admission charged.

Mud Island: In downtown Memphis you may want to try out the unique walking path at a place with the dubious name of Mud Island. For a fee, a ferry will take you to this small man-made island with a 5-block-long scale model of the Mississippi River Valley, complete with a 1-acre pond (the "Gulf of Mexico") with a sandy beach, which functions as the largest swimming pool in the city.

Restaurants

Blues City Cafe, 138 Beale St., Memphis; (901) 526-3637. This cafe offers a taste of a different, vibrant world coexisting next to this natural one.

Lodging

Campground facilities at the park.

3 Shiloh Monuments Hike at Shiloh National Military Park

The Monuments Hike focuses on the Battle of Shiloh, honored here. You may want to begin with a tour by a park ranger, learning the significance and history of the battle. This hike follows the loop road, which runs through the center of the park and takes in most of the significant monuments. Walking it, you will be awed by the scale of the battle in a way that driving by at 30 miles per hour could not. On this hike, one is struck by the apparent reality that a small and relatively insignificant act can change the course of a war and the history of a nation. Since the sun can be punishing on a hot day, and Tennessee has plenty of those, you might want to take this walk late in the day, so that stretches of the hike will be shaded and cooler.

Start: Monuments Loop Trailhead
Distance: 3.2-mile loop
Hiking time: About 1.5 hours
Difficulty: Easy
Trail surface: Paved
Best seasons: Spring or fall (because of punishing summer heat)
Other trail users: Cars, bicycles
Canine compatibility: Leashed dogs permitted, except in the Shiloh National Cemetery

Fees and permits: None
Schedule: Park open from dawn to dusk and visitor center open from 8 a.m. to 5 p.m. daily, except Thanksgiving, Christmas, and New Year's Day.
Map: USGS quad 13NE, Pittsburg Landing
Trail contact: Park Visitor Center, 1055 Pittsburg Landing Rd., Shiloh, TN 38376; (731) 689-5696

Finding the trailhead: Take TN 22 south for 7 miles after it intersects with US 64, turn left into the park entrance, and follow Corinth-Pittsburg Landing Road past the visitor center., where you may want to stop for a tour, or to see the famous graveyard. Continuing on, make the first left onto Hamburg-Savannah Road. After 0.9 mile turn right (it will be your first right) onto the access road for the Manse Cabin, and park here in the parking lot. **GPS:** N35 07.948' / W88 19.923'

The Hike

Shiloh Military Park is a necessary stop for anyone with even a budding interest in the Civil War. The Battle of Shiloh was waged for two days, on April 6 and April 7, 1862. The Shiloh confrontation engaged Confederate and Union armies from all over the country in an all-out battle to control a crucial river supply route. With 110,000 soldiers engaged in the battle and over 23,000 casualties, this was one of the most significant battles of the Civil War. In fact, there were more soldiers killed in the battle than in all previous American wars combined.

The park was established directly on the original battle site in 1894. You will likely be impressed with the magnitude of the struggle from the moment you drive in the entrance and begin to pass stone marker after stone marker on the carefully manicured grass shoulder, commemorating various exercises or movements in the battle.

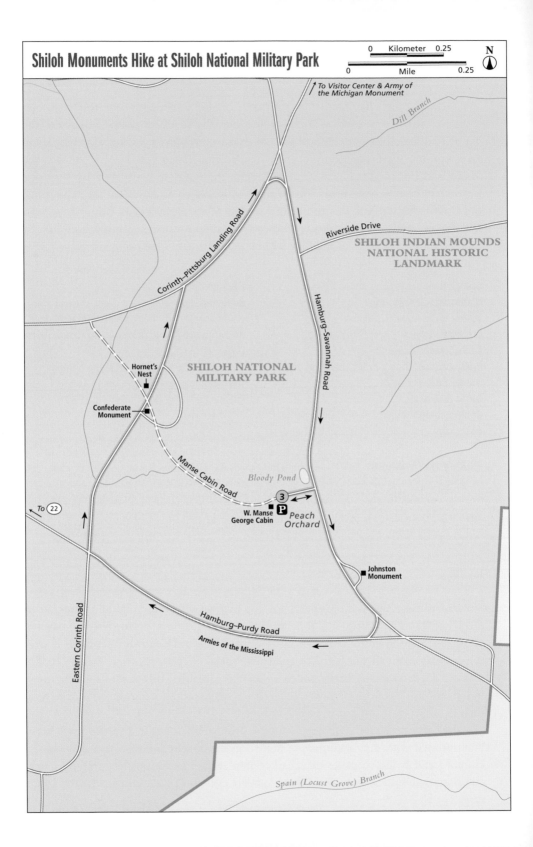

Shiloh Monuments Hike at Shiloh National Military Park

0   Kilometer   0.25
0   Mile   0.25

N

To Visitor Center & Army of
the Michigan Monument

Dill Branch

Corinth–Pittsburg Landing Road

Riverside Drive

SHILOH INDIAN MOUNDS
NATIONAL HISTORIC
LANDMARK

Hamburg–Savannah Road

Hornet's
Nest

SHILOH NATIONAL
MILITARY PARK

Confederate
Monument

Manse Cabin Road

Bloody Pond

3

To 22

W. Manse
George Cabin

P

Peach
Orchard

Johnston
Monument

Eastern Corinth Road

Hamburg–Purdy Road

Armies of the Mississippi

Spain (Locust Grove) Branch

The park headquarters contain a museum with an explanation and video reenactment of the battle. A large monument stands near the museum, marking Ulysses S. Grant's last line of defense during the battle. Nearby is the sobering sight of acres and acres containing thousands of soldiers' mostly unmarked graves.

In the case of Shiloh, the Union was stationed at Pittsburg Landing, an important supply depot, and was warned of Confederates marching on it from the south, but General Grant at first tended to ignore these warnings. This mistake could have cost the Union the war. Had Grant's men not fought valiantly to counter the attack and received reinforcements in the nick of time, the War Between the States may have had a different ending. April 6, 1862, saw 44,000 Confederate soldiers, led by General A. S. Johnston, collected at Corinth, Mississippi, waiting to attack the 40,000 men in General U.S. Grant's Army of the Tennessee at Shiloh Church. Johnston attacked (and was killed in the battle), and Grant regrouped at Pittsburg Landing, with fifty-three guns defending from the hills around the landing. The next morning, 15,000 Union reinforcement troops arrived, and Confederates attacked again, only to be repelled, with 15,000 dead. On April 8, Grant sent General W. T. Sherman after the Confederates, but they were protected by forces led by Colonel Nathan Bedford Forrest (see the description of this remarkable soldier at Hike #8), and the Union forces abandoned the pursuit.

Miles and Directions

0.0 Start from the Manse Cabin, approximately in the middle of the park. After you examine the cabin and the large field alongside it, with a plaque explaining the history of the battle at that site, return to the Hamburg-Savannah Road.

0.1 Turn right onto Hamburg-Savannah Road (the road you drove in on). Pass the large Johnston Monument. (Confederate General Johnston was the only high-ranking officer to ever be killed in action.) On this stretch you will walk past Civil War cannons and many monuments honoring the Army of the Mississippi, which includes armies from all states touching the Mississippi, including Tennessee, Ohio, Missouri, Iowa, Louisiana, and Mississippi.

0.4 Turn right onto Hamburg-Purdy Road.

1.1 Turn right onto Eastern Corinth Road.

1.5 Pass Sunken Road, which connects with the Manse Cabin's access road and provides a shortcut through the middle of Shiloh Military Park. Here you also find Confederate Monument, which is unique in that Shiloh is primarily a Union graveyard and memorial, though thousands of Confederates were buried here in large trench-type graves. The monument is very large and includes realistic figures, providing a human touch in otherwise formal "graveyard" memorial grounds.

1.6 Just after this point is a monument called Hornet's Nest, named for the battle that raged there. You can sometimes see deer at play here, in sharp contrast to the otherwise somber tone of the scene.

1.8 Turn right onto Corinth-Pittsburg Landing Road.

2.1 Turn right onto Hamburg-Savannah Road, at the large statue honoring the Army of the Michigan and past the Hurlbut monument.

Manse Cabin, the designated trailhead for the Monuments hike, was here prior to the bloody conflict at Shiloh, which engaged 110,000 soldiers and left over 23,000 dead.

2.4 Pass the turn for Riverside Drive and the Indian Mounds Trail.

3.0 Pass Bloody Pond, so named because of the soldiers, both Confederate and Union, who used this water for drinking and washing wounds during the battle, turning its water red.

3.1 Turn right to head back to the Manse Cabin and end your journey through history.

3.2 Arrive at the Manse Cabin and the end of your hike.

Hike Information

Local Events/Attractions

Corinth Civil War Interpretive Center, 501 West Linden St., Corinth, MS 38834; (662) 287-9273.

Hike Tours

Visitor center has interesting guided tours that explain history and facts about the Battle of Shiloh.

4 Riverside and Indian Mounds Loop Trail at Shiloh National Military Park

This nearly flat hike passes Indian mounds several centuries old and is appropriate for all ages and abilities. These earth mounds are all that remain of a large city built by "Mound Builder" Indians, who lived in the area of West Tennessee before the advent of white settlers. Their society included at least six communities, of which the one at Shiloh was the largest. Since the residents moved out of this area nearly 800 years ago, it's uncertain whether they were related to the later Choctaw, Creek, or Chickasaw tribes.

Start: Indian Mounds Trailhead behind Shiloh Indian Mounds National Historic Landmark
Distance: 1.1-mile loop
Hiking time: About 40 minutes
Difficulty: Easy
Trail surface: Wood chips, dirt
Best seasons: Fall or spring (to avoid summer heat)
Other trail users: Hikers only

Canine compatibility: Leashed dogs permitted, except in the Shiloh National Cemetery
Fees and permits: None
Schedule: Park open from dawn to dusk. Visitor center open from 8 a.m. to 5 p.m. daily, except Thanksgiving, Christmas, and New Year's Day.
Map: USGS quad 13NE, Pittsburg Landing
Trail contact: Park Visitor Center, 1055 Pittsburg Landing Rd., Shiloh, TN 38376; (731) 689-5696

Finding the trailhead: Take TN 22 south for 7 miles after it intersects with US 64, turn left into the park entrance, and follow Pittsburg Landing Road to the visitor center. To get to the Indian Mounds Trailhead from the visitor center, return on the Corinth-Pittsburg Landing Road and make the first left onto Hamburg-Savannah Road. After 0.3 mile turn left onto Riverside Drive and park in the large parking area after the meadow, in front of the Shiloh Indian Mounds National Historic Landmark. The trailhead is behind the landmark, a white stone structure with information about the Indian Mounds and the residents who built them. **GPS:** N35 08.484' / W88 19.610'

The Hike

Spend some time at the interpretive center before you begin this hike, to add to your appreciation of the "ancientness" of what you are seeing. The native residents of this chiefdom may have selected this location because it was high on a bluff and safe from the flooding of the Tennessee River, and also because the steep ravines on two sides and the bluff next to the river made the village less accessible to raiders. They were primarily agricultural people whose staple was corn, but they also grew melons, pumpkins, beans, peas, sunflowers, and tobacco, and gathered berries, fruits, and nuts. The large, flat-topped mounds were the bases for ceremonial lodges and chieftains' lodges. Depressions in the ground mark the locations of 800–plus–year–old round huts made of mud and logs and branches (called *daub* and *wattle*) that were common

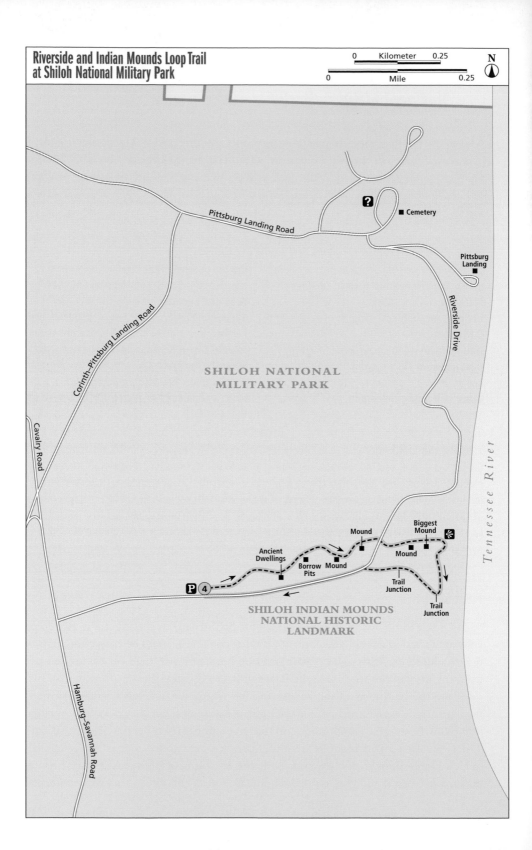

**Riverside and Indian Mounds Loop Trail
at Shiloh National Military Park**

0 Kilometer 0.25

0 Mile 0.25

N

Pittsburg Landing Road

? ■ Cemetery

Pittsburg
Landing ■

Corinth–Pittsburg Landing Road

Riverside Drive

**SHILOH NATIONAL
MILITARY PARK**

Cavalry Road

Tennessee River

Mound ■
Biggest
Mound ■

■ Ancient
Dwellings
Mound ■
Borrow
Pits ■ Mound ■
■ Mound

P (4)

Trail
Junction

Trail
Junction

**SHILOH INDIAN MOUNDS
NATIONAL HISTORIC
LANDMARK**

Hamburg–Savannah Road

Well-defined mounds and remnants of housing structures still mark the location of a major center for Mound Builders who lived in complex societies here centuries before Europeans arrived.

for these Indians. Because the Shiloh battleground was set aside as a cemetery in 1866 and was later included in the national park, this area has never been disturbed by farming. Archaeologists first excavated at Shiloh in 1899 and found the site's most famous artifact, a large stone pipe in the shape of a kneeling man, which is on display in the Tennessee River Museum in Savannah, Tennessee. (See "Local Events/Attractions" below.)

Miles and Directions

0.0 Start from behind the Shiloh Indian Mounds National Historic Landmark on Riverside Drive. Head straight ahead into the trees, past the information boards.

0.1 Reach the remnants of native *daub*-and-*wattle* (mud and stick) dwellings, which have lasted over 800 years. These are small, round mounds about 1 foot high and between 10 and 20 feet in diameter.

0.2 Pass the Borrow Pits, where earth was dug up and used to create the impressive mounds you are about to see.

0.3 Approach and walk around your first mound. These formations are very obviously not naturally made, and took tremendous effort at the time. It is believed they were so important because they were ceremonial.

0.4 Pass more mounds and reach the largest of these. (You may also see a large community of squirrels, who have moved in.)

0.5 Reach the overlook onto the Tennessee River. It is believed that this location was selected for the central community in this chiefdom because its view of the river and the land formation made it more easily defensible.

0.6 Reach the river, after passing behind the back of the mounds, and reach a trail junction with a sign directing you to the right.

0.7 Reach another junction, and continue straight onto the road. (There should be a path on the opposite side of the road, paralleling it, but it was not well marked, so this hike finishes along the road, which has virtually no traffic.)

1.1 Complete your hike in front of the historic landmark.

Hike Information

Local Events/Attractions

Tennessee River Museum, 495 Main St., Savannah, TN 38372; (731) 925-2364.

Buford Pusser Home and Museum, 12 miles from the park. A famous lawman who served as sheriff here from 1964 to 1970, Pusser was the target of many death threats, and his dedication made him become a symbol of "law and order." His life was the basis of the three *Walking Tall* movies, which glorified the life of the lawman. 342 Pusser St., Adamsville, TN 38310; (731) 632-4080; bufordpussermuseum.com.

5 Pinson Mounds Nature Trail at Pinson Mounds State Archaeological Park

The Pinson Mounds Nature Trail covers most of the major formations at Pinson Mounds in a 3.1-mile hike and also provides a wooded walk and boardwalk access to an overlook over the Forked Deer River, winding past many of the fifteen sacred ceremonial mounds found on the site.

Start: The trail starts at the park museum and heads on the paved road straight back toward Saul's Mound.
Distance: 3.1-mile loop
Hiking time: About 2 hours, with stops to examine the mounds and cool off on a bench once in a while
Difficulty: Easy
Trail surface: Paved and dirt, with the portion closest to the museum wheelchair accessible
Best season: Year-round
Other trail users: Hikers only
Canine compatibility: Leashed dogs permitted

Fees and permits: None
Schedule: Trails and shelters open daily 7 a.m. to sunset. Museum and office Mon to Sat from 8 a.m. to 4:30 p.m. and Sun 1 to 5 p.m. Museum closed on weekends during the winter (Nov 1 through Mar 15) and museum and office are closed on all federal holidays from Nov through Good Friday.
Map: USGS quad 446SW, Beech Bluff
Trail contact: Pinson Mounds State Archaeological Park, 460 Ozier Rd., Pinson, TN 38366; (731) 988-5614

Finding the trailhead: Take US 45 south from I-40 at Jackson, Tennessee, to Pinson, and turn left on Ozier Road/TN 197 (at the park sign) and follow Ozier Road 2.5 miles to the park entrance on the right. (You will pass the exit on the way to the entrance.) **GPS:** N35 29.815' / W88 40.939'

The Hike

Pinson Mounds contain the largest mound group in the United States, an area of 1,200 acres, dating from the Middle Woodland period. These mounds were used between AD 1 and AD 500 by Indians who predated all the known Indian tribes in the United States. The mounds were used for ceremonial purposes and burials and apparently were the destination of pilgrimages from as far away as Louisiana and Georgia, based upon pottery fragments found at the site. In total the site contains at least fifteen earthen mounds, a geometric enclosure, related earthworks, and crematory areas and has teams of archaeologists working on portions of the site periodically.

The park has approximately 6 miles of trails, which make up for in interest what they may lack in hiking challenge. Its trails are primarily wide, smooth paths that lead from one burial mound to another, making them ideal for visitors using wheelchairs.

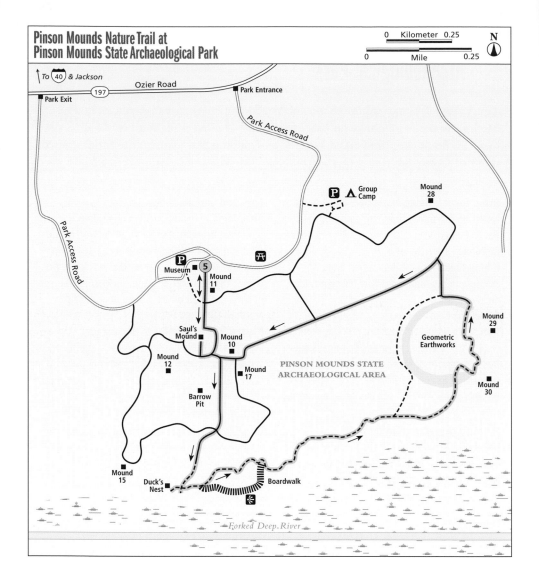

Pinson Mounds Nature Trail at
Pinson Mounds State Archaeological Park

0   Kilometer   0.25

0   Mile   0.25

N

To 40 & Jackson

Ozier Road

197

Park Entrance

Park Exit

Park Access Road

Park Access Road

Group
Camp

Mound
28

Museum

5

Mound
11

Saul's
Mound

Mound
10

Geometric
Earthworks

Mound
29

Mound
12

Mound
17

PINSON MOUNDS STATE
ARCHAEOLOGICAL AREA

Mound
30

Barrow
Pit

Mound
15

Duck's
Nest

Boardwalk

Forked Deep River

Hiking to the top of Saul's Mound may work up a bit of a sweat, but basically, the park is easily navigated.

A very well-presented museum gives an in-depth and sophisticated view of the archaeological activities that have taken place at Pinson Mounds and offers a video presentation that provides a visual explanation of ongoing activities. Guides are available to answer any questions.

The place has an almost chapel-like reverence to it. The areas between most of the mounds have been cleared and have green, manicured grassy expanses, or have been left to their native wild grasses. The mounds themselves, dating back nearly twenty centuries, are an impressive reminder of the presence of civilized residents, which

A section of the Pinson Mounds loop trail, which includes sections of pavement, gravel, dirt, wood steps, and boardwalk spurs, before returning to its beginning.

predated by centuries not only the subsistence farmers and hunters of the 1700s and 1800s, but even the Native American tribes that we readily recognize and associate with this region, such as the Choctaw and Chickasaw.

Miles and Directions

0.0 Start at the museum's back entrance. A board a couple of hundred steps from the open-air pavilion will show you where you are going.

0.2 Head directly south to arrive at Saul's Mound. At 72 feet, this mound is the second-tallest in the United States and the tallest within Pinson Mounds, constructed between AD 1 and AD 300. The mound provides the best view of the park and usually has its share of visitors scrambling up its 155 steps to enjoy a beautiful view of the tranquil meadow and the mounds. At the base again, head right.

0.3 Pass the Barrow Pit on the right. On your left you will pass Mound 17. The Barrow Pit is the source of most of the earth used to construct Saul's Mound. Continue south and then curve right (west) from here.

0.6 A spur trail to the right takes you to Duck's Nest, a circular embankment constructed between AD 1 and AD 300. Archaeologists have determined that the fire pit in the center of Duck's Nest was used only once.

0.7 Back on the main trail, you can fork to the right here onto the boardwalk, which runs over lowlands to reach an overlook on the Forked Deer River, a good spot for observing birds. The boardwalk loops back to meet the main trail at 0.9 mile. Head left to stay on the mail trail, passing through a wooded area.

1.3 Arrive at Mounds 29 and 30 and the Geometric Earthworks that surround the mounds, known as the Citadel. Before you reach the mounds, a dirt path will fork off to the left, which will lead to the west side. If you take this path, you will be missing Mounds 29 and 30, which are at the eastern end of the circular earthworks. The earthen enclosure was not constructed for defense purposes, but the actual purpose is not known. Mound 29, constructed between AD 1 and AD 200, stands 9.5 feet tall and is located exactly 3,350 feet from Saul's Mound. Two other mounds have been discovered to be located the same distance from Saul's Mound. After this the path becomes gravel.

1.8 The path rounds these mounds, passes through the gap between the earthworks and Mound 29, and then turns left on the path to loop back west and return to Saul's Mound. You will pass through an open field, which will be in the direct sun for a while if the weather is good, until you pass the group camp on your right, and then finally get to a bench in the shade. Pass another junction, and you are back in the sun.

2.9 Arrive at Saul's Mound after passing Mound 10, which stands 4.3 feet tall and contains a hearth that was used for ceremonial purposes. At this point the path joins the one that led you out from the museum, and you will retrace your steps for 0.2 mile to complete the hike.

3.1 Arrive at the museum to conclude your exploration.

Hike Information

Local Events/Attractions

Archaeofest is held at Pinson Mounds State Park on the third weekend in September. This is a Native American celebration that includes craft demonstrations in leatherwork, basketry, and jewelry making and storytelling.

Casey Jones Restaurant and Museum in nearby Jackson (13 miles away, at 30 Casey Jones Ln., Jackson, TN) tells the colorful story of Casey Jones the railroad man, who gave his life for his comrades. An admission fee is charged.

6 Lakeshore Trail at Chickasaw State Park

The 1.9-mile Lakeshore Trail is a local favorite. This loop trail begins at the foot-bridge that crosses Lake Placid, which is no longer functional but still creates a picturesque image reflected in the lake. The trail varies between dirt, sand, and boardwalk as it makes its way around the lake, at times passing through marshy areas and at other times traversing small rises that provide a lake view.

Start: Footbridge at Lake Placid
Distance: 1.9-mile loop
Hiking time: About 45 minutes
Difficulty: Easy
Trail surface: Dirt and sand
Best season: Any time of year
Other trail users: Hikers only

Canine compatibility: Leashed dogs permitted
Fees and permits: None
Schedule: 8 a.m. to 10 p.m. year-round
Map: USGS quad Silerton
Trail contact: Chickasaw State Park Headquarters, 850 Lake Levee Rd., Henderson, TN 38340; (731) 989-7629

Finding the trailhead: From I-40 at Jackson, exit onto US 45, heading south through Jackson, approximately 17 miles to Henderson. Turn right onto West Main Street/TN 365, and continue onto West Main Street/TN 100 for 6 miles until you turn left into the park entrance onto Lake Levee Road. Make an immediate left onto Cabin Lane, and park in the parking lot near the Bathhouse. Walk past the swimming area toward the wooden footbridge. When you arrive at the water's edge, the trail will begin to your left, heading toward the cabins, and will pass in front of them into the woods. **GPS:** N35 23.420' / W88 46.183'

The Hike

Chickasaw State Park, together with the accompanying state forest, comprises over 14,384 acres and has some of the highest terrain in West Tennessee. The park uses nearly all its area for recreation, with extensive offerings for horseback riding, including trails, rental horses, and even the Wrangler Campground, with nearby stables so campers can stay near their horses. Fishing is also popular on Chickasaw's two lakes, Lake Placid and Lake LaJoie, both of which have bass, catfish, and bream. Canoes, kayaks, fishing boats, and pedal boats can be rented.

The park has over 6 miles of trails, including the Lakeshore Trail, featured here. The Forked Pine Trail, at 0.6 mile, and the Friend's Trail, at 1.5 miles, both connect within 0.3 mile from the Lakeshore Trailhead and make nice add-ons to that hike for those who want something longer. The Fern Creek Trail, at 0.8 mile, starts out of the RV campground and passes by Brewer's Cabin, offering another alternative. The park also offers thirteen cabins, both one- and two-bedroom, with wood-burning fireplaces. The cabins are stocked with wood from October through March.

Lakeshore Trail at Chickasaw State Park

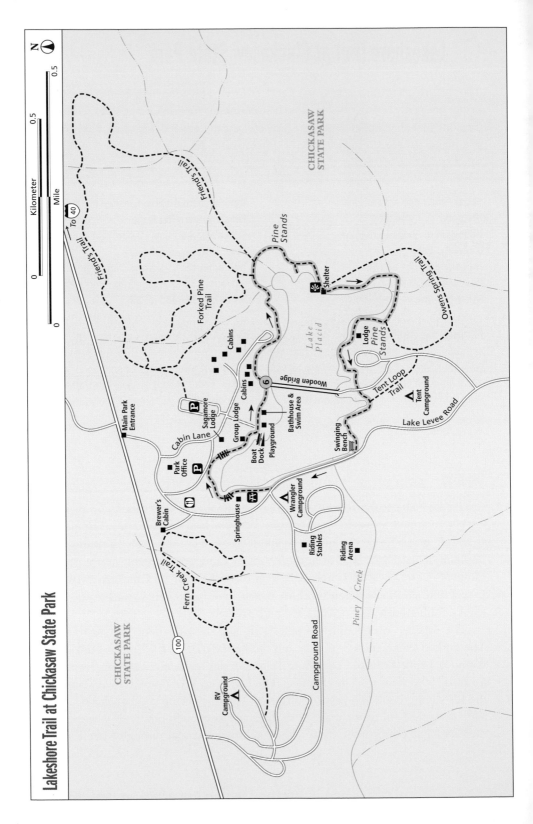

Main Park Entrance

Cabin Lane

Sagamore Lodge

Group Lodge

Cabins

Cabins

Brewer's Cabin

Park Office

Springhouse

Playground

Boat Dock

Bathhouse & Swim Area

Wooden Bridge

Swinging Bench

Wrangler Campground

Tent Campground

Lake Levee Road

Tent Loop Trail

Riding Stables

Riding Arena

Campground Road

RV Campground

Fern Creek Trail

Friend's Trail

Forked Pine Trail

Pine Stands

Lake Placid

Lodge Pine Stands

Shelter

Owens Spring Trail

CHICKASAW STATE PARK

CHICKASAW STATE PARK

Piney / Creek

To 40

100

N

Kilometer

Mile

0

0.5

0.5

0

0.5

View across Lake Placid to the unique wooden footbridge, which is no longer functional but is still picturesque.

Miles and Directions

0.0   Start from the lake edge in front of the wooden bridge, to the left of the swimming area (as you face the water). The trail heads to your left toward the cabins, and then continues over a sandy surface along the lake's edge.

0.3   Arrive at the junction with the 0.7-mile Forked Pine Trail, which heads to the left.

0.4   Arrive at the junction with the 1.5-mile Friend's Trail, which also heads left.

0.5   Reach what appears to be a fork but in fact is a short spur trail to the right that leads to the lakeshore, but affords no view. The trail continues south and then curves west (right).

0.6   Reach a small, well-maintained shelter with a bench where you can enjoy the lake view and take a moment to relax and enjoy the tranquil scene. It's located at the opposite side of the lake from where you began.

0.7   Arrive at the junction of the 0.8-mile Owens Spring Trail almost immediately after the shelter. The trail turns sharply left (south) and continues to follow the narrow southern finger of Lake Placid.

0.8   After curving to the right around the tip of the finger, you reach the Junction of the Tent Loop. (You will meet the other end of this loop before you finish the hike.)

0.9 After passing through another beautiful stand of pine, you reach the junction of the Spur Loop, arriving at the other end of the loop at the lodge in a few hundred feet.

1.0 Arrive at the other end of the bridge, where you began the hike.

1.1 Junction with the other end of the Tent Loop.

1.3 A nice feature just as you reach the road is a wood swing, self-standing, which is somewhat in the open and gets a breeze as you sit and contemplate the lake on your right. The road on your left creates the western boundary of Lake Placid. Now you will have to climb up to the roadway and walk on the shoulder until you pass onto the dirt trail.

1.5 Pass onto the dirt trail to your right and continue following the lake's edge.

1.6 From this point on, you are in "civilization" again, first passing through the picnic area, followed by an interesting feature—the old Springhouse—built around a spring that undoubtedly was an important source of water for local residents at one time. Pass the old Springhouse and continue along the lake's border, with the parking lot to your left.

1.7 Pass the boardwalk, fork to the left around the lodge, and pass by the playground.

1.9 Arrive at the parking lot near the trailhead.

7 Fairview Gullies Loop at Natchez Trace State Park

One of the more interesting (and perhaps shortest) hikes at the Trace is the 1-mile Fairview Gullies Loop (park materials show it as a 3-mile loop), through an area shown in the 1930s photographs at the Park Office Museum as a poster child of the level of degradation that was faced by President Theodore Roosevelt and the New Deal in restoration efforts. The photographs show an area of washed-out, barren soil, riddled with deep gullies of erosion, which could support almost no life at all. The trail now leads over ferns and other undergrowth, through firs and beech trees, and wanders down steep ravines caused by the erosion of the sandy clay hills. The contours, under their green cover, demonstrate just how severely these lands were damaged at one time.

Start: Fairview Gullies Loop Trailhead
Distance: 1.0-mile loop
Hiking time: About 1 hour
Difficulty: Easy
Best season: Autumn
Trail surface: Dirt
Other trail users: Hikers only
Canine compatibility: Leashed dogs permitted

Fees and permits: None
Schedule: Unrestricted (park office hours are Mon–Fri from 8 a.m. to 4:30 p.m.)
Map: USGS quad 21SW, Holladay
Trail contact: Natchez Trace State Park, 24845 Natchez Trace Rd., Wildersville, TN 38388-8329; (731) 968-3742 (use also for camping information)

Finding the trailhead: Enter the park from I-40 from the north (exit 116 South) to Camden Road/Natchez Trace Road (US 114) and immediately look for the trailhead on your left (before you reach the park office). The trailhead is well marked, though you need to be looking for it. There is a small parking lot for hikers' convenience. **GPS:** N35 48.675' / W88 15.345'

The Hike

This park was named for the Natchez Trace, which was a long trail that ran at one time all the way from Natchez, Mississippi, to Nashville, and was the return route for river boatmen. Originally, this trail was known as the Chickasaw Trail of Peace. The park is bisected by a section of the Natchez Trace Parkway, which follows much of the same route as those early traders. Natchez Trace State Park's 7,000 acres, inside 48,000 acres of state forest and wilderness area, is heavily forested, has three major lakes, and is riddled with dirt side roads that lead to small homesteads once staked along the Natchez Trace Road, many with family graveyards from the 1830s to the mid-1900s. The park has mapped the locations of twenty-five of these homestead/graveyards.

The park offers over 50 miles of trails, including a 40-mile backpacking trail, and 13.5 miles of smaller hiking trails along the lakes and streams, ranging from 0.5 mile

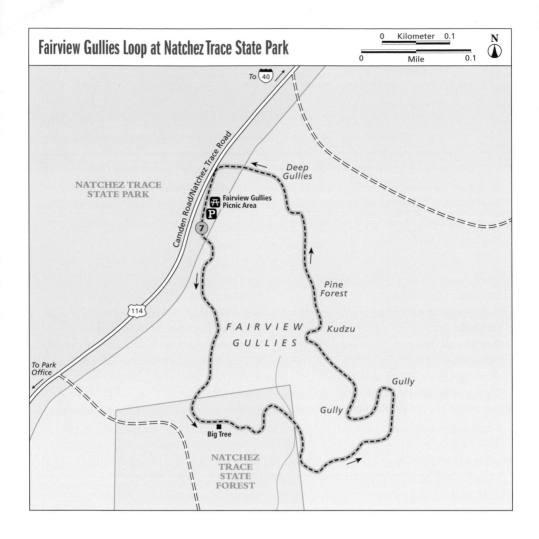

Fairview Gullies Loop at Natchez Trace State Park

to 4.5 miles in length. Cub Creek Trail, a 3.5-mile hike, is a favorite, and is included in "Additional Great Hikes" at the end of this chapter.

This short but interesting loop tells two stories about the history of this section of Tennessee. Not only does it demonstrate the severe erosion caused by early farming practices, it also illustrates what happens when good intentions run awry. To address this erosion, the government brought in Japanese kudzu, a fast-growing and very hardy vine, to provide ground cover and reduce the erosion. However, once it took hold, the kudzu rapidly spread throughout the park and beyond. Much of Natchez Trace Park now looks almost surreal, with trees on either side of the road covered with kudzu.

Areas of this hike are simultaneously beautifully green and oddly eery. You can almost feel the kudzu vines, which are completely covering trees in many places, sucking the life out of the forest, notwithstanding their vibrant greenness and graceful

Hills and gullies gutted by erosion in the early 1900s, and now cloaked in the eerie, fantasy-like vines of Japanese kudzu, an invasive plant originally introduced to help, which carries its own risks.

lines. Kudzu is also known as "Minute Vine," "The Vine that Ate the South," and "Wonder Vine." Kudzu is herbicide resistant and is not killed by fire or mowing. A park flyer on kudzu concludes: "Kudzu was a mistake. Kudzu is probably here to stay."

Kudzu notwithstanding, the Natchez Trace reclamation effort has been called a "triumph" of the New Deal because it has been transformed from one of the most eroded and abused lands of Tennessee to a forested park well utilized by local residents.

Miles and Directions

0.0 Start from the parking lot at the well-marked Fairview Gullies Loop Trailhead, on the main road through the park, known as "the Trace."

0.2 You will pass a big tree and a large gully that indicates the area's sad history.

0.3 Cross the state forest boundary. Over the next quarter mile, the trail becomes a little steeper, and you hike over a series of small gullies.

0.6 Arrive at an open area, covered with kudzu, and you are able to recognize easily its invasive (though pretty) nature. You may have to cut through the kudzu with a stick! You will hike over one of the larger gullies like those you were just observing.

0.8 The heaviest area of kudzu ends, and you can enjoy the pine forest.

0.9 Reach a service road and turn left, and in a few feet you can see the impressive gullies that brought on this kudzu invasion, so sharply eroded that they rise to peaks, now softened by the cover of kudzu.

1.0 Reach the pavement of the Trace, turn left, and walk briefly alongside it until you return to your starting point.

Hike Information

Local Information

Natchez Trace has four lakes for fishing and boating, a swimming beach, and a ball field, firing range, and archery range.

Local Events/Attractions

The park offers **"Race on the Trace"** (a 5-mile run) in January, a Gospel Music Festival in June, and various horseback-riding events throughout the year.

Mills Darden Lane, Lexington, TN. In nearby Lexington, Mills Darden Lane residents are proud that their lane's namesake was Mills Darden, reputedly the fattest man in recorded history, weighing over 1,000 pounds. (Tennessee is full of these interesting and possibly dubious claims to fame.) Thirteen yards of cloth were required to make him a coat, and twenty pall bearers were needed to put him to rest. However, his size was not only lateral. It turns out that he was 7 feet 6 inches tall! Curiously, the man sired at least eleven children with two wives. He was known to eat two dozen eggs, a comparable number of biscuits, and several pounds of bacon for breakfast. One might wonder how a man of such ample stature supported such a large family. Conveniently, he was an innkeeper.

Lodging

RV campsites are available year-round on the lake. Tent camping is comfortably priced and only available Apr 1 through Oct 31. Nice cabins are also available near the RV camping for very reasonable prices.

Restaurants

The **Pin Oak Lodge,** located right in the park, has forty-seven rooms and Southern buffet-style meals that are hearty and affordable.

Organizations

Natchez Trace Parkway Association (natcheztrace.org), a volunteer group operated by donation, has been a friend to the Natchez Trace Parkway for more than eighty years.

8 Combination Trail at Nathan Bedford Forrest State Park

Nathan Bedford Forrest Park contains five trails, totaling approximately 25 miles, varying from the 0.25-mile Polk Creek Nature Trail to the 20-mile Tennessee Forrest Trail, used for overnight camping. The hike described here combines the Polk Creek, Beech Grove, and Tennessee Forrest trails, taking advantage of riverfront views, after a loop through a pretty forest, and ending, after a steep climb, at Kelley's all-time favorite Tennessee museum, the Folklife Museum, at the top of Pilot Knob.

Start: Trailhead behind the main park office on Pilot Knob Road

Distance: 3.6 miles out and back

Hiking time: About 2.5 hours

Difficulty: Moderate

Trail surface: Dirt and pavement

Best season: Year-round

Other trail users: Only hikers on trails, but the trail will cross roads on occasion

Canine compatibility: Leashed dogs permitted

Fees and permits: None

Schedule: Dawn to dusk. Museum open 8:30 a.m. to 4:30 p.m. daily, with an hour break for lunch from 11 a.m. to noon.

Maps: USGS quad 30-SW, Johnsonville; 30-NW, Harmon Creek

Trail contact: Nathan Bedford Forrest State Park, 1825 Pilot Knob Rd., Eva, TN 38333; (731) 584-6356

Finding the trailhead: Take exit 126 on I-40 and travel north on US 641 for 15 miles to Camden. Turn right on US 70 East (do not take the 70 bypass) at the traffic signal. Follow the signs to the park. (You can also take US 70 all the way from Nashville, and look for signs.) Within the park, continue to the Main Park Office on Pilot Knob Road. **GPS:** N36 04.954' / W87 59.116'

The Hike

A sign at the entry of the Folklife Museum declares in neat, blue letters: "Welcome to Pilot Knob and the Tennessee River Folk Life Center." The sign continues: "No one knows who named Pilot Knob. It's been called that for as long as anyone can remember." One is left to ponder that bit of useful information while wandering inside to explore the museum's offerings.

Local personality and color isn't something you pick up only in the museums of Tennessee. The people themselves express the traditions, styles, and personality of the region. The Nathan Bedford Forrest State Park was a pleasant surprise because of the friendliness and accommodation of the people who worked there. The Folklife Museum was closed the day we arrived, but a nice park ranger arranged for the maintenance man to open the museum for a private showing.

The museum has a "Liar's Bench" on the balcony overlooking Kentucky Lake, where recorded storytellers tell tall tales at the push of a button. Old Tennesseans

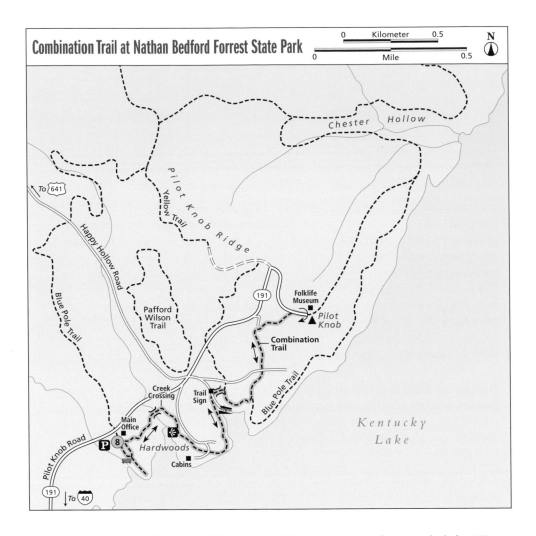

Combination Trail at Nathan Bedford Forrest State Park

Kilometer 0 0.5

Mile 0 0.5

N

Chester Hollow

To 641

Pilot Knob Ridge

Yellow Trail

Happy Hollow Road

Blue Pole Trail

Pafford Wilson Trail

191

Folklife Museum

Pilot Knob

Combination Trail

Blue Pole Trail

Creek Crossing

Trail Sign

Main Office

Kentucky Lake

Pilot Knob Road

P 8

Hardwoods

Cabins

191

To 40

describe their recollections of Tennessee River showboats that traveled the Mississippi River system at the turn of the century, entertaining locals who had precious little else to break up their routines. The enthusiasm in the cracking voices is unmistakable as they list out the names of the most memorable: the Orange Blossom, the Serendipity, the Fancy New Sensation. Another feature is the worn, wooden mussel boat named *Betsy*. This water-going equivalent to the "House That Jack Built" was originally equipped with modified farm equipment. Eventually, one of its creators lived on the boat, with a Coleman stove, army cot—"the works," according to the plaque at *Betsy*'s side, which explains more fully: "*Betsy* may not have had a refrigerator or air conditioner, but now *Betsy* really was his dream boat."

The museum also explains the mission of the Tennessee Valley Authority and the damming of the Tennessee River to create Kentucky Lake, which spreads below the museum. And of course, perhaps most importantly, it introduces visitors to the park's colorful namesake, General Nathan Bedford Forrest, and the story of his conquest of a naval munitions station in the Civil War.

WHO WAS NATHAN BEDFORD FORREST?

One thing to remember in West and Middle Tennessee is that local heroes are as likely to be those who fought for the severing of the Union as those who fell in with President Abraham Lincoln's ranks, such as Lincoln's successor Andrew Johnson, who is honored in his hometown of Greeneville in northeast Tennessee, and is the namesake for Johnsonville State Historic Park, across the river. Nathan Bedford Forrest was easily the most colorful of the Confederate generals. Despised and viewed as unbeatable by his Union foes, Forrest was able to take a band of rattle-tag Tennessee farm boys and turn them into the strategic force he used to make Civil War–style surgical strikes on the Union forces.

Pilot Knob overlooks the site of an ambush by General Forrest of a Union naval supply depot located across the river. In a carefully strategized plan that covered several weeks, with forces that never numbered over 3,000 (but were estimated at 12,000 to 20,000 by the Yankees at times), he managed to overcome and destroy a supply depot with more than $6.7 million in supplies, and to debilitate four gunboats, fourteen steamboats, and seventeen barges and capture 150 prisoners. His losses for this victory were two killed, nine wounded, and two guns lost. The battle is known as the only one in history in which a cavalry unit took a naval installation.

One of Forrest's greatest victories occurred at Brice's Crossroads when his 2,500 troops defeated 8,000 Union troops. He inflicted hundreds of casualties on the enemy, captured a large supply train, and took 1,618 prisoners. Forrest's name had achieved such notoriety that one of his lieutenants got the Union garrison at Union City to surrender in 1864 by signing Forrest's name to the surrender request and parading around fake cannons in front of the fort (a favorite Forrest trick).

The plaque at Pilot Knob concludes with a statement about Forrest's notoriety: "The battle was, however, entirely typical of Nathan Bedford Forrest, whose generalship led General Sherman to say 'That devil Forrest must be hunted down if it costs 10,000 lives and bankrupts the Federal Treasury!'" In April of 1865 Forrest's command was the last large force to surrender east of the Mississippi River.

View from the top of Pilot's Knob, behind the Folklife Museum. It was from here that General N. B. Forrest and his ragtag army surveyed and held the river valley for the Confederates.

Miles and Directions

0.0 Start behind the park office, at 1825 Pilot Knob Rd., with a small loop trail called the Polk Creek Trail.

0.1 Arrive at a bench, in a pretty forest, and continue to the lakefront.

0.2 Enjoy the view at the lakefront, and return on the short loop trail to the back of the park office.

0.3 Start at the trailhead sign (this is the Beech Grove Trail) and head into the woods to your right as you leave the Polk Creek Loop. You will see some white blazes in this section of the trail.

0.5 Cross a creek on a small bridge and continue through the woods.

0.6 You will catch a view of the water on the left as you walk through a hardwood forest.

0.7 Reach a paved road, and see lakefront cabins in front of you and to your right. Cross the road and find a park sign trail marker to show you where to reenter the woods.

1.1 After following the lakefront and taking in some open views, reach a cul-de-sac with a boat ramp, and continue up the road briefly to see a trail marker on the right, and reenter the woods. You are now on the 20-mile trail briefly.

1.2 Arrive at a junction, with a trail going off to the left. Head right to stay on the connector trail which closes a loop on the 20-mile trail.

1.3 Cross a road and arrive at the junction for the Blue Pole Trail. Follow it steeply uphill.

1.4 Cross another road and continue a steep climb on the Blue Pole Road.

1.6 Reach the upper road, turn right at the sign, and continue a steep climb.

1.8 You have reached the Folklife Museum. From here you can retrace your steps back to the park office. (For a slightly shorter return you can follow Pilot Knob Road 1.2 miles back to your car.)

3.6 Arrive back at the park office.

Option: The Yellow Trail (described in "Additional Great Hikes") connects with the Combination Trail behind the Folklife Museum. If you want to continue into a bit more solitude, this is a beautiful little trail that's easy to follow and will loop you back to the museum. It also connects to the Five-Mile Trail and the 20-Mile Trail.

Hike Information

Local Events/Attractions

Tennessee Folklife Festival, held every Sept.

Lodging

Park has campgrounds, improved and primitive, comfortably priced. Rustic cabins overlooking Kentucky Lake are also available for rent.

9 Johnsonville Redoubts Trail at Johnsonville State Historic Park

This 1.9-mile loop trail is an ideal place to get a feeling for the Union resistance to confederate insurgents during the Civil War. Johnsonville was the scene of a fairly embarrassing defeat for the Union Army, which is detailed across the river at the Nathan Bedford Forrest State Park. Here is where a superior Union army, guarding a supply depot along the Kentucky River, ended up being trounced by a small, poorly equipped Confederate force commanded by the brilliant general Nathan Bedford Forrest. Capitalizing on some design errors in the redoubts you will be passing, Forrest's men were able to take by surprise and completely overwhelm the Union forces at two redoubts, one at the top of the mountain and one near the bottom.

Start: Trailhead by the entry gate
Distance: 1.9-mile loop
Hiking time: About 1.5 hours
Difficulty: Easy
Trail surface: Dirt
Best season: Winter, to avoid ticks
Other trail users: Hikers only

Canine compatibility: Leashed dogs permitted
Fees and permits: None
Schedule: Dawn to dusk
Map: USGS quad 30SW Johnsonville
Trail contact: Johnsonville State Historic Park, 90 Nell Beard Rd., New Johnsonville, TN 37134; (931) 535-2789

Finding the trailhead: If heading east from Memphis on I-40, turn off onto US 70 at Jackson, and follow it to New Johnsonville, just after the bridge over Kentucky Lake. Make the first exit at the sign for the historic park, and follow the signs to the entrance. Park at the entrance gate along a snow fence with a cannon. The trailhead is on the left side as you drive in, starting at the entry gate. **GPS:** N36 03.623' / W87 57.667'

The Hike

Johnsonville State Historic Park, with 1,500 acres and 10 miles of hiking trails, is located directly across the Kentucky River from Pilot Knob in New Johnsonville. Johnsonville was the site of the supply depot that was destroyed by General Nathan Bedford Forrest's confederate soldiers in 1864, and has had an extensive history and significance to the region. The original town was flooded in the creation of Kentucky Lake and remains underwater today. What remains of the town is contained in the state park, with a view of the river, some original foundations, a museum, commemorative plaques, and earthworks that soldiers used for protection in defending the supply depot.

The road into the park makes an exceptional drive in fall, with the dark tree trunks and bright leaves contrasting against the grass-covered hillsides. A narrow road

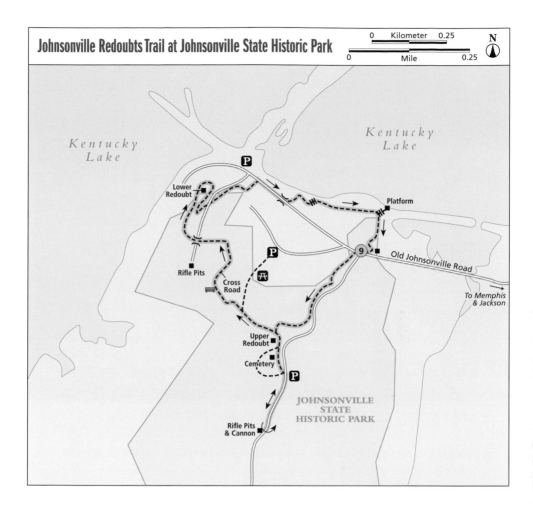

winds into the low area next to the river and then up the hill to a small overlook. There you will find some gravesites and redoubts. No view exists here like the one from Pilot Knob across the river, but the location is more peaceful. It appears that this park facility has not received the same public investment as its cousin park across the water. Nevertheless, this park has more of an authentic feeling of history and a quieter and less commercial setting than its sister park, and for those interested in Civil War lore, the Johnsonville Redoubts Trail provides an interesting glance into the past, and a wide variety of flora and fauna.

The Johnsonville Redoubt Trail passes two "redoubts" used to defend the city, along with other historic sites. (A redoubt is no more and no less than an earthen mound used to shield soldiers in battle.) The trail begins on the left side of the main entrance and heads uphill through forest to the hilltop and the first redoubt, which is at the side of the small but interesting Crockett Cemetery, with some rifle pits and cannon along the road at the summit. You then begin to return the way you came,

Snow fence and cannon at the entrance to Johnsonville State Historic Park.

and veer left to hike directly to the lower redoubt, which now has little view because the area's trees have matured much since those days more than a century ago when this lower redoubt was intended to keep watch on the goings-on below at the river depot.

The small town of Johnsonville was named for Tennessean Andrew Johnson, who was elected governor of the territory in 1862 and went on to become president when Lincoln was assassinated. It was a major supply depot after the Union completed the railroad to this location during the Civil War. After it was destroyed by General Forrest, it revived again and became a major supply depot for forty years, until major flooding of the river caused more problems. In 1945 the area was bought for Kentucky Lake, and the town ceased to exist, with much of its remains now underwater. The residents were moved to nearby New Johnsonville.

A plaque at the top of the hill, dedicated to the memory of Johnsonville, reflects its diminished status over time: "Today, only a few pieces of concrete, the railroad bed and a few leveled building sites remain to remind the visitors that for a hundred years Johnsonville was home for many families."

Miles and Directions

0.0 Start at the sign to the right at the entry gate. Cross the road, and the trail goes uphill to the left side as you drive in.

0.3 After a gradual and steady climb, with some descending also, you will arrive at the Upper Redoubt and Crockett Cemetery.

0.4 An interesting plaque tells something of the story of Old Johnsonville.

0.5 A small overlook provides a view of the valley below.

0.6 Examine rifle pits and cannons of Civil War vintage at the top of the hill, which is now forested but at one time gave a comprehensive view of the valley below. Retrace your steps past the cemetery and upper redoubt to double-back for 0.2 mile until you descend to the Lower Redoubt.

0.8 Turn to the left from the trail you ascended on to continue straight down an old roadbed toward the Lower Redoubt.

1.0 Pass a bench and cross a road.

1.1 Cross a bridge and continue to descend gradually to the redoubt.

1.2 Reach the Lower Redoubt clearing, and explore the enclosure. The Lower Redoubt is an interesting structure and is much easier to recognize than the Upper Redoubt, which has been overtaken by forest in the intervening years (rather than by the "Forrest" of military fame).

1.4 After leaving the lower redoubt, you will go downhill to the paved park road.

1.6 Arrive at and cross the road, and then cross the meadow and a small stream to steps on the far side, next to the river.

1.7 Ascend steps and reenter woods to follow the shoreline toward the entrance gate.

1.8 Arrive at wooden platform at river's edge before turning right to mount steps.

1.9 Complete the hike at the gate at the opposite side of the road from the trailhead. Some interesting plaques near the trailhead explain the history of this place and give this small park its charm, at least for Civil War buffs!

Employees of Homeplace 1850 actually weave, tend cattle, farm, knit and sew, and basically live just as settlers did over a century ago, while visitors wander through this "living museum," a remarkable step back in time.

camping and/or hiking facilities. The Tennessee side of the recreation area contains over 200 miles of hiking trails, 40 miles of bike trails, 30 miles of horse trails, a special area set aside for off-road vehicles, camping facilities, a 200-acre buffalo range (with American bison actually grazing their ponderous way across it), and a nineteenth-century living-history museum called Homeplace 1850.

Land Between the Lakes provides plenty of opportunity to get away for hours and not see another soul. Because of its isolation and lack of development, it is an ideal spot for researching characteristics of managed and unmanaged forest communities. University scientists and students at LBL research biotic inventories, community structure, and rare and endangered species. LBL is a fertile area for research because of its tremendous biological diversity. Seventy-one species of amphibians and reptiles have been found at LBL, including twenty-four varieties of snakes and eleven varieties of frogs. Similarly, over 1,000 species of flowering plants can be found here, and LBL hosts more than 250 species of birds. The biological diversity in LBL is due to the great range of habitats, from floodplains to dry ridgetops.

WALKING BACK IN TIME: HOMEPLACE 1850

Homeplace 1850, located within Land Between the Lakes, gives a fascinating glimpse into life in the mid-1800s. The 20-acre compound contains homes and several work barns, including a carpentry shop and tobacco barn, all complete with period tools, dishes, looms, furnishings, stoves, and other elements of everyday life in the years prior to the War Between the States.

It is the people that make the Homeplace so fascinating. Wearing accurate reproductions of clothes from the era, "residents" arrive each day to carry out the responsibilities of a working farm in 1850. Here you may find a long-skirted grandmotherly woman with a dirty apron cooking biscuits, stoking the wood-burning stove, warming soup on the warming shelf, and cutting vegetables in her daily routine of feeding an extended "family" of thirteen or so. In another room a young woman is busy at a loom, weaving cloth from yarn spun from the sheep at the Homeplace. She proudly displays an intricate coverlet that she completed last year, among other duties.

Outside one of the barns, a young man explains how his two oxen, Clay and Calhoun, have been yoked together for most of their lives, always with Clay on the left. A creature of habit, an ox is unable to pull anymore if there is a change in placement. In the carpentry barn a tall, professorial man with old-fashioned round glasses displays his tools and describes how they built their homestead with wood they split into boards, using tools available in 1850 wherever possible. He has "lived" at the Homestead for ten years and was with another living-history museum for years before that. Essentially, this man has lived in a version of the 1800s most of his life, and his knowledge of the times is testimony to that. In a way that is distinct from traditional museums, the Homeplace gives a sense of shifting reality, almost as if you had actually stepped back in time.

Miles and Directions

0.0   Start from the trailhead across the street from the South Welcome Center.

0.1   You will begin with a view of a meadow, after which the trail begins a gradual ascent, continuing to climb until it begins to descend at 0.4 mile.

0.5   Begin to climb again, and pass through a pretty stand of tall, straight trees.

0.7   Reach the crest of a small hill, and continue over undulating landscape for the next mile, seeing some red blazes during a level section.

1.7   Reach Marker 13 and turn right to stay on the trail, though it appears that another trail continues almost straight ahead. Again you will be descending.

1.9 Reach a gravel section and the trail levels off again.

2.0 Arrive at a small spring and cross a small creek. Shortly after, you will pass Marker 12, which will reassure you that you are on the right trail.

2.1 Follow the edge of a pretty meadow, most likely in cultivation (like most of the meadows within LBL).

2.3 Leave the meadow and begin following a creek in the woods.

2.4 Cross a dry creek bed, arrive at another meadow, and follow the edge of it.

2.6 Leave the meadow and make a sharp left, and you will shortly be going in and out of a dry creek bed.

3.0 Reach another meadow, obviously used for cultivation, then continue and follow the right side of the meadow, basically in a straight line.

3.2 Return to the woods and continue.

3.6 Make a sharp right at Marker 10. Continue on the trail.

4.1 Arrive at Marker 2, with a yellow post. Turn right onto Fort Henry Road to return to the trailhead. You may feel the urge to go on, however. If you do, the North–South Trail begins at this location and continues north for 65 miles into Kentucky, ending at the Golden Pond Visitor Center.

4.3 Turn right again at the Trace.

6.5 Arrive back at the South Welcome Center.

Hike Information

Local Events/Attractions

Special events held at LBL include craft festivals and other events, and planetarium and moonshine displays at the **Golden Pond Visitor Center,** about 15 miles north of the Kentucky-Tennessee line.

The **Woodland Nature Station** on the Kentucky side of the Trace features live plant and animal exhibits, video presentations, and special programs.

Homeplace 1850 can be found near the Tennessee-Kentucky border 13.7 miles from US 79 on the Trace. It is open daily from 10 a.m. to 5 p.m. from Apr through Oct, and in Mar and Nov only Wed through Sun. Homeplace is closed from Dec through Feb. A small admission fee is charged.

Lodging

Piney Campground is at the south end of LBL, and camping (and campfires) are generally permitted within the LBL trail system.

Additional Great Hikes

A   Cub Creek Trail at Natchez Trace State Park

Cub Creek Lake makes a pleasant stop within the Trace. Picnic and camping areas line the lake, and some trails combine to follow most of its perimeter. A picturesque footbridge crosses a narrow end of the lake, from Camping Area #1 to the boat dock, and provides a serene view across the middle of the lake, which is beautiful when the water reflects the autumn colors. In the fall you can enjoy not only the beautiful variations in color, but also the smells of fall and the sound of the leaves underfoot.

The lakefront 3.5-mile Cub Creek Trail is not as heavily utilized as one might think, and it affords many moments of quiet solitude. The trail follows the lakefront, intersects with the Deer Trail, a 4-mile trail leading through the center of the undeveloped area of the Trace, and ends at the cabins on the southeast side of the lake, perhaps 2 miles from Camping Area #1 by road. A shuttle here may avoid traveling the park's campground roads or retracing your steps to the trailhead.

Finding the trailhead: Take I-40 southwest of Nashville for 100 miles, or take I-40 for 35 miles east of Jackson, and turn south on Natchez Trace Road. Pass the park office and the Check-In Station, both on the right. Bear left at the next intersection, and turn left again at the park office and grocery, at a three-road intersection. Make the first left, pass Camping Area #1, and park at the lodge, at the end of the road. (You can also park at Camping Area #1, and cross the footbridge past the docks and up the hill to the lodge.) The trailheads for the 1.0-mile Fern Trail and the Cub Creek Trail are on the north side of the parking lot. **GPS:** N35 46.938' / W88 15.059'

B   Yellow Trail at Nathan Bedford Forrest State Park

The Yellow Trail first follows the Pilot Knob Ridge along the Kentucky Lake for less than a mile, then heads down a steep ravine, into a hollow (or "holler") to 320 feet in elevation, and meanders through the woods along the hollow for a good distance, where it forks. You can fork right and continue on the Orange, Red, or Blue Trail, each of which follows along the other side of the hollow, or turn left and climb back up the backside of the ridge. Along this trail you will see many species of mosses, ferns, shrubs and wildflowers in season. Mountain laurel can be found on the higher ridges. You eventually will come out on a dirt road above the home of one of the rangers. This road crosses the top of the ridge to return to the paved road. The last quarter mile or so of the hike is along the paved road back to the museum parking lot. This road-walking sounds worse than it is, because the road itself is narrow, lined with trees (which in autumn means filled with color), and is not heavily traveled.

Finding the trailhead: Take exit 126 on I-40 and travel north on US 641 for 15 miles to Camden. Turn right on US 70 East (do not take the 70 bypass) at the traffic signal. Follow the signs to the park. Within the park, continue to the Folklife Museum on Pilot Knob Road. **GPS:** N36 04.954' / W87 59.116'

C   North–South Trail at Land Between the Lakes

This long, relatively level hiking trail of 65 miles passes right through the center of LBL, in a north–south direction (not surprising, given its name). It starts at the South Welcome Station on the Trace (TN 453) and runs northward over the Kentucky-Tennessee line, continuing along the shore of Kentucky Lake to the North Welcome Station. Along the way the trail passes streams and small ponds and approximately eleven small cemeteries of settler/squatter families who lived in this area for generations.

From the South Welcome Station, the trail runs north and then west, parallel to Blue Springs/Fort Henry Road until it meets the Fort Henry Trails connector. It then turns north (or right), and the Fort Henry Trails connector bears off to the left. The trail continues north, passing by Morgan Cemetery just before crossing marker #8 at a gravel road and coming to a shelter shortly thereafter. The trail soon curves right (Fugua Cemetery is on the left), then back to the left to cross another road just south of the Lookout Tower. The trail continues almost due north and crosses Ginger Creek Road, then winds left and right and begins to curve east toward the Trace. It crosses the Trace at marker #7, approximately 1 mile north of the Buffalo Range and Homeplace 1850, and then follows the backside of the Cedar Pond picnic area, where there is another shelter, just before the southern segment of the North–South Trail ends at the Kentucky line. The short segment of the trail east of the Trace might be confusing due to some spur trails. If you end up crossing over the road along Laura Furnace Creek, then you have gone approximately 1 mile past the Kentucky state line.

Finding the trailhead: From Nashville take I-24 north and exit to Clarksville. Take US 79 west to Dover, and continue past Dover for 5 miles to the park entrance on the right, at the turn onto the Trace. Park at the South Welcome Station or the picnic area. **GPS:** N86 31.253' / W87 57.440'

Nashville and Middle Tennessee

Middle Tennessee," as one of Tennessee's three Grand Divisions, extends from the Tennessee River to the west to the north–south dividing line between the central and eastern time zones. The Division contains 41 percent of the state's area and 36 percent of the state's population, making it the lowest-density division of the state. However, for the purposes of this book, Middle Tennessee comprises the area from the Tennessee River to the Cumberland Plateau (which has been divided between the North and South Cumberland). Geographically, this area is characterized by rolling hills, with higher terrain in all directions. The lower area is known as the Central Basin, with Nashville in its northwest corner. Within the center of the basin is the remnants of a formation called the Nashville Dome, which is an area of uplifted strata. The Central Basin runs 45 to 60 miles east of Nashville and 80 miles to the south, nearly to the Tennessee-Alabama state line. Surrounding it is an escarpment of higher elevation, known as the Highland Rim, which ranges in elevation from below 1,100 feet to 1,400 feet above sea level, except where broken by outlying ridges of the Cumberland Plateau. The area mostly contains ridges, valleys, and low hills. East of Nashville, within the eastern portion of the basin, are the "cedar glades," also known as "limestone glades," which contain plant life that is completely unique to this region—they're found nowhere else on the planet. These glades are created where soil has washed away from open areas of limestone rock, leaving unique environments for plant growth.

Nashville, the capital of Tennessee, dominates Middle Tennessee. Nashville is also known as Music City because it has grown into a major center for the country music industry. As a prize shipping and transportation crossroads, Nashville, after the Battle of Nashville, fell to Union troops in the Civil War and stayed occupied throughout, thus avoiding the bloody conflicts that occurred elsewhere.

The hilly country that characterizes Middle Tennessee affords many hiking opportunities, even within Nashville itself and its immediate environs. Lovely hikes can be found along lakes, through Cedar Glades, and near historic Indian Mounds built more than an 1,000 years ago by the area's early residents, the Woodland mound builders, which were succeeded by the Mississippian mound builders.

11 Eagle Point Overnight Trail at Mousetail Landing State Park

This 6.7–mile lollipop loop trail has two nice shelters along the way, is well marked with blue blazes, and is a great trail to break in new overnight hikers. Sections of the trail are mossy and soft underfoot, and the view from Shelter #2 is amazing and worth the wait.

Start: Next to the playground near the Ranger's Station
Distance: 6.7-mile lollipop loop
Hiking time: About 5.5 hours
Difficulty: Moderate
Trail surface: Dirt with rocks and roots, and sections of soft moss
Best seasons: Spring or fall
Other trail users: Hikers and backpackers only

Canine compatibility: Leashed dogs permitted
Fees and permits: None
Schedule: 7 a.m. to 10 p.m. daily (Overnight hikers should register with the park office.)
Map: USGS quad Jeannette
Trail contact: Mousetail Landing State Park, 3 Campground Rd., Linden, TN 37096; (731) 847-0841

Finding the trailhead: From Memphis take I-40 to exit 126, turn south on TN 69, go 14 miles to Parsons, then head east on TN 412 for 6 miles and cross the Tennessee River. Turn left onto TN 438, and find the park entrance on the left in 2.5 miles.

From Nashville, take I-40 West to exit 143. Take a left onto TN 13 south, and go 19 miles to Linden. Turn right onto TN 412, go 12 miles and turn right onto TN 438, then follow it 2.5 miles to the park entrance. Once at the park entrance, follow the road to the first left, and then to the crossroads with the Ranger Station. **GPS:** N35 39.393' / W88 00.315'

The Hike

Mousetail Landing State Park is located on the eastern banks of the Tennessee River. Its 1,247 acres contain a profusion of animal life, and it is a favorite spot for birders. Mousetail Landing received its name during the 1800s when one of the area's tanning companies caught fire. There were so many mice fleeing the burning tannery that the area was named Rattail Landing. Later, when a new tannery was built, it was known as Mousetail Landing because of its smaller size. The park has a 3-mile trail and the Eagle Point Overnight Trail, which is sometimes hiked as a large loop, finishing around the lakefront, in 8 miles. (The hike featured here is a lollipop loop trail that is more easily identified.)

Miles and Directions

0.0 Start from the trailhead near the playground and park office. Trail is well marked with blue blazes. The trail heads north with some mild inclines and declines, until you reach the start of the lollipop.

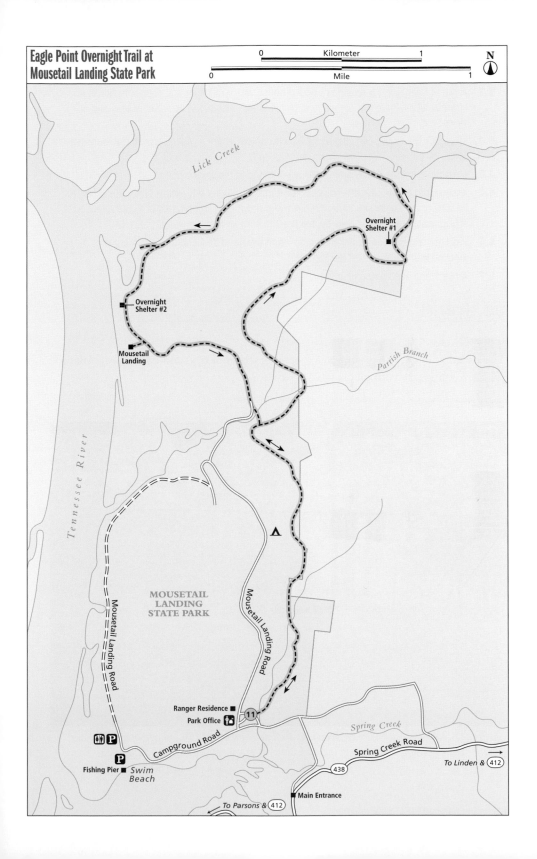

Eagle Point Overnight Trail at Mousetail Landing State Park

0   Kilometer   1

0   Mile   1

N

Lick Creek

Overnight Shelter #1

Overnight Shelter #2

Mousetail Landing

Parrish Branch

Tennessee River

MOUSETAIL LANDING STATE PARK

Mousetail Landing Road

Mousetail Landing Road

11

Ranger Residence

Park Office

Campground Road

Fishing Pier

Swim Beach

Spring Creek

Spring Creek Road

To Linden & 412

438

Main Entrance

To Parsons & 412

1.3 Meet the start of the lollipop loop. A sign indicates Shelter #2 to the left. Head right toward Shelter #1.

2.7 Arrive at Shelter #1, a screened wooden house with a dirt floor and eight wire bunks and stove facilities. There is a fire ring and picnic table outside, but no water access and no views.

3.4 Meet Lick Creek and continue along the shore west where it widens toward the Tennessee River.

4.2 Meet the Tennessee River and continue south along the shore.

4.6 Ascend into Shelter #2. It is basically the same as Shelter #1, except that it has a beautiful view of the Tennessee River and has water down the hill a bit. This is a great place to stay, to watch the barges pass by and see the sun set over the water.

5.4 Pass the original Mousetail Landing, and turn inland to descend and again arrive at the junction with the stem trail leading back.

6.7 Arrive at trailhead and park office.

Hike Information

Lodging

The park has twenty-five campsites (twenty with hookups) and twenty-one lakeside primitive campsites with picnic tables.

Shelter #2 along the Eagle Point Overnight Trail appears magical in late afternoon light and provides beautiful sunset views over the river. Photo courtesy of Darrial Marshall

12 Overnight Trail at Montgomery Bell State Park

This pleasant overnight trail takes you around the circumference of the park and past or near most of its highlights, such as the Ore Pit Loop, Lake Woodhaven, and Lake Acorn.

Start: Trailhead at the warehouse parking area
Distance: 10.5-mile loop
Hiking time: 4 to 5 hours
Difficulty: Moderate
Trail surface: Dirt, gravel
Best season: Any time of year
Other trail users: Hikers and runners only
Canine compatibility: Leashed dogs permitted (please clean up after dog)

Fees and permits: No fees; permit required from park office for overnight stay
Schedule: Dawn to dusk year-round
Map: USGS quad 48SE, Burns
Trail contact: Montgomery Bell Park Office, 1020 Jackson Hill Rd., Burns, TN 37029; (615) 797-9052

Finding the trailhead: From Nashville or Memphis take I-40 to exit 182 (Fairview/Dickson TN 96 exit). Turn left (west) onto TN 96. Stay on TN 96 until it dead-ends at US 70. Turn right (east) on US 70, off-ramp provided. Stay on US 70 approximately 3 miles. Park entrance is on the right. From the park office near the US 70 main entrance, the road forks. Take the right fork (go straight) toward the campground. Pass the campground entrance on the right and cross the bridge. Take the left fork past the ranger's residence and turn left to the warehouse parking area at the trailhead.
GPS: N36 05.525' / W087 17.110'

The Hike

Montgomery Bell State Park covers 3,782 acres in Dickson County. The park honors Montgomery Bell, who began a business with a furnace to process iron ore and went on to build a small empire within the county. The park is situated on top of old ore pits and even contains the remains of the Old Laurel Furnace, vintage 1815. Both the ore pits and the furnace are located along the Montgomery Bell Overnight Trail.

The park has 19 miles of trail in eight trails, six of them a mile or less long. The longest one is the Montgomery Bell Overnight Trail, which winds around the periphery of the park, passing along two of the park's three lakes and accessing three overnight shelters along the way. The park also has ninety-four campsites and rents cabins individually. Group Camp One has forty-seven rustic cabins, which can sleep 120 people. Also available are an inn and restaurant, an eighteen-hole golf course, and a swimming beach on Acorn Lake. Fishing is permitted on all three lakes, and Acorn Lake has paddleboats, canoes, kayaks, and johnboats for rent. Only Lake Woodhaven allows private boats.

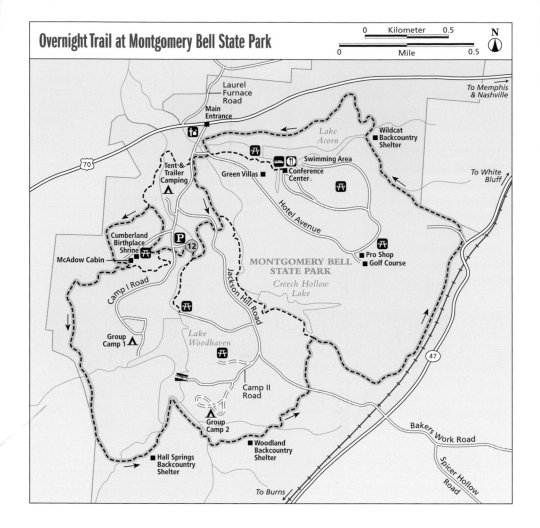

Overnight Trail at Montgomery Bell State Park

Miles and Directions

0.0 Start from the warehouse parking area.

0.1 Cross the road to Group Camp 1 and continue down to a small stream. The remains of Laurel Furnace, which was built in 1815 to produce iron, are about 50 yards downstream from this point. Follow the Ore Pit Trail uphill from here.

0.6 Arrive at a small rest shelter.

0.9 After the pit area the trail makes an abrupt turn to the left and heads south, continuing downhill.

1.2 Pass a log house replica of the home of Samuel McAdow, one of the founders of the Cumberland Presbyterian Church. After passing the cabin, cross the creek and reenter the woods, following an old roadbed west and crossing the stream three times.

1.9 After heading uphill, cross a fire access road next to another small rest shelter, and continue on an old roadbed.

Geese and kids become swim partners at the swimming area on Lake Acorn.

2.6 Pass by the entrance of Hall Cemetery, and continue across the cemetery entrance and back into woods. Continue to follow the MB Trail and old roadbed, turning left shortly after the cemetery.

2.9 Pass in front of and to the left of the Hall Springs Backcountry Shelter (Campsite 1), which contains a platform for camping. (Water should be treated here before consumption.)

3.1 Pass an old wooden bridge overlook (bridge to nowhere), and continue along the stream past multiple beaver dams, where you can observe a beaver if you move quietly.

3.3 Arrive at Lake Woodhaven and follow the lakeshore right for a short distance, enjoying the nice view.

3.4 The trail turns sharply to the right and crosses several bridges, passing through hardwood and pines forests.

4.3 Junction with a spur trail on the right, which leads in 0.3 mile to the Woodland Shelter (Campsite 2, 4.6 miles from the trailhead), which also has a camping platform and a spring about 50 yards down the path in front of the shelter.

4.6 After passing the spur trail, continue on the main trail through open upland forest, and cross a paved road.

5.0 Descend to the upper end of Creech Hollow Lake and the junction with the Creech Hollow Trail. Bear right to continue on the Overnight Trail.

5.6 The trail intersects with a dirt road, where you will turn left and follow the dirt road about a mile or so.

6.6 Intersect with the rear entrance to the park, and turn left to follow the gravel road about 50 yards to a sign, turning right to reenter the forest.

7.7 Arrive at Wildcat Shelter (Campsite 3), a camping shelter with a camping platform, after following the park boundary for some distance and descending to follow a small stream. (Lake Acorn is only a short distance away, making this a good site for fishing.)

7.8 Cross a stream, after following it east from the shelter, and ascend a hill.

8.1 At the crest of the hill, bear left and merge into what remains of the old Nashville-Dickson Highway. This road leads downhill to the old park office, about 1 mile away.

9.2 Head in front of the old office and cross the bridge. Then follow the paved road for a short distance until you find the trail again as it enters the woods on the other side of the street. Enter the woods and follow this section of trail across a small creek.

9.4 Reach junction where turning right exits the trail, and turn left to continue on the Overnight Trail.

9.6 Pass another sandstone pit, which has a nice stand of pine trees growing in it, and at the other side of the pit, ascend wooden steps to pass through a mixed forest.

9.9 Meet the junction with the Creech Hollow Trail and turn right to come to a paved road and reenter the trail on the other side. You will ascend and descend a couple of hills.

10.5 Arrive at the junction with the Spillway Trail on the left and a bridge on the right. Cross the bridge and follow the trail out to the front of a park building to complete the hike.

Hike description was prepared in collaboration with Eric Runkle, park ranger at Montgomery Bell State Park.

13 Ganier Ridge–Lake Trail Combination at Radnor Lake State Park

This hike combines the Access, Ganier Ridge, and Lake Trails to create a 2.7-mile loop. The Ganier Ridge Trail has a number of wood- and stone-stepped sections and a more challenging ridgetop climb, combined with the more tranquil lakefront hike on the Lake Trail, with benches on which to sit and take it all in along the way. Though the trail does not afford views, except in the winter, it is a pleasant, serene walk that is popular with joggers because of the steep inclines, steps, and the well-worn trail.

Start: Trailhead at the East Parking Lot off Otter Creek Road
Distance: 2.7-mile lollipop
Hiking time: About 1.5 hours
Difficulty: Moderate
Trail surface: Dirt and rock
Best season: Year-round
Other trail users: Joggers and hikers only. (**Note:** Supposedly jogging is prohibited, but you are almost certain to encounter some.)
Canine compatibility: Dogs permitted on leash in the park, but prohibited on trails
Fees and permits: None

Schedule: Daily 6 a.m. to dusk. Visitor center open daily 8:30 a.m. to 4 p.m., closed for lunch noon to 1 p.m.
Map: USGS quad: Oak Hill
Trail contact: Radnor Lake State Park, 1160 Otter Creek Rd., Nashville, TN 37220; (615) 373-3467
Optional: If you prefer, after completing the Ganier Ridge Trail portion of the loop, when your trail joins the Lake Trail, you can turn right instead of left to continue to follow the Lake Trail to the northwest until you reach the Spillway and the Nature Center in 0.8 mile.

Finding the trailhead: From Nashville take I-65 south to exit 78A (Harding Place) and head west on Harding Place/TN 255 to US 31/TN 6/Franklin Pike. Turn left (south) and continue for 1.4 miles to Otter Creek Road. Turn right onto Otter Creek Road and continue approximately 1.3 miles to the East Parking Lot. The hike starts at the trailhead for the Access Trail at the East Parking Lot off Otter Creek Road, on the east side of Radnor Lake (the opposite side from the Spillway and Nature Center). **GPS:** N36 03.509' / W86 47.555'

The Hike

Radnor Lake State Park provides a unique and convenient opportunity to get away within the Nashville metropolitan area. Its trails are full of wildlife, including a wide variety of bird species, making it popular for bird watching. Its 1,332 acres have been declared a Class II Natural Area, entitled to special protections. Though it has only 6 miles of trails, they are well designed to give hikers the natural experience they seek. Deer come very close to the trail on the Ganier Ridge Trail, and the new Barbara J. Mapp Aviary Center, opened in May 2015, houses birds of prey, both flighted and

Ganier Ridge–Lake Trail Combination at Radnor Lake State Park

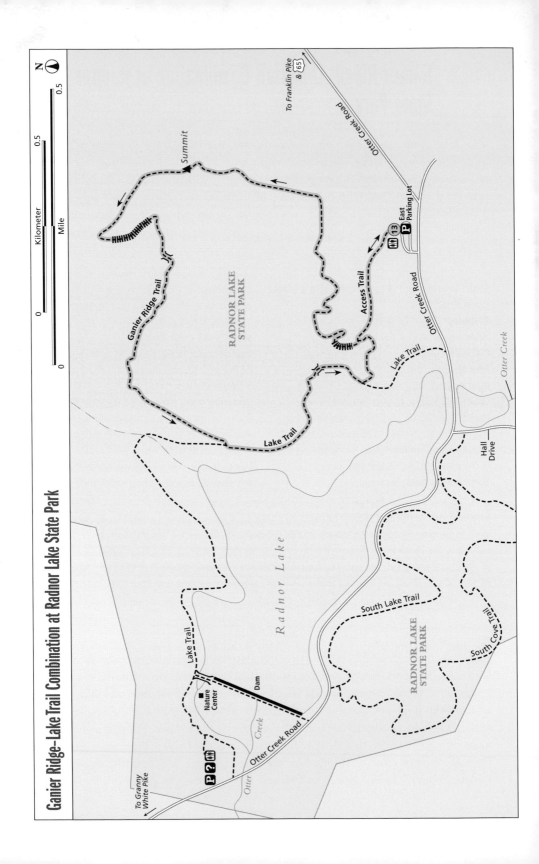

The Ganier Ridge Trail at Radnor Lake State Park offers solitude literally in the middle of the Nashville metro area.

unflighted, and gives visitors comfortable access for bird watching along its board-walks, on Wednesdays and Saturdays. Access is restricted so as not to overstress the birds, so call to confirm the schedule before you come.

Miles and Directions

0.0 Start from the East Parking Lot on Otter Creek Road, past the southeast corner of Radnor Lake. Begin walking on the Access Trail.

0.2 Reach the junction with the Ganier Ridge Trail, and head to the right and uphill. Climb steadily, up some stairs in about 0.1 mile, until you reach the ridgetop.

0.5 Arrive at the ridgetop and continue to climb gradually up the ridge, passing a few benches and high points before the trail begins to climb more steeply again.

0.9 You are at the highest point along the ridge, where you will have some views in winter, although truly this is not a trail for finding views. Along this stretch you might see a few deer, which could offer a nice photo opportunity. After the summit you begin a gradual descent.

1.2 A section of stairs helps with the descent, and the trail flattens out after the stairs end.

1.4 Pass over a bridge and through a stand of mature trees.

1.9 Junction with the Lake Trail. If you choose to head right, you will return to the lakefront and follow it to the northwest until you reach the Spillway and the Nature Center. Continue to the left.

2.3 Arrive at the junction with the Access Trail, just after crossing another bridge. The Lake Trail will head to your right, but you will continue left on the Access Trail.

2.5 Once again reach the junction with the Ganier Ridge Trail, and continue to the right on the Access Trail.

2.7 Continue a gradual decline until you reach the trailhead again, at the East Parking Lot.

Hike Information

Local Events/Attractions

Volunteer Days are held on the fourth Saturday of each month except December and are a great way to meet others who appreciate a natural setting.

Organizations

Friends of Radnor Lake has extensive information on its activities at radnorlake .org.

14 Couchville Lake Trail at Long Hunter State Park

This loop trail is paved, level, 8 feet wide, and is ideal for hikers in wheelchairs or those who are interested in less rigorous hikes. The trail winds past wildflowers and a great variety of hardwoods and other trees, and provides its share of shorebirds and waterfowl as it opens up at various points. It also has periodic, strategically located benches to rest upon as a hiker makes his or her way around the lake and passes by sinkholes under hardwood forests. This trail can be a feast of sights and smells in the autumn also, with the leaves changing and falling underfoot. Approximately 0.5 mile down the loop, you will cross a picturesque 300-foot footbridge, which provides an open view over the lake. This trail is particularly popular with female joggers, because there is always some company on the trail, and it is seen as a safe location for an after-work walk or jog.

Start: Couchville Lake Pier and picnic area boat ramp
Distance: 2.3-mile loop
Hiking time: About 1.25 hours
Difficulty: Easy
Trail surface: Paved (barrier-free)
Best season: Year-round
Other trail users: Hikers and joggers only (no dogs or bikes)

Canine compatibility: Dogs not permitted
Fees and permits: None
Schedule: Daily 7 a.m. to sunset
Map: USGS quad 311-SE, La Vergne
Trail contact: Long Hunter State Park, 2910 Hobson Pike, Hermitage, TN 37076; (615) 885-2422. (Park office open 8 a.m. to 4:30 p.m., with an hour-long lunch from 11:30 a.m. to 12:30 p.m.)

Finding the trailhead: Take I-40 east of Nashville to the Mount Juliet exit (exit 226-A), and head south 5.6 miles on SR 171 to the park entrance. Alternatively, you can take I-24 east to Old Hickory Boulevard, exit 62, then north on SR 171 for 8 miles to the park entrance. From the park entrance, follow SR 171 through the park and turn at the first left, 0.5 mile after the entrance, which is the turn for the visitor center. Continue to the left until the road dead-ends at the Couchville Lake Pier and picnic area. The trail starts at the side of the boat ramp. **GPS:** N36 05.645' / W86 32.627'

The Hike

Long Hunter State Park contains over 2,600 acres of land located along the southeast side of 14,000-acre J. Percy Priest Lake. It was named for early explorers who were known as "long hunters" due to the length of their excursions. The park is divided into three units: Couchville, Bakers Grove, and Bryant Grove. The large lake itself was created in 1968 by the US Army Corps of Engineers by impounding the Stones River for flood control and hydroelectricity, and the park was created four years later.

The park contains over 25 miles of hiking trails, ranging from walks of a few hundred yards to the 5.5-mile Volunteer Trail, in the Bakers Grove unit, which ends

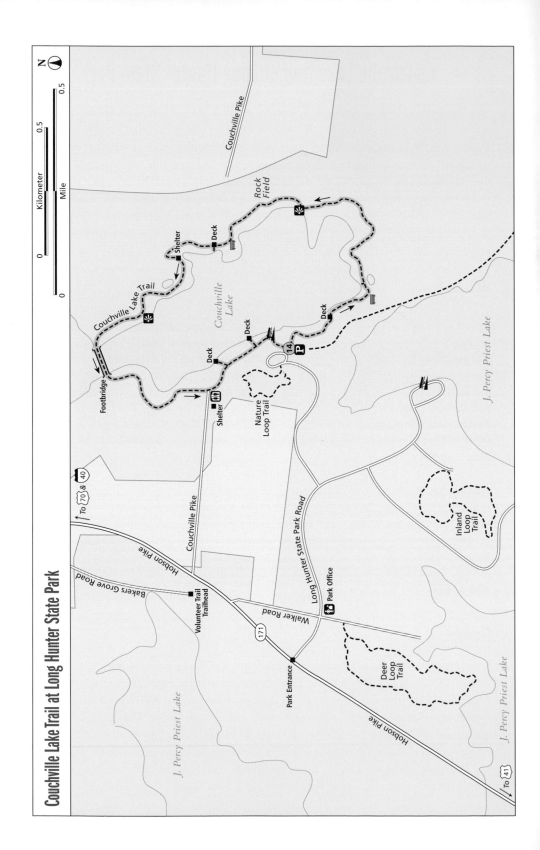

Couchville Lake Trail at Long Hunter State Park

Couchville Lake not only hosts a nice hike but also provides entertainment for kayakers, fishermen, and other boaters.

at a backpackers' campsite area. The 0.75-mile Inland Loop Trail, off the J. Percy Priest Lake boat ramp, is enjoyed for its thick hardwood forest and spring wildflowers. The 0.25-mile Nature Loop, off Couchville Lake, wanders through a cedar glade that contains many species of rare and endangered wildflowers. The more rigorous Bryant Grove Trail starts at the Couchville Lake boat ramp and heads south along the shore of J. Percy Priest Lake, ending at the shelter at the end of Barnett Road.

The paved, barrier-free Couchville Lake Trail is the most popular of the park's trails, no doubt due to its scenic views of the 110-acre Couchville Lake as it follows the shore around to the start. The trail begins to the right of the boathouse as you face the water and hugs the lake throughout, with periodic open decks. Benches and shelters afford unobstructed views of the water. Also barrier-free are the boating area, picnic area, and restrooms of Couchville Lake, and the Bryant Grove Picnic Area and Visitor Center.

Miles and Directions

0.0 Start from the trailhead, just to the right of the boat docks, as you face the water. (This trail description follows the lake counterclockwise.)

0.2 Arrive at the first of the decks that jut out into the water and afford you a relaxed lake view and fishing access. A bench is located shortly after the deck.

0.3 Pass the second deck and encounter a pond alongside the lake.

0.7 There is a very nice lake view at this point, on the opposite side of the lake from the boathouse.

0.8 Pass through a rock field and continue.

1.0 Arrive at another bench, followed by another deck. The trail then takes a U-turn and doubles back along the shore.

1.2 Arrive at a shelter, followed by another pond.

1.4 You are given another beautiful lake view here.

1.6 You arrive at the picturesque bridge that crosses the north end of Couchville Lake. This wooden structure is quite picturesque and makes for beautiful photographs in the fall with the trees in full color reflected in the lake. After crossing the lake on the bridge, you will make a sharp left to double-back along the lake toward the boathouse.

2.0 You reach the third deck, followed by a fourth deck 0.1 mile after, which make nice sunning spots on crisp autumn days.

2.3 The trail ends just past the boathouse.

Hike Information

Local Events/Attractions

On Halloween the trail converts to a "dark and twisting trail of terror," as children 8 and older test their nerves against witches, vampires, ghosts, and goblins reputed to be "more horrible than you can imagine," according to promotional flyers.

Both Couchville Lake and J. Percy Priest Lake are open to fishing, and rental boats are available. Typical fish include bass, rockfish, stripe, crappie, and catfish. Picnic areas are located throughout the park, and Bryant Grove has a swimming area.

15 Hidden Springs Trail at Cedars of Lebanon State Park and Forest

The longest hiking trail in the park, this hike is well worth the exploration because of the large number of rare species of plants likely to be encountered along the trail, although most of the endemic species of flowers can be seen only from March through June. This loop trail, marked with white blazes, can be followed in either direction and passes over mostly level ground. It makes a broad loop into state forest land and returns back to the trailhead. The rare glade anemone and a summer-flowering glade orchid are both found in the cedar glades.

Start: Trailhead across the street from the parking area on Stables Road
Distance: 4.7-mile loop
Hiking time: About 2.5 hours
Difficulty: Easy
Trail surface: Dirt
Best season: Spring, to see the flowers
Other trail users: Hikers only, but crosses horse trails and roads
Canine compatibility: Leashed dogs permitted
Fees and permits: None
Schedule: Daily 8 a.m. to 10 p.m.
Map: USGS quad 314-SE, Vine
Trail contact: Cedars of Lebanon State Park, 328 Cedar Forest Rd., Lebanon, TN 37090; (615) 443-2769

Finding the trailhead: From Nashville take I-40 east to the Lebanon exit (exit 238) at US 231/TN 10. Exit south onto US 231 (Murfreesboro Road), and follow it to the park entrance on the left, at Cedar Forest Road. Continue down Cedar Forest Road until just past the Limestone Sinks Trailhead and turn right onto Stables Road. Park in the parking area to your right. The trailhead for the Hidden Springs Trail is across the street. **GPS:** N36 04.618' / W86 18.980'
Special considerations: This trail can be muddy after a big rain, but it has plenty of colorful rewards in the late spring in the form of wildflowers special to this karst region.

The Hike

The 900-acre park is bordered by the 8,056 acres of the Cedars of Lebanon State Forest and Natural Area and contains the largest eastern red cedar forest remaining in the United States. The park is also one of the recreational areas along the Trail of Tears State Scenic Route. This area was badly abused by farmers prior to the 1930s, with the forest heavily cut (primarily for the pencil industry), burned, and damaged by overgrazing. The US Department of Agriculture established a reforestation project in the area in 1936 and replanted 792,000 eastern red cedar trees to help with erosion control and restoration of the forest. The area was developed as a state park and state forest, and in 1955 the federally managed land was deeded to the State of Tennessee for that purpose.

Hidden Springs Trail at Cedars of Lebanon State Park and Forest

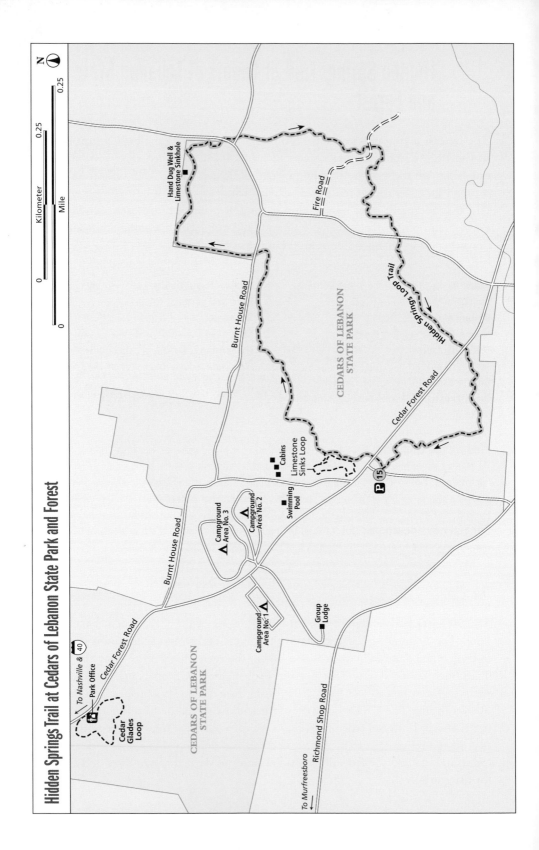

Wildflowers abound in the cedar glades, showcasing the unique vegetation found in a karst region.

The area is interesting ecologically and geologically because it contains cedar glades, also known as limestone glades, which are a companion to cedar forests and support a wide variety of plants and animals. Cedar glades are the rocky barrens between stands of cedar, which are very dry and host many varieties of plants that do not survive elsewhere in the area. There are nineteen species of plants endemic to the cedar glades of middle Tennessee, and seventeen of these can be found in the park, including the Tennessee purple coneflower, which is on the federal endangered species list. The limestone concentrations here create geologic features known as "karst" topography, named after the Karst region in Yugoslavia, which has these types of formations. Karst formations include caves, sinkholes, and disappearing streams, all created over millions of years as water runs through and erodes porous limestone.

The park and forest have a surprising lack of maintained trails, in light of their nearly 9,000-acre total area. Only 8 miles of hiking trails and 12.5 miles of horse trails can be found in the park and forest combined, although the forest has several forestry roads running through it, which are used as fire trails.

The trail passes through cedar forests and glades and oak-hickory forest, past sinkholes and caves. Trees along the trail include shagbark hickory, eastern red cedar, fragrant sumac, honey locust, pin oak, hackberry, and post oak, with dogwood and redbud flowering in the spring. Wildflowers found along the trail include purple glade violets, glade flamethrower,

Tennessee milk vetch (cream-colored flowers), the white-flowered sandwort, St. John's-wort, Gattinger's lobelia (a mint), pale-blue glade phlox, the golden groundsel, wild rose, blackberry lilies, three species of glade cress (white or yellow flowers), and others. If the loop is taken to the left, it crosses horse trails and Burnt House Road during the first 1.5 miles, then climbs over another ridge, passes a hand-dug well and a large limestone sink-hole believed to have housed a moonshine still, and crosses Burnt House Road again and more roads and trails before reaching the trailhead again to complete the loop.

Miles and Directions

0.0 Start from the trailhead across the street from the parking area on Stables Road. and head left on the trail.

0.1 Pass along the outside edge of the Limestone Sinks Loop. The trail then curves right and climbs to 700 feet.

0.6 Cross a horse trail twice, then follow a ridge before descending and making a hard left.

1.3 Cross Burnt House Road, then climb over another ridge.

1.9 Reach a hand-dug well next to a stream, which is in the area of the Hidden Spring, since there is an underground stream directly under the surface streambed. It is believed there was once a moonshine still here in a limestone sinkhole, and that a person could walk over the still without seeing it. Within the exposed limestone rock that you can see in this area are the fossil remains of aquatic sea life from the Ordovician period, such as varieties of shellfish and coral. From the well, a short spur trail to the left leads to the limestone sinkhole.

2.1 Turn sharply right, cross Burnt House Road, and pass into the state forest.

2.8 Cross a fire road.

3.2 Cross the Susie Warren Trail.

3.7 Again cross the horse trail.

3.8 Cross Cedar Forest Road and continue on the south side. Just after Cedar Forest Road, a short spur trail to the right leads to a small pond. The main trail crosses the horse trail two more times before reaching the trailhead again.

4.7 Complete the loop and arrive again at the trailhead.

Hike Information

Local Events/Attractions

The **Stables at Cedars of Lebanon** provide guided trail rides, overnight boarding, and barn birthday parties. You can also bring your own horse. The park also has an Olympic-size swimming pool.

In April the park hosts an **Annual Wildflower Pilgrimage,** and in August the area enjoys both the **Watertown Jazz Festival** and the **Wilson County Fair.**

Lodging

Cedars has 717 campsites with hookups and thirty tent campsites, in addition to a group lodge that sleeps eighty people.

16 The Enclosure Wall Trail at Old Stone Fort State Archaeological Park

Old Stone Fort State Archaeological Park is a gem of a small park. Even though it was set aside primarily to protect a walled enclosure constructed by the Native Americans, situated the way it is, high on the bluffs at the confluence of the Duck and the Little Duck Rivers, it has a lot more to see than the walled enclosure. There are numerous waterfalls and cascades scattered along both sections of creek, and the stone ruins of several old mills also, which once harnessed the power of the waterfalls. Also, in the lower portion of the park, down near the confluence of the two rivers, there are several stands of large, mature hardwoods to explore in the area often referred to as the "moat." This small park has it all!

Start: Behind the Park Visitor Center, which is a recommended stop, beside the dugout canoe
Distance: 1.7-mile loop
Hiking time: 2 hours
Difficulty: Easy, but there are bluffs that are a little more challenging.
Trail surface: Earthen trail
Best season: Great year-round

Other trail users: Hikers only
Canine compatibility: Leashed dogs permitted
Fees and permits: None
Schedule: 8 a.m. to sunset, year-round.
Map: USGS 7.5' quad: Manchester
Trail contact: Old Stone Fort State Park, 732 Stone Fort Dr., Manchester, TN 37355; (931) 723-5073

Finding the trailhead: Take I-24 northwest from Chattanooga or southeast from Nashville to the city of Manchester. From the courthouse in Manchester, head northwest on US 41 for 0.5 mile to the park entrance on your left (south). Turn into the park, and proceed to the parking lot at the visitor center. You will pass two other roads on the way: The first leads to a nice campground with an old iron truss bridge entrance, and the second road will take you to a quiet picnic area. The trail starts to the left around the visitor center. **GPS:** N35 29.170' / W86 06.150'

The Hike

This hike brings the hiker into contact with the remains of a Native American walled enclosure believed to have been constructed around 2,000 years ago. Since the wall was built at the junction of the Little Duck and the Duck Rivers, the trail passes numerous waterfalls and other views. The area was also a bustling industrial center in the late 1800s, and the stone ruins of an old paper mill can also be seen.

Stories of who had built the massive walls variously had Prince Madoc the Welshman, wandering tribes of Phoenicians, and even one of the Lost Tribes of Israel as the builders. And even the purpose of the enclosure was debated over the decades: Situated high on the bluffs at the confluence of the Duck and the Little Duck Rivers, it is easy to surmise that it had a defensive purpose as a fortification. However,

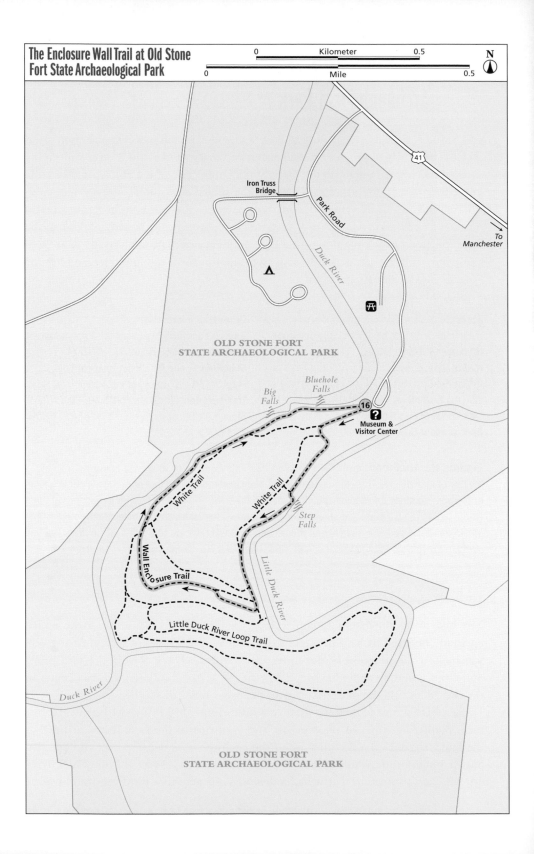

The Enclosure Wall Trail at Old Stone Fort State Archaeological Park

Kilometer
0   0.5

Mile
0   0.5

N

Iron Truss Bridge

Park Road

Duck River

To Manchester

41

OLD STONE FORT
STATE ARCHAEOLOGICAL PARK

Bluehole Falls

Big Falls

16

Museum & Visitor Center

White Trail

White Trail

Step Falls

Wall Enclosure Trail

Little Duck River

Little Duck River Loop Trail

Duck River

OLD STONE FORT
STATE ARCHAEOLOGICAL PARK

The delicate falls found along the Enclosure Wall Trail.

as archaeological surveys of the walls and the fort progressed, and an even broader understanding of the complexity of prehistoric Native American culture unfolded on a regional basis, it has been widely accepted that Native Americans constructed the fort.

The reasons for its construction cannot be definitively answered, and the original idea that it was a defensive site has not been totally debunked. But the most widely held idea now is that it was a trading and ceremonial center. It could have been used as a trade site by regional groups, perhaps with the trading periods coinciding with periods of the spring or fall equinox, or summer solstice, which the alignment of the entrance complex seems to suggest. The visitor center is a great stop, with good interpretive exhibits.

Miles and Directions

0.0 Start the hike just outside the visitor center, beside the dugout canoe. It is advised to do this loop trail in a clockwise direction because the good interpretive signs along the trail seem to be written to do the trail in that direction. Almost immediately, you will enter the "Eastern Gateway" to the Old Stone Fort, one of the most important features of this archaeological area.

0.1 Bear left (north) at the second interpretive sign. You will quickly come up on the bluffs above the Little Duck River, also known as the Bark Camp Fork.

0.2 There is a set of steps across the Walls. These will also give you a better view of the Little Duck River.

0.3 Climb down to the fall on the Little Duck. However, be advised that the last stretch is actually a climb down among the rocks that takes some agility. It is advised to stay on the trail.

0.4 The trail follows the bluffs above the river, and there are several sheer drops. Be careful!

0.6 Arrive at the junction for several other trails. This also begins a 2,000-foot stretch of wall, which is the longest in the fort.

0.7 The Moat, once thought to be a moat such as those found in European forts, is off to your left, below the Walls. It is now thought to be a natural, abandoned river channel that once connected the Duck River to the Little Duck River. There are also some mature trees scattered down in this area.

1.0 An old road cuts through the Wall. This old road goes back over a hundred years, to when this area was a bustling industrial area. However, today this cut is the junction for three trails: the Moat Trail, the Backbone Trail, and the Forks of the River trail. Stay on the Wall Trail.

1.1 Arrive at Big Falls on the Duck River. At this point you can take a side track down to multiple views of the waterfalls and the cascades above.

1.3 You have a choice to stay straight or cross back over the Wall on a set of steps. You will have a better view of the river if you cross the Wall.

1.4 You will come upon the elaborate ruins of the Main Mill. There were several mills in this area, some dating to before the Civil War. This large mill converted old clothing into paper and was called the "Ragmill."

1.5 A side trail leads to an overlook of the surprisingly beautiful Bluehole Falls.

1.7 Back to the Dugout Canoe and the beginning of the hike.

17 The Downstream and Upstream Trails at Rock Island State Park

The Upstream and the Downstream Trails at Rock Island State Park give some great views of the scenic Twin Falls and access to the Caney Fork River. Most of the time, you can see the kayakers play around in the rapids below the Twin Falls. Because of the multiuse aspect of this trail, expect to see a variety of users, including kayakers, fishermen, and families just out for a saunter. And in season, some of the fern displays along the trail are great. The Upstream Trail also has some nice bluffs.

Start: Twin Falls Parking area across the river from the main park, on the White County side of the rivers
Distance: 2.7-mile double loop, for both the Upstream Trail and the Downstream Trail
Hiking time: 2 to 3 hours . . . lots to see!
Difficulty: Moderate, due to lots of rocks and tree roots, and a small scramble on the Upstream Trail
Trail surface: Rock, earthen, and a portion of an old roadbed
Best season: The Twin Falls are beautiful any season!

Other trail users: Kayakers, fishermen, some swimmers in season on the Upstream Trail. The Downstream Trail is closed to swimming, and swimming is not advised on either trail.
Canine compatibility: Leashed dogs permitted
Fees and permits: No overnight parking and no fees required
Schedule: Daytime use only
Maps: USGS 7.5' quad Doyle and Campaign
Trail contact: Rock Island State Park, 82 Beach Rd., Rock Island, TN 38351; (931) 686-2471 or (800) 713-6065

Finding the trailhead: From Nashville or Knoxville take I-40 to Cookville and head south on US 70S/TN 111 toward McMinnville. Just past Sparta, when the road forks and TN 111 heads left, take the right fork and stay on US 70S. Follow the park signs and turn right onto TN 136. When Route 287 forks to the left and heads toward the center of the park, stay right on TN 136 instead. Cross the Caney Fork, and immediately after crossing the river, turn left (west) on Powerhouse Road. Pass the renowned Foglight Restaurant on your left. Stay straight 2.2 miles to the Powerhouse parking area. **GPS:** 35 48.533' 85 38.003'

The Hike

Rock Island State Park's 883 acres is located at the confluence of the Caney Fork and Collins Rivers and is notable for its numerous waterfalls and associated bluffs. Its ten three-bedroom cabins are some of the nicest in the state park system. One of the main features of the area is the Great Falls Dam, built in 1915 and 1916 and managed by the Tennessee Valley Authority since 1939. It is a true hydroelectric dam, which impounds the Caney Fork River just below its junction with the Collins and Rocky Rivers. By backing up these rivers and then diverting the water through

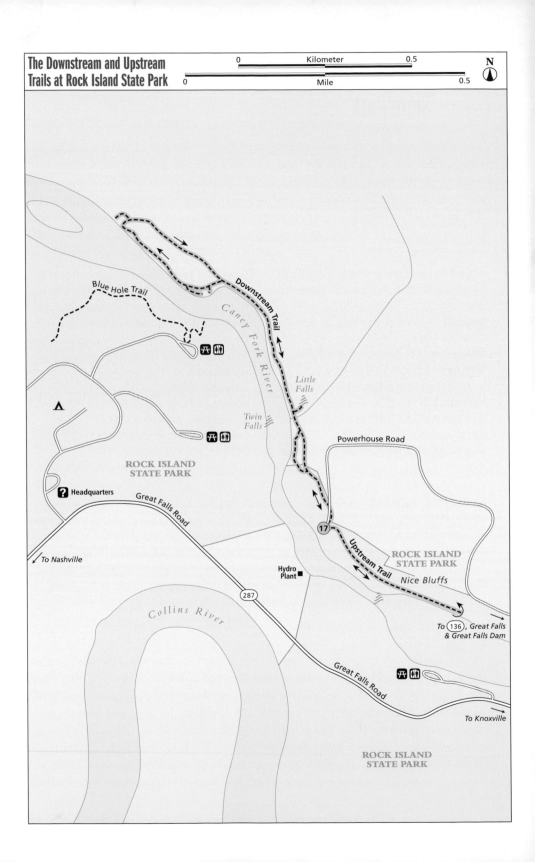

The Downstream and Upstream Trails at Rock Island State Park

0
Kilometer
0.5

0
Mile
0.5

N

Blue Hole Trail

Caney Fork River

Downstream Trail

Little Falls

Twin Falls

ROCK ISLAND STATE PARK

? Headquarters

Great Falls Road

To Nashville

Powerhouse Road

17

Upstream Trail

ROCK ISLAND STATE PARK

Nice Bluffs

Hydro Plant

287

Collins River

To 136, Great Falls & Great Falls Dam

Great Falls Road

To Knoxville

ROCK ISLAND STATE PARK

The Twin Falls at Rock Island State Park is a favorite area for kayakers.

massive turbines, the plant generates electricity that is fed into the TVA power grid. An inadvertent effect of the Great Falls Dam was the creation of Twin Falls, where water from the impoundment has found its way through passages in the rock and gushes out of the bluff just downstream of the powerhouse. Many small trails run throughout the park.

The 1.7-mile Downstream Trail winds down along the river and gives excellent views of Twin Falls and Little Falls. Across the road and slightly southward is the trailhead for the 0.5-mile Upstream Trail (1 mile round-trip). It follows a highly sculpted bluff line and gives some great views of the Caney Fork gorge and its cascades below. Both trails, while short, have beauty spots along them. Bluffs and drop-offs are found throughout the trails, with uneven and sometimes slick rocks. The trails, for the most part, are marked with white or blue metal blazes, but at one place on the Upstream Trail, you may have to search for the correct route. White blazes generally signify the main route, with the blue blazes signifying side routes.

Safety note: Postings throughout the park warn about the unpredictable water levels and power due to discharges from the dam through the turbines. When running, the turbines create strong currents downstream. After heavy rains TVA sometimes must discharge water through the main dam, causing water to rise rapidly in the upper gorge area. Swimming is prohibited from the powerhouse discharge down to the beach/boat launch area (citations may be issued), and swimming is discouraged in the upper gorge area. If TVA's warning sirens sound, hikers and swimmers near the river should seek higher ground immediately.

Miles and Directions

0.0   Start at the powerhouse parking lot. Several trails start from the parking lot. The Downstream Trail starts at the west end of the parking lot.

0.1   Immediately you will find a nice overlook of Twin Falls.

0.2   Arrive at the junction with the side trails up to "Little Falls." You can see the falls well from the trail; however, going up the steps of the side trail is worth the effort. The falls have a sinuous texture, and the rock underneath the falls looks like the "flowstone" that you might see in caves. Go back to the main trail.

0.4   You come to a fairly nice staircase.

0.6   Begin the loop trail by heading left. You'll come to a nice overlook of the Caney Fork River. Just past this overlook, the woods are carpeted with euonymus, an escapee from overseas that will often outcompete the native plants.

0.7   A blue side trail marked to the left (South) in a short distance takes you down to a broad flat rock, like a plaza, that overlooks the river. It is worth seeing, so take this side trip and then go back to the main trail.

0.8   Numerous small waterfalls are visible on the opposite bank of the river and scattered up and down the hillsides.

1.0   A blue side trail leads off to the left (west). If you take it, at 1.1 miles it leads you down to an area by the river, which looks like a popular fishing spot.

1.1   Return to the main trail, continuing on the loop.

1.3   Back to the beginning of the loop.

1.6   The single-track trail merges with an old road.

1.7   You arrive back at the Twin Falls Parking area. To continue on to the Upstream Trail, just walk across the parking lot, and bear to the right (south) toward the river.

1.8   A great view of the Great Falls Hydroelectric Plant powerhouse is here, with steps to the river (an access point for the kayakers) to another good overlook of Twin Falls.

1.9   To start the Upstream Trail, you cross the blacktop road onto a gravel road, and cross a cable (which blocks the trail to vehicles).

2.1   You reach a confusing junction. The trail seems to drop off to the right, but it actually climbs a short distance up to a ledge, which then continues on under a rock overhang. A small but pretty cascade flows at least part of the year, coming over the lip of this overhang. Also, the fern display in summer is great on the east side of the overhang.

2.2   The trail ends at a large body of water, which appears to be a large quarry site, probably where rock was quarried to make the original dam or associated structures back around 1917. Head back toward the parking lot along the route you came.

2.7   Arrive at the parking lot and the start of the hike.

18 River and Ridge Combination Trail at Burgess Falls State Park

This very accessible area also has surprisingly beautiful waterfalls and cascades. The moderate-to-strenuous hike rambles along the Falling Water River as it falls deeper and deeper over cascades and waterfalls. This short trail has a lot of scenery packed into a short distance. A dam and lake are still there from days when a power plant was here. You will also see the remains of pipeline that moved water from the lake to the turbines used to generate electricity. This area is very popular, so you might want to schedule your trip during a weekday, especially in the morning, to avoid having trouble finding a parking spot, and to miss the crowds.

Start: Begin at the parking lot by the shelter and playground.
Distance: 1.8-mile double loop (includes side trail to base of Big Falls)
Hiking time: About 2 hours, with stops to take photos!
Difficulty: Moderate, unless you take the trail to the base of the High Falls, which is strenuous.
Trail surface: Natural materials, and gravel, with lots of steps on the river portion

Best season: Year-round
Other trail users: Hikers only
Canine compatibility: Leashed dogs permitted
Fees and permits: None
Schedule: Open 7 days a week from sunrise until sunset
Map: 7.5' quad: Burgess Falls
Trail contact: Burgess Falls State Park, 4000 Burgess Falls Dr., Sparta, TN 38583; (931) 432-5312

Finding the trailhead: Take I-40 from Nashville or Knoxville, and take exit 286 (at Cookeville) and head south on Route 135. Go approximately 8 miles, and the park entrance is marked on the right (west side of the road). It is only a couple of hundred yards to the lower (main) parking lot.

From Sparta, head north on US 70S/TN 111 approximately 5 miles. You will see the signs for Burgess Falls Road. Take that exit, and head west approximately 8 miles. The route is well signed. **GPS:** N36 02.634' / W85 35.684'

The Hike

The Burgess Falls hike is surprising in that you find so many beautiful things in such a short distance. This area has a lot of beauty in a very accessible area, and people have found out about it. On most weekends in the spring and summer, the parking lots are full. You can have more peace (and parking) if you schedule a trip during a weekday, especially in the morning.

When you drive in, you have the option of parking at the upper (overflow) parking area or driving down to the main parking lots. A nice picnic area is sandwiched between the two parking areas. Parking at the upper lot gives a good view of the

River and Ridge Combination Trail at Burgess Falls State Park

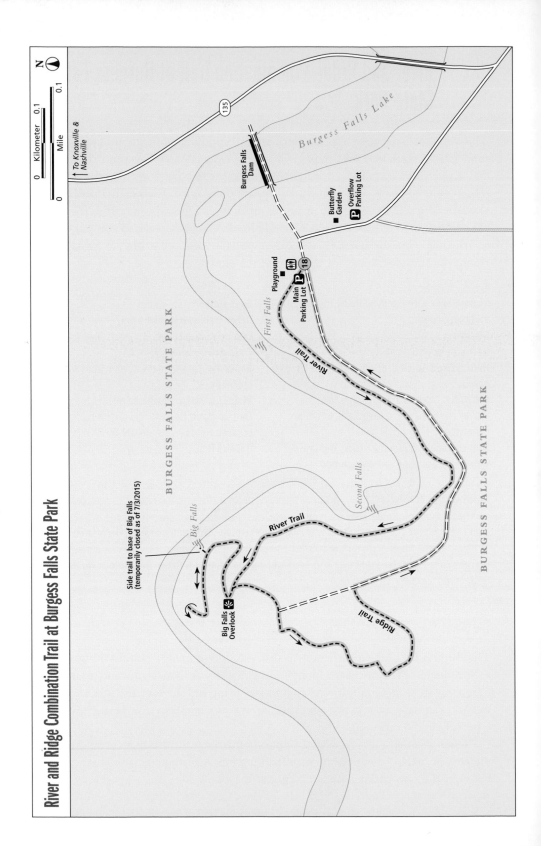

The Big Falls are a popular hiking destination at Burgess Falls State Park.

Butterfly Garden, a garden planted specifically with native plants that will attract butterflies. An annual butterfly celebration usually happens in June. Parking at the upper lot also will bring you by the dam that was used to create Burgess Falls Lake. This dam was used to generate hydroelectricity for the city of Cookeville but was closed in 1944 after the Tennessee Valley Authority took over electricity production for the area.

The River Trail begins at the lower (main) parking lot, where a nicely done kiosk contains lots of historic photos that detail the building of the dam, pipes, and turbines in the 1920s. Also, there is a nice playground here and a pavilion with restrooms. The trail passes the First Falls, the Second Falls, and the Big Falls, any one of which would be worth the journey. This hike concludes with the short but view-rich Ridge Trail, before it delivers you back to the parking lot.

Miles and Directions

0.0 The trail starts on the west side of the main (lower) parking lot.

0.2 As the River Trail follows the river, you will almost immediately encounter a number of beautiful cascades. The First Falls, 30 feet high, is just downstream.

0.5 The Second Falls overlook gives a grand view of the 80-foot Second, or Middle, Falls. A fairly steep stairway begins just past the overlook on this main trail.

0.6 You reach the Big Falls Overlook, which gives a nice upper view of the impressive, 136-foot Big Falls (also known as the Lower Falls). At this point you can take the trail to the base, which will add 0.5 mile round-trip. Because of the steepness, with lots of steps, and the unevenness of the rocks at the bottom, this portion should be considered strenuous. From this overlook, you also can head directly back along the Service Road Trail to the parking lot (0.5 mile), or continue on the Ridge Trail, which will add 0.2 mile to the overall hike. Continue to the base.

0.9 Reach the base of the Big Falls. The rocks at the base are slick, and the waterfalls themselves may have strong currents in winter and spring. Be careful.

1.1 Return to the overlook from the base. Backtrack on the main trail about twenty paces, and bear right (south) to begin the Ridge Trail. In about one hundred more paces, you will enter a large gravel turnaround for park service vehicles. The trail continues on off to the south side. Almost immediately, the Ridge Trail starts offering some great views of the Falling Water River Gorge.

1.3 The Ridge Trail turns away from the gorge through the woods and then hits the old service road. Bear right (east) to head back to the parking lot.

1.8 Arrive back at the parking lot. (Subtract 0.5 mile if you didn't go to the base of the falls.)

Hike Information

Local Events and Attractions

The **Annual Butterfly Garden Celebration** looks at both the native plants of the area and the butterflies that feed off of them.

Lodging

Several chain hotels can be found in Cookeville, 8 miles away.

Restaurants

Cookeville is a college town, boasting a wide variety of great eateries . . . you shouldn't go hungry! Local favorites include **Char Steak House** (on the square) and **Crawdaddy's** on Broad. Sparta has several good restaurants, including **Yanni's** (off of West Bockman), **Mrs. Miranda's Tea Room** (near the Square), and **El Tapatio**, a Mexican restaurant, which also has two locations in Cookeville . . . they stay busy!

19 Lake Trail at Standing Stone State Park

The 4.7-mile Lake Trail, within Standing Stone State Park, a "New Deal" park near Cookeville, takes you around the lake and also shows off some of the WPA handiwork of the park, especially the dam. Birdlife and other wildlife abound around the lake.

Start: Park headquarters
Distance: 4.7-mile loop
Hiking time: 2 to 3 hours
Difficulty: Moderate, but there are some switchback areas on the trail
Trail surface: Forest trail for most, with one stretch of road
Best season: Reports are that the spring wildflowers are great!

Other trail users: Hikers-only on trail
Canine compatibility: Leashed dogs permitted
Fees and permits: None
Schedule: Be off the trail by dark.
Maps: USGS 7.5' quad Hilham. Cloudhiking .com has a good map with a trail description.
Trail contact: Standing Stone State Park, 1674 Standing Stone State Park Hwy., Hilham, TN 38568; (931) 823-6347

Finding the trailhead: From Cookeville take TN 111 north 20 miles to Livingston. From Livingston take TN 85 west 8 miles to Hilham. At Hilham turn right (north) on TN 136, which is Standing Stone Highway. It will carry you right into the park. Or you can take TN 136 (North Dixie) due north out of Cookeville. This route is somewhat shorter, curvier, and nicer. To find the Park Office, go across the Dam, and the Office is about ½ mile up hill, on the right. **GPS:** N36 28.258' / W85 24.919'

The Hike

Standing Stone State Park is a wonderful little 855-acre state park that is surrounded by the much larger 11,000-acre Standing Stone State Forest. The park is situated on a hilly area of the eastern Highland Rim and has many creeks and valleys that sculpt the uneven terrain. This park and forest were set aside during the Great Depression, and as such, Standing Stone is another of the New Deal parks that Tennessee has to be proud of. The work building the road, cabins, Tea Room, and some of the other structures was primarily handled by the Works Project Administration (WPA), although some work was also done by the Civilian Conservation Corps (CCC). The dam, which impounds Mill Creek and creates the lake, is a marvel to behold and worth the trip to the park just to admire. The elaborate dam was created stone by stone, with the limestone quarried from a hillside clearly visible from the dam. The dam itself is best appreciated from the public area just below the dam, where you will also find a suspension bridge.

The handiwork of the WPA is visible in many areas along the hike. The hike starts up near the office, down in the cabin loop. Some of the cabins are original WPA-era, others are more recent. The described hike starts out and returns to the park office

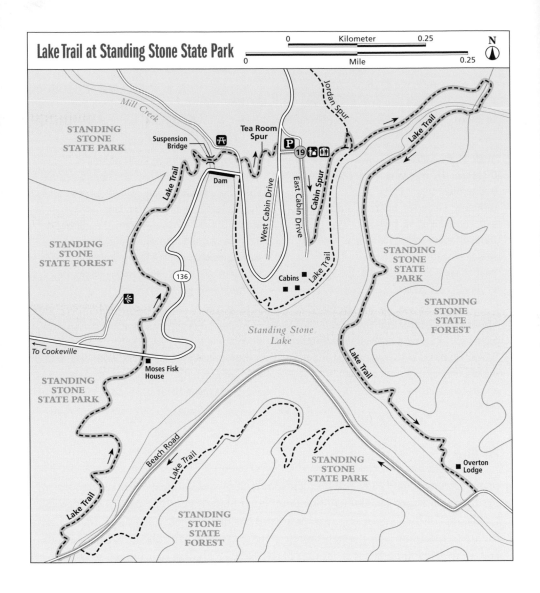

Lake Trail at Standing Stone State Park

STANDING STONE STATE PARK

Mill Creek

Suspension Bridge

Tea Room Spur

Lake Trail

Dam

P 19

Jordan Spur

Lake Trail

West Cabin Drive

East Cabin Drive

Cabin Spur

STANDING STONE STATE FOREST

STANDING STONE STATE FOREST

136

Cabins

Lake Trail

STANDING STONE STATE PARK

STANDING STONE STATE FOREST

Standing Stone Lake

To Cookeville

Moses Fisk House

Lake Trail

STANDING STONE STATE PARK

Overton Lodge

Beach Road

Lake Trail

STANDING STONE STATE PARK

Lake Trail

STANDING STONE STATE FOREST

N

via the Tea Room, another Depression-era building and example of the WPA handi-work. The bench, or platform, that the trail itself is located on was apparently cut out and graded by the WPA also, judging by its width and the work that went into it. However, the tread of the trail today has been partially reclaimed by the surrounding forest and is much narrower.

Standing Stone State Park and Forest were apparently named for a large stone that some described as a "dog-shaped monolith," originally around 12 feet in height. The stone was important in that it was reported to be the boundary between two Native American tribes. It was later moved, and reduced in size, and is mounted on a pedestal in Monterey, Tennessee.

The dam that creates Standing Stone Lake was built by the WPA during the Great Depression.

Lots of wildlife was visible during this hike, one of the more interesting critters being the large gars that you could see coming to the top of the lake. Great blue herons, kingfishers, wood ducks, and other birds were visible. Another hiker related that the wildflowers are great along the trail in the spring.

Miles and Directions

0.0   Start at the park headquarters and begin the hike by walking down the East Cabin Drive.

0.2   The trail diverges from the East Cabin Drive between cabins.

0.4   This cabin spur trail joins up with the main Lake Trail.

0.8   The Lake Trail crosses a bridge over Mill Creek. Along this trail there is a lot of evidence of WPA handiwork.

1.9   Follow the Lake Trail to Overton Lodge. The lodge is rented to park visitors . . . be respectful and move quickly around the building over to the road if the lodge appears occupied. When we were there it was empty, and we took a snack break on the picnic table outside and enjoyed the lake view. A nice auto bridge connects Overton Lodge to the Beach Road.

After leaving Overton Lodge, cross the bridge via the road. On the south side of the bridge, you can either hit the hiking trail that parallels the road or just walk the road. The road appeared underused and had a great view of the lake and a picnic shelter. We just followed the road and enjoyed it.

3.1 After following the Beach Road for about 1.2 miles, you will leave the lake, cross a bridge, and start heading away from the lake. The Lake Trail picks up again on the right (north) side of the road, just across the bridge. Get back on the trail.

3.7 You will come out on the main park road, just beside the Moses Fisk house. We took a look around the house. The trail continues just across the road. This next stretch of trail has a lot of big trees but also a lot of switchbacks. As usual, please stay on the trail and don't cut the switchbacks.

4.4 After descending through some switchbacks, you will come out at a pretty suspension bridge that crosses Mill Creek just below the dam. This is a great place to admire the handiwork of the dam, with its individually quarried, then laid, limestone rocks. This popular spot has a picnic shelter and some other amenities.

4.5 The boat dock nearby appears to date from the Depression era also. Backtrack a little to hit the Tea Room spur trail, which has its own switchbacks.

4.6 Arrive at the Tea Room, another reminder of the great work of the CCC and the WPA.

4.7 Arrive back at the parking in front of park headquarters, where we began our hike.

Additional Great Hikes

D   Recovery Trail at Dunbar Cave State Park

Dunbar is a 110-acre park located in a residential neighborhood of Clarksville, with trails winding through the park around the lake. While the park may not be the place for a rugged encounter with nature, the looped 1.9-mile Recovery Trail is very pleasant and passes by the mouth of Dunbar Cave. Cave tours, with a naturalist or ranger, are only offered during May, June July, and part of August, due to the impact of the White Nose Syndrome on the cave's bats and the Park's efforts to reduce stress on the bats. The cave contains remarkable Native American Mississippian cave art that dates back to at least the 1300s, including religious symbols and a warrior figure. The hike essentially carves a wide curve through the woods on the back side of Swan Lake, after following its shore for a while, and returns to the lake to meet the Lake Trail, where you will turn right and follow the lakeshore back to the visitor center.

During a quiet afternoon, not far from the cave entrance, I ran into a young fisherman with four lines in the water and two catfish already caught. When I asked how many more he wanted before he would call it a day, he said he expected to catch "a mess." While he was describing a 17-pound buffalo fish he had caught at this spot, a line pulled, and he landed another cat. Before he had time to get that one off the line, another one was biting. That one fought like the dickens, even after he landed it on the shore to kick itself out. It looked like he was well on his way to reaching the "mess" he wanted. I said goodbye and continued on my way.

Finding the trailhead: Take I-24 to the exit for US 79, and follow US 79 into Clarksville. In Clarksville turn left onto Dunbar Cave Road and continue for approximately 1 mile to the park entrance, on the left. The trailhead is at the north end of the parking lot.

E   Limestone Sinks Trail at Cedars of Lebanon State Park

This is one of two very good educational nature trails available at Cedars of Lebanon. The short but extremely interesting 0.5-mile self-guided nature trail provides an introduction to karst topography and plant forms, and is designed to capture the interest of children. A trail guide is available at the park office for this self-guided nature trail, which provides explanations of the unique characteristics of limestone sink geology and ecology found here. The trail description explains that the dryness of these areas is due to the porous nature of the rock, which does not retain water, allowing prickly pear cactus and other desert-type species to grow. The trail guide material explains the succession and reclamation by the cedar forest of lands that had been logged and over-farmed, and helps with identification of mosses, lichen, and several varieties of trees and bushes. The half-mile trail also passes a limestone sink that clearly demonstrates the dramatically erosive character of limestone.

Finding the trailhead: Take I-40 east from Nashville for approximately 31 miles to exit 238 (the Lebanon exit), and turn onto US 231 south. Follow US 231 south 6 miles to the park entrance on the left. After passing the park office, take the right fork at the first fork in the road. You will pass the swimming pool on the left, before the road merges with another park road. The trailhead is near the point where these two roads converge.

F   The Cedar Glades Trail at Cedars of Lebanon State Park

This 0.7-mile loop trail provides an opportunity to explore cedar glades, examine limestone formations, and enjoy the great variety of rare wildflowers, plants, and trees that reside in this karst region within the park. The hike begins to the right as you face the park headquarters and passes through a remarkable variety of natural life found in a cedar glade in a short distance. Informative plaques along the way describe what you are seeing in this unique karst region. The trail bends to the right and then the left, reaching the first cedar glade in 250 feet, then turns right and reaches the first park plaque at 0.1 mile. The trail then heads sound and at 0.2 mile crosses a footbridge. It continues to curve gradually right until you reach an informative marker with photographs of different types of wildflowers that can be seen in the small meadow to your left. The trail turns sharply left at this point and straightens out, entering a mixed hardwood forest at about 0.3 mile, followed by an open meadow. At this point you curve to the right again and reach a limestone sinkhole at 0.4 mile, curving left again to enter another open meadow shortly thereafter. Another plaque explains "Longmeadow" at 0.5 mile. A final sharp right returns you to the trailhead at 0.7 mile.

Finding the trailhead: From Nashville take I-40 east to the Lebanon exit (exit 238) at US 231/ TN 10. Exit south onto US 231 (Murfreesboro Road), and follow it to the park entrance on the left, at Cedar Forest Road. Continue down Cedar Forest Road until you see the park headquarters.

The North Cumberlands

P ossibly the most unique landform in Tennessee is the Cumberland Plateau and mountains, which straddle the state, running from the southwest to the northeast, 135 miles long and approximately 55 miles wide within Tennessee. It was these Cumberlands that stood in the way of the westward migration of the early Europeans. They could easily navigate through the Appalachians to the east along river ways. But as the pioneers moved westward, they came to the Cumberlands, which stood in their path like a 1,000-foot wall. Explorer Thomas Walker had found a northerly path through them in 1750: the famous Cumberland Gap, which he named after his benefactor, the Duke of Cumberland. Without the Gap, these pioneers had the option of following rougher trails like the Avery Trace. And if these early pioneers tried to avoid this tortuous terrain by following the Tennessee River, the Cumberlands still got a jab at them when they hit "the suck," a treacherous area on the river where the Cumberland Plateau had narrowed the river down into some dangerous rapids.

The South Cumberlands are the true plateau area, with their rolling plateau top averaging around 1,750 feet above sea level (abs). However, north of I-40, the landforms are completely different. The North Cumberlands experienced a lot more folding and faulting and true mountain building. Whereas the South Cumberland area may struggle to have points higher than 2,000 feet, the North Cumberlands have numerous peaks over 3,000 feet, with the highest being Cross Mountain at 3,500 feet. And while the South Cumberlands area is known for caves and waterfalls, the North Cumberlands are remarkable for the abundance of natural arches and tall, smooth, colorful bluff lines and escarpments. Big South Fork and Pickett are both great places to explore and discover natural bridges and beautiful bluff lines. And looking at topographic maps of places like the Big South Fork, or Pogue Creek, where there are few trails, one can only imagine the number of geologic wonders still to be found in these places. The North Cumberlands is a rich place for exploration!

Caution: Black bears are becoming more common in the Cumberlands, especially in the North Cumberlands around the Big South Fork and Frozen Head. Please follow precautions when in bear country, including proper storage of food and disposal of food scraps when camping. (See this book's introduction for a note on what to do if you encounter a bear.)

20 Natural Bridge–Hazard Cave Combination Loop at Pickett CCC Memorial State Park

This is a wonderful park that contains a myriad of good trails that traverse bluffs, arches, rock formations, and nice old-growth forest. Although the park itself is small, it is surrounded by the much larger Pickett State Forest, where some of the trails are located. Much of this core area of the park is listed on the National Register of Historic Places because of the preservation of the handiwork of the Civilian Conservation Corps (CCC) workers.

Start: Park headquarters
Distance: 2.9-mile loop
Hiking time: 1.5 to 2 hours
Difficulty: Moderate due to elevation changes
Trail surface: Rock and forest trail
Best season: Any time of the year
Other trail users: Hikers only
Canine compatibility: Leashed dogs permitted
Fees and permits: None required for this day-use area, but backpackers must register.
Schedule: Trail closed from sundown until sunup

Maps: There is a good, free map, done by students from MTSU, available in the park headquarters. USGS 7.5' quad: Sharps Place
Trail contact: Pickett State Park, 4605 Pickett Park Hwy., Jamestown, TN 38556; (931) 879-5821 or (877) 260-0010
Other: Black bears are becoming common at Pickett. When camping be sure to follow precautions, especially when it comes to food storage.

Finding the trailhead: From Nashville take I-40 east to Crossville, exit 317, and head north on US 127 for 34.5 miles to Jamestown. Stay on the bypass east, around town, and get off at TN 154 and head northeast 12 miles to the park headquarters, across from the CCC museum. Find the trailhead to the south, across from Cabin 8. **GPS:** N36 32.998' / W84 47.995'

The Hike

Pickett State Park and Forest was donated to the state by the Stearns Coal and Lumber Company in 1933. The park was actually designated as 865 acres, situated inside of the 20,887-acre state forest. Many people consider Pickett to be the first state park in Tennessee because it was donated directly to the state as "Pickett State Park and Forest" in 1933, four years before the state park system itself was organized. In 1934 a CCC camp was set up, and the CCC boys moved in to start work on trails, cabins, bridges, and a Recreation Hall. (One of the authors actually met one of the CCC workers, now long since retired, who helped build this park he now camped in!) Most of the building material was local, with some beautiful rock work created with the sandstone. A lake was impounded in Thompson Creek and is called Arch Lake because it goes under a natural rock arch, or bridge.

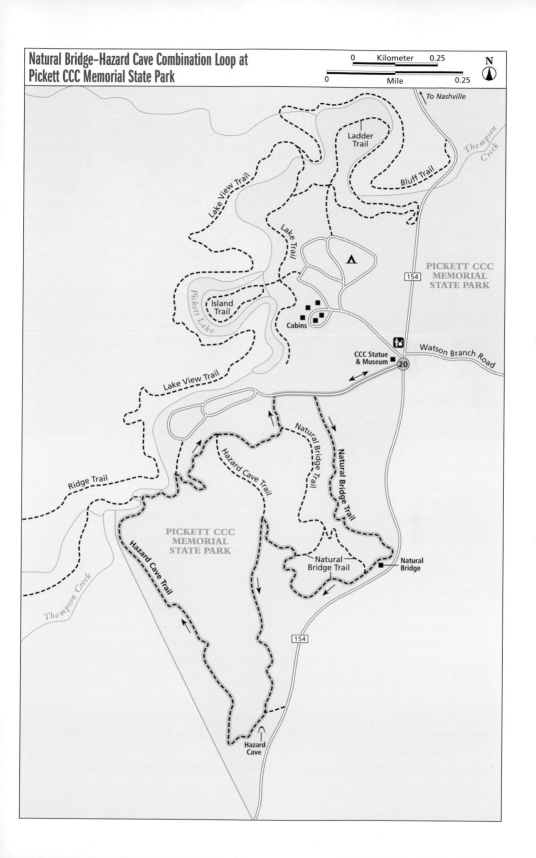

Natural Bridge–Hazard Cave Combination Loop at Pickett CCC Memorial State Park

0   Kilometer   0.25

0   Mile   0.25

N

To Nashville

Ladder Trail

Bluff Trail

Thompson Creek

Lake View Trail

Lake Trail

PICKETT CCC
MEMORIAL
STATE PARK

154

Island Trail

Pickett Lake

Cabins

CCC Statue
& Museum

20

Watson Branch Road

Lake View Trail

Ridge Trail

Hazard Cave Trail

Natural Bridge Trail

Natural Bridge Trail

PICKETT CCC
MEMORIAL
STATE PARK

Thompson Creek

Hazard Cave Trail

Natural
Bridge Trail

Natural
Bridge

154

Hazard
Cave

Pickett was renamed a few years back in memory of the CCC boys who were instrumental in setting aside this wonderful area.

Although there have been some additions and changes since the original CCC days, the park retains its rustic CCC atmosphere. The cabins, recreation hall, old park headquarters, and other facilities blend so well into the natural surroundings that they illustrate what "parkitecture" is all about. The original park headquarters was turned into a CCC museum and sits across from the newer park headquarters. The developed area of the park is now listed with the National Register of Historic Places because of its excellent preservation and illustration of the CCC handiwork.

The hike described is actually a mixture of several trails. Indeed, leaving on foot from the headquarters area, you can explore a variety of areas, see some great natural features, and discover some CCC handiwork. This described hike visits the park's Natural Bridge and Hazard Cave.

Miles and Directions

0.0 Start the hike at the Park Headquarters. This is a great place to get maps, and the hike will carry by the CCC Museum.

0.2 One place to join the Natural Bridge Trail is across from Cabin 8, which is 0.2 mile west of the park headquarters.

0.4 There is a nice rock overhang with a bench.

0.6 You are at the Natural Bridge but standing on top.

0.8 There are some more beautifully sculptured bluffs, and a short distance past, there is a small cave on your left.

0.9 Meet the junction with Hazard Cave Trail. Bear left.

1.0 At another junction bear left again.

1.4 There is a junction with some concrete steps descending downward. There are actually two sets of steps, and these steps are carrying you to the base of a beautiful bluff called Hazard Cave.

1.5 Hazard Cave.

1.9 The trail, and a set of steps, takes you to a nice little rock canyon, unusual even for the Cumberland Plateau.

2.2 You come up in short order on two trail junctions: first with the Ridge Trail (bear right), and then with the Lake View Trail. Stay straight, but notice the nice rock and wood bridge over the creek—undoubtedly the work of the CCC boys. You have the option in this area to head off to explore on several different trails.

2.3 You will come out on a picnic area with a shelter. It is easy to miss the trail, but bear to the right (east). If you join the road, you have gone too far. Almost immediately there is another junction. Bear left.

2.6 An old historic structure, now abandoned, appears at this point. Could it have been a well house or a pump house from the CCC days? The trail brings you out onto the road in front of the Recreation Hall, which is another great example of the CCC handiwork. Take some time to explore this area. This was the focal point of the park back in the early days. Turn right (east) on the road to get back to the trailhead.

2.7 Arrive at the trailhead in front of Cabin 8.

2.9 Back to your car and the park headquarters.

21 Pogue Creek Canyon Overlook Trail at Pogue Creek Canyon State Natural Area

This trail was constructed in 2014 in one of Tennessee's newest state natural areas. The trail stays on top of the Cumberland Plateau but winds around by several nice rock formations, bluffs, and rock houses before ending out on the spectacular overlook of Pogue Creek Canyon.

Start: Trailhead/parking on TN 154
Distance: 1.8-mile lollipop loop
Hiking time: About 2 hours
Difficulty: Moderate due to uneven footing in some places
Trail surface: Forest trail and rock
Best season: Any time of year
Other trail users: Hikers only
Canine compatibility: Leashed dogs permitted

Fees and permits: None required, but day-hiking-only at this point.
Schedule: Sunup until sundown, no overnight parking or camping. (Go to the main Pickett State Park, just down the road for camping.)
Maps: USGS 7.5' quads Sharps Place, Pall Mall, Jamestown
Trail contact: Pickett State Park, 4605 Pickett Park Hwy., Jamestown, TN 38556; (931) 879-5821 or (877) 260-0010

Finding the trailhead: From Nashville take I-40 east to Crossville, exit 317, and head north on US 127 for 34.5 miles to Jamestown. Stay on the bypass east, around town, and get off on TN 154 and head northeast as if you are heading to Pickett State Park, but at about 10 miles out of Jamestown, and before you get to Pickett State Park, you will see the parking area on the left. **GPS:** N36 31.326' / W84 49.053'

The Hike

Pogue Creek Canyon State Natural Area, over 3,000 acres in all, was acquired in 2006 from the Nature Conservancy to protect the spectacular views of Pogue Creek Canyon and to protect several species of plants found only on the bluffs and rock outcroppings in this area of the Cumberlands.

In the summer of 2014, an AmeriCorps NCCC team moved in and constructed the 1.75–mile trail that is described in this hike. Although it is a short hike, it has a great vista of Pogue Creek Canyon. The trail also winds down alongside several nice bluff and rock overhang areas. More trails are planned for the future—however, because of the rough terrain, it is going to be a slow process. More work is also planned for this area to further protect the viewshed and the habitat of these rare plants.

Miles and Directions

0.0 Start at the parking lot and kiosk, constructed in 2014, directly off of TN 154. The kiosk has both interpretive information and trail information.

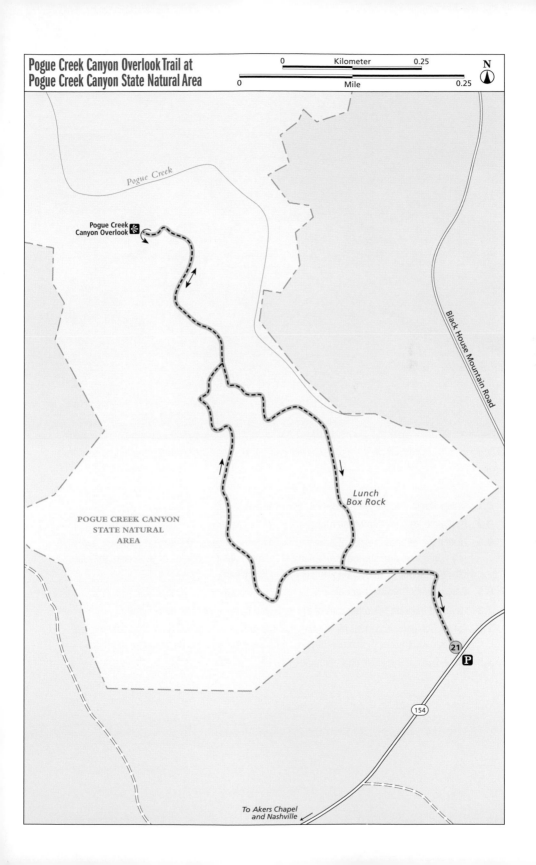

Pogue Creek Canyon Overlook Trail at
Pogue Creek Canyon State Natural Area

0   Kilometer   0.25

0   Mile   0.25

N

Pogue Creek

Pogue Creek
Canyon Overlook

Black House Mountain Road

POGUE CREEK CANYON
STATE NATURAL
AREA

Lunch
Box Rock

21

P

154

To Akers Chapel
and Nashville

The view from Pogue Creek Canyon is great, and plans are to build more trails down into the canyon.

0.1 Turkey Roost Rockhouse (actually a rock overhang).

0.2 Begin the loop portion of the trail.

0.5 Notice the abundant beds of boxwood huckleberry. Because these large beds are actually connected and started from an initial "parent" plant hundreds of years ago, they are considered one of the oldest living plants in Tennessee.

0.9 Pogue Creek Canyon Overlook.

1.3 Heading back on the other part of the loop, you come by a nice, damp grotto.

1.5 Lunch Box Rock is named for the fact that the AmeriCorps NCCC team that constructed this trail would take their lunch breaks here. Circle back to the beginning of the loop.

1.8 Arrive back at the kiosk and trailhead.

22 Northrup Falls Trail at Colditz Cove State Natural Area

Colditz Cove is a beautiful state natural area located near the community of Allardt, a couple of miles off of TN 52. It is best known for the beautiful Northrup Falls, but it also has some tremendous rock overhangs that line the cove on both sides of the waterfalls. To get a decent view of the waterfalls, you don't have to descend down into the cove itself. However, the trail down into the cove winds through rock gardens and underneath bluffs, loops behind the waterfall itself, and is worth the extra energy.

Start: At the kiosk just off Northrup Falls Road
Distance: 1.5-mile lollipop loop
Hiking time: About 1.5 hours
Difficulty: It is an easy walk out to the first overlook. However, the trail that winds down into the cove has some uneven footing, which makes the trail moderate in difficulty.
Trail surface: Forest trail, rocks in some areas
Best season: Year-round
Other trail users: Hikers only

Canine compatibility: Leashed dogs permitted
Fees and permits: None required, but there is no overnight camping.
Schedule: Day use only, area closes at dark
Map: USGS 7.5' quad Burrville
Trail contact: Pickett CCC Memorial State Park, 4605 Pickett Park Hwy., Jamestown, TN 38556; (931) 879-5821 or (877) 260-0010
Other: No alcohol, no camping, no hunting, and no wheeled vehicles

Finding the trailhead: From Nashville take I-40 east to Crossville, exit 317, and head north on US 127 for 30 miles. Follow signs to Allardt on TN 296. Turn right (east) through Allardt and continue 4.5 miles. Turn right (south) onto Northrup Falls Road, and go 1.2 miles to the parking lot/trailhead on your right. **GPS:** N36 21.449' / W84 52.150'

The Hike

Colditz Cove is a beautiful state natural area that is noted for the stunning Northrup Falls. The falls were named for a family that lived in the area and harnessed the creek at one time for a water mill. Although the upper area around the parking lot is somewhat nondescript plateau, once you follow the trail down into the cove, you descend into a wonderland of water, rocks, and trees.

Miles and Directions

0.0 Start the hike at the trailhead kiosk and parking area. The trail is marked with white plastic blazes.

0.1 The trail crosses a small footbridge.

0.3 You reach a T-junction in the trail and a decent overlook of Northrup Falls from above. The trail from here on will have uneven footing. Bear to the left (south) to continue on. This area of the trail has numerous steep bluffs with drop-offs. Be cautious, and if you have children hiking with you, keep them close by.

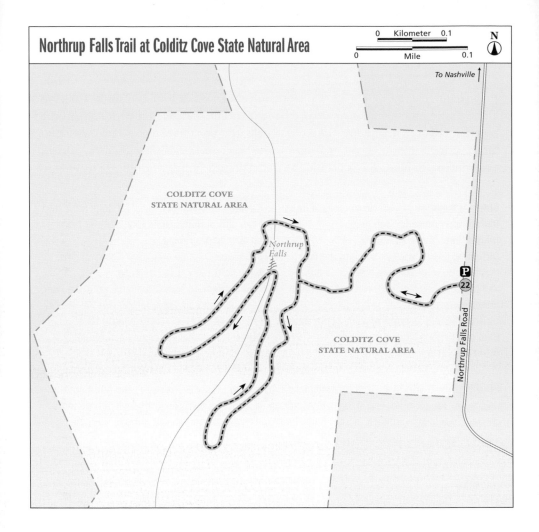

0   Kilometer   0.1

0   Mile   0.1

N

To Nashville ↑

COLDITZ COVE
STATE NATURAL AREA

*Northrup
Falls*

P
22

Northrup Falls Road

COLDITZ COVE
STATE NATURAL AREA

0.5 The trail starts descending into the cove and winds between rock gardens and under numerous bluffs and rock overhangs in this area.

0.7 There is a very nice large rock overhang just before you get to Northrup Falls. The trail is not well marked in this area, and you should pick your way among the boulders. The trail winds through this rocky area and then goes behind the waterfalls on its loop. Be especially careful in this section if there is ice on the trail.

1.1 Cross a footbridge over the creek above the falls.

1.2 You have arrived back at the T junction, at the beginning of the loop.

1.3 There is a shortcut back to the parking lot, but resist temptation and stay on the marked park trail. Always stay on the marked trails for your safety and also to protect the area from shortcuts.

1.5 Arrive back at the parking lot and kiosk.

Northrup Falls at Colditz Cove is a nice, accessible waterfall. The loop trail winds down underneath some nice bluffs and behind the falls before coming back out on top.

The view from the observation tower at Frozen Head offers a 360-degree panorama.

set aside the Brushy Mountain Coalfield in 1894 to mine coal for the state office buildings. Brushy Mountain Prison itself can be seen to the south from the lookout tower.

Later, a large portion of the Brushy Coalfields was transferred over to the Division of Forestry as Morgan State Forest. As part of the forest, in 1935, a CCC camp was established, and the CCC boys built trails and bridges throughout the area. Look carefully, and you can see their handiwork. In the early 1970s the area was designated a state natural area, and management of that area was turned over to state parks. Minimal development was done, with some rustic campsites along the road, picnic areas and shelters, playgrounds, and a visitor center, all laid out as to not degrade the area's formal designation as a natural area.

Miles and Directions

0.0 Start at the trailhead in the picnic area The trail starts as the Old Mac Mountain Trail. The trailhead is also the start for the Judge Branch Trail. Soon you will encounter a plaque on the right side of the trail in memory of CCC workers Ralph Farmer, Wolford Hall, and Frank Hatcher, who were all killed here.

0.2 Junction with North Old Mac Trail. For the South Old Mac Trail, stay straight.

0.3 Junction with the Interpretive Loop trail (to right). Stay straight and when you reach another junction, turn left for the South Old Mac Trail. This trail will be blazed with yellow-painted blazes.

0.6 Old CCC dynamite shack.

1.1 Junction with the Judge Branch Trail. Go straight (Judge Branch Trail splits off to the right).

1.2 There is a small creek with a cascade.

1.5 Cross another small branch with some stacked rocks. (Perhaps there was a small bridge here back in the CCC days?)

1.6 There is an overlook at the point, in the bend in the trail. Again, if you look carefully, you can see the handiwork of the CCC boys.

3.1 You leave the single track and join an old road. A hundred yards or so past this junction, you encounter another larger junction where several roads converge. It is also the site of the Tub Springs Campsite, which is just to the north and off the old road about 50 yards. Bear right, and follow the old road to the right (south), and start the climb toward the Lookout Tower. From this junction, it is 0.5 mile on up to the tower.

3.6 You will find the Lookout Tower and another tower for cell phones. The lookout tower is actually the remains of an old fire tower that was reconfigured, stabilized, and strengthened to provide hikers a view of the surrounding mountains. The map indicates this point is 3,324 feet above sea level.

4.0 Back down the old road, and this time divert over to see the Tub Springs. The springs are covered with a rock house, and there is a rock grill just a few feet away. While some of this is the work of the CCC boys, some of this is the work of prisoners who were brought up from Brushy Mountain Prison. Backtrack a short distance onto the old road you came in on, then stay straight (north) to find the North Old Mac Trail.

4.3 Leave the old road and start following the North Old Mac Trail, which is marked with red-painted blazes.

5.4 Junction with Panther Branch Trail. Instead of heading back on the North Old Mac Trail, which is a good trail and about 1 mile closer to the parking area, opt to turn right (north) onto the Panther Branch Trail in order to see a couple of nice waterfalls. This choice will also have you walking back to your car along the blacktop park road for about a mile, but it is a great overview of the park. Turn right (northeast) onto Panther Branch Trail.

6.0 The trail starts actually paralleling Panther Branch, and it is steep in places.

6.3 There is a really unique long cascade here. But be careful, the footing is slick.

6.4 The trail actually flattens out some and becomes gentler.

6.5 The trail crosses a wooden bridge across Panther Branch.

6.7 You come onto Panther Branch Campsite. There is also a nice bench with a roof there.

6.8 You cross a long footbridge. Immediately on the other side, you join the Emory Gap Side Trail, and if you bear to the right (east) at this junction, it is 0.5 mile up to the pretty Emory Gap Waterfalls. Go left (west) to continue. At this point Panther Branch Trail starts following an old roadbed and becomes easy walking. You cross several bridges, most wide enough for cars. Some of the abutments appear to have been there a long time—possibly more of the CCC work.

7.1 Debord Falls. There is an observation area and another trail that will take you to the bottom of the falls. Notice the huge hemlock tree and how it has been circled with some large "belts." Are these scars from sapsucker woodpeckers?

after a heavy rain, you may not see the volume pick up appreciably, where you would if the falls were fed strictly by surface runoff.

The cave, most often called Lost Creek Cave, is noted for its large passages and is another spectacular feature of this sink. For most of the cavers in Tennessee, visiting Lost Creek Cave is almost a rite of passage. However, as tempting as entering the cave might be, there are regulations that control its entry: Because of the presence of the white-nose syndrome, the cave is closed during the hibernating time of the bats. And to enter it at other times of the year requires an access permit, which can be obtained by contacting Fall Creek Falls State Park, which manages the natural area.

To get the full impression of this magnificent karst area, it is recommended to follow the trail from the parking area down to the waterfalls. An old trail, marked, ascends back out of the sink on the north side. It will bring you out back on the county road, passing several other small cascades and springs. Once hitting the county road, head back south toward the parking area. You will cross directly over the cave entrance. If you continue south on the road, you will come up onto another trailhead on the left of the road (east). It is 0.5 mile up this fairly flat trail to the Rylander Cascades, another water feature that emerges out of a cave and then disappears again. At this point you are standing only a couple of miles due west of Virgin Falls. Park officials hope that someday there will be a trail system linking these two beautiful areas.

This area, with its waterfalls and large cave, has been called by various names, including Ben White Cave and Falls and Dodson Cave.

Miles and Directions

0.0   Start from the parking lot. The trail, with steps, starts just to the right of the kiosk.

0.1   Arrive at Lost Creek Falls. Pivot 180 degrees around and you can see the looming entrance to the well-known Lost Creek Cave. The trail out of the sink begins about twenty paces back toward the cave entrance and to the north.

0.3   Meet the junction with the county road. Once on the road, make a hard right (south). This road crosses directly overhead of the cave entrance. The view from the road, looking westward, gives a good idea of the shape of this massive karst feature.

0.5   You will come back to the original entrance to the parking area. Keep straight on the county road.

0.7   Arrive at the junction with the Rylander Cascades Trail.

1.1   Enjoy the beautiful Rylander Cascades, and then return the way you came.

1.8   Arrive back at your car and the starting point.

The water for Lost Creek Falls comes out of one cave, flows over the precipice, and disappears into another passage. Fog and mist are common in the summer.

31 Gorge Overlook/Trail to Base of Fall Creek and Woodland Trail at Fall Creek Falls State Park

This is a wonderful 3-mile round-trip hike that highlights some of the scenic gems of this park. Starting at the park's interpretive center, the hike crosses a suspension bridge that is just above cascades. The trail then wanders a short distance through nice woods to several overlooks of both waterfalls and canyons, takes you over to an overlook of one of the highest waterfalls in the eastern United States, and then continues on for a better view of the gorge and waterfalls to the base.

Start: Betty Dunn Nature Center at Fall Creek Falls State Park

Distance: 3.1-mile lollipop loop

Hiking time: 3 hours

Difficulty: Strenuous, due to the elevation changes

Trail surface: Forest trail, several bridges, and a steep section through a rocky area

Best season: Year-round

Other trail users: Hikers only

Canine compatibility: Leashed dogs permitted

Fees and permits: None

Schedule: The park opens at sunrise and closes at 10 p.m., but you must be off the trails by dark.

Map: USGS quad: Sampson

Trail contact: Fall Creek Falls State Park, 10821 Park Road, Spencer, TN 38585. (423) 881-3297, (423) 881-5708, or (800) 250-8610

Finding the trailhead: From Nashville take I-40 for 75 miles to exit 288, just past Cookeville, onto TN 111 south. You will see park signs on TN 111 just south of Spencer. From Chattanooga take TN 27 north for 21 miles to the TN 111 split. Proceed on TN 111 north another 36 miles, until you see park signs to turn right onto Archie Rhinehart Parkway/TN 284, and follow it approximately 9 miles to the park. Upon entering the park, take the first right turn and follow it approximately 4 miles around to the Betty Dunn Nature Center. There are good interpretive exhibits there, plus maps. **GPS:** N35 39.758' / W85 21.010'

The Hike

Fall Creek Falls State Park is one of the most popular state parks in the southeastern United States, and this hike illustrates why. You will find waterfalls, canyons, cascades, rocky crags, and forest, and you will get an eyeful on this relatively short hike.

Fall Creek Falls State Park was actually first set aside by the National Park Service, with the land acquisition beginning in 1935 with 16,000 acres. The intent was to later turn it over to the state, but when some park officials saw the roaring waterfalls and deep gorges, they had second thoughts and almost kept it as part of the national park system. But in 1944 it was turned over to the state. In the late 1960s, the look of the park changed quite a bit, with an influx of development: an inn and restaurant, twenty cabins, an eighteen-hole golf course, the Betty Dunn Nature Center, the

33 Byrd Lake Trail/Pioneer Short Loop at Cumberland Mountain State Park

This is a gentle hike that takes the hiker around Byrd Lake and to some of the main features of this Depression-era r the hike gives an opportunity for wildlife viewing natural features can be enjoyed, including a small w white pines and hemlock trees, and some nice rock f

Start: Park headquarters
Distance: 3.0-mile loop
Hiking time: About 2 hours
Difficulty: Moderate
Trail surface: Earthen, rock, a couple of bridges, with a sidewalk toward the end
Best season: Any time of year
Other trail users: Hiking only

Canine c
Fees and
Schedule:
Maps: Clo
USGS 7.5
Trail conta
Park, 24 C
484-6138

Finding the trailhead: From Knoxville take I-40 west to ex Orchard, make a right onto Market Street and left onto US 70 south onto Cox Valley Road. Go 3.4 miles, turn right onto TN 6 and south onto US 127, which will take you to the park entra west to the park headquarters, which is on the right. **GPS:** 35

The Hike

Cumberland Mountain State Park is a beautiful 1,720 aside around 1938 to provide recreation for the fam stead Project. This New Deal project was set up un Act to provide support for local families struggling Depression, aggravated by the closing of several loca

The dam, which is constructed of locally quar considered the largest masonry project ever built by t (CCC). And just downstream of the dam is the Mill nally built to provide a mill for the Homesteads fam mill itself were never installed, and today it is mana Today, the park, along with much of the original F National Register of Historic Places.

This 3-mile hike will take you around Byrd Lak CCC circa 1935. On the hike, you will see lots of ev of the CCC and the Works Progress Administration (

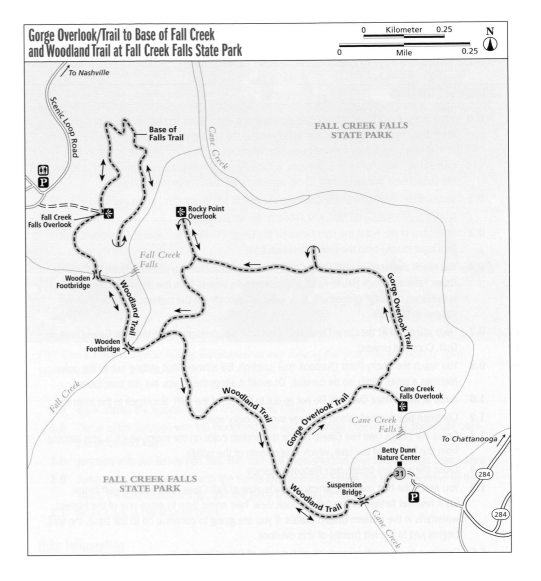

Village Green area, miles of paved roads, and numerous ranger residences were all built. In the early 1990s, to protect the park's watershed and viewshed from development and mining activities, park staff rallied support and acquired another 10,000 acres to better protect the park's scenery and resources.

It is its diversity that makes Fall Creek such a remarkable park. You can hike or rock-hop through some of the wildest areas in Tennessee, breathe in the mist from stunning waterfalls, and then follow up your exploration with a meal at the park's restaurant, or even crash in one of the comfortable hotel rooms. And it looks like the opportunities for outdoor recreation will continue to increase. Adjoining the park is another 28,000 acres of public land, some of it donated to the state by the

12.0 You arrive at the junction with the Turkey Pen Trail. Contin[...]

12.1 The Gorge Overlook Trail rejoins the trail you are on at th[...] again.

12.2 Meet the junction with the Trail to Campground C. Turn le[...]

12.3 Cross the suspension bridge over Cane Creek.

12.3 You arrive at the Betty Dunn Nature Center, named for th[...] Winfield Dunn.

12.4 Look for a side trail out to the Cane Creek Gulf Overlook[...]

12.5 Follow the sidewalk out to the road, and then bear left ([...] the Paw Paw Trail.

12.7 You will reach another side trail to an overlook of Cane C[...] Pass another nice overlook of Cane Creek Falls, from a [...]

12.8 Backtrack back to the Paw Paw Trail.

12.9 Begin the Paw Paw Loop. Bear right (east).

13.4 You are at the junction of the Paw Paw Trail and the Lowe[...]

13.8 Cross the Park Road near the north entrance to the parl[...]

14.0 Reach the trail junction of the Upper and Lower Loops. E[...] where the hike began. **Note:** This 14-mile distance inclu[...] Millikan's Overlook. The actual trail is 13 miles long.

THE CUMBERLAND TRAIL

The idea for having a trail that traversed the length of the Cumberland Plateau and Mountains was probably first articulated in the mid-1960s and was advocated by outdoors writer Evan Means, Nashville banker and avid hiker Bob Brown, Mack Prichard, and others, who started lobbying the state government for long-distance trails. The Tennessee Trails Association was formed in 1968 to be the advocacy arm of this push for trails. With the passage of the Natural Areas Act, the Scenic Rivers Act, and the Scenic Trails Act under Governor Winfield Dunn, the mechanism was put in place for the creation of the Cumberland Trail.

The Tennessee Trails Association obtained its 501(c)(3) nonprofit designation in 1975 in order to help obtain easements and leases for the Cumberland Trail on the bluffs above Lake City and across Brady Mountain. Work on this trail hit setbacks with budget constraints under the McWherter administration around 1990, and was revived under the leadership of Justin Wilson, deputy governor for environment and policy under successor Governor Sundquist. Today the Justin P. Wilson Cumberland Trail State Park is up and running and directly manages almost 30,000 acres. Its trails cross over 200,000 acres of other units of public land. The Cumberland Trail Conference (cumberlandtrail.org), a nonprofit group, was formed to actually build the trail. At this writing 190 miles of trails out of a planned 300 miles have been built. It may be decades before the vision of Evan Means, Bob Brown, and others is fully realized. However, in the meantime, the areas that have been set aside are amazing in their beauty and complexity. Get out and discover them!

0.6 Arrive at the wooden footbridge that crosses the lake to the boathouse. This is a good place to take a shortcut, if you want. The steps to the left (south) lead to the recreation hall and pool. Continue straight to stay on the described hike.

0.8 Cross a small wooden bridge.

0.9 You will start encountering some of the large white pine trees that are found along the trail.

1.0 There is a small waterfall just off the trail. It is probably seasonal, although it was flowing well at the time we hiked here.

1.1 The trail passes through a thicket of mountain laurel and rhododendron, which are typical shrubs of the Cumberland Plateau.

1.4 Pass a small rock overhang, or "rock house," to the left of the trail, and a large hemlock tree on the right of the trail.

1.5 Enjoy some nicely laid rock steps, probably Depression-era in origin. Then arrive at a trail junction, with kiosk.

1.6 Cross over a suspension bridge.

1.8 Notice that the trees are smaller on this south-facing slope. Although there are probably several factors involved, "south slope" trees are typically smaller than "north slope" timber.

2.2 You will find a nice rocky spot overlooking the lake. Take a break.

2.4 The trail emerges behind the park cabins. Some of these cabins are Depression-era, and others are more recent.

2.5 Take a detour down to the boathouse area. The boathouse and dock area is also Depression-era. This is the same footbridge you saw earlier.

2.7 The CCC Bathhouse has been newly renovated, and contains a small museum and a meeting area for the park. The restaurant is just down the sidewalk.

2.8 Cross the bridge and notice the fine stone work.

3.0 You reach the end of the hike, back at the headquarters parking lot.

36 North Chickamauga Creek Trail at North Chickamauga State Natural Area

The North Chickamauga Creek Gorge is a very important hiking and recreation area located just 15 miles north of Chattanooga. The trail is great and is a portion of the North Chickamauga Creek Segment of the Cumberland Trail. However, expect lots of swimmers in the summer, coupled with a lack of parking and crowding. Spring or fall trips can be somewhat calmer.

Start: Parking lot off of Montlake Road
Distance: 4.8 miles out and back
Hiking time: 3 to 4 hours
Difficulty: Moderate to strenuous, due to elevation change, and uneven footing in places
Trail surface: Old rail grade in one section, switchbacks, and nice stairway near top
Best season: Good year-round hiking, but crowding and lack of parking in summer
Other trail users: Hikers mainly, but in the summer lots of swimmers in the creek
Canine compatibility: Leashed dogs permitted

Fees and permits: None required for day use. For backpacking, please call (423) 566-2229 or register at friendsofthecumberlandtrail.org.
Schedule: Sunrise to 7 p.m. (If you get locked in, call the Hamilton County Sheriff Department to let you out, but you may be ticketed.) HCSD should be notified at (423) 622-0022 if you are leaving a car overnight.
Maps: The Cumberland Trail Conference has good maps at cumberlandtrail.org.
Trail contact: Cumberland Trail State Park, South Trail Office, 1838 Taft Hwy., Signal Mountain, TN 37377; (423) 886-2951

Finding the trailhead: From Chattanooga take US 127 28 miles to Dunlap. From Dunlap head east 6.2 miles to the Lewis Chapel Road exit. Take the exit and head south (Lewis Chapel Road turns into Poe Road). Follow Lewis Chapel/Poe Road 10 miles until it dead-ends into Montlake Road. Turn right on Montlake Road and go 4 miles to the turnoff for the parking lot, which will be on the right (west) side of the road. **GPS:** N35 14.259' / W85 14.065'

The Hike

The North Chickamauga Creek Gorge is a beautiful canyon just north of Chattanooga. Its major feature is the gorge itself, cut out of the east flank of the Cumberland Plateau (or more specifically, Walden's Ridge) by North Chickamauga Creek. The gorge is remarkable for its sheer sandstone bluffs, the tumbling creek that bisects the area, and the lush forest cover.

The natural area measures 7,093 acres, and its core area was first set aside as a pocket wilderness area by Bowater Pulp and Paper Company. Later, the North Chickamauga Creek Conservancy added to the acreage, and when Bowater Pulp and Paper divested itself of its land holdings in 2006, the pocket wilderness and some associated acreage was purchased by the state in order to protect the area and to pro-

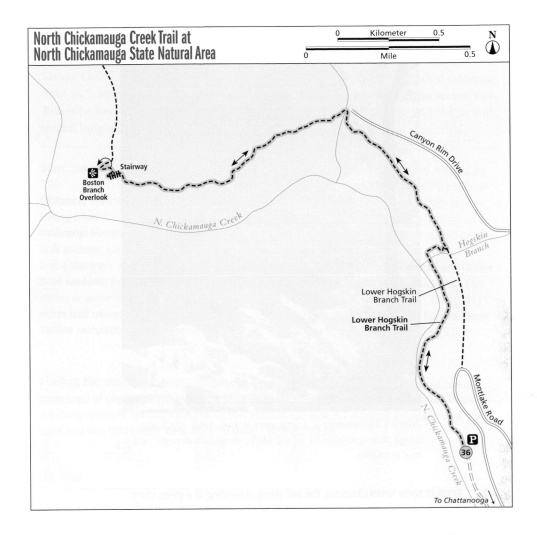

North Chickamauga Creek Trail at
North Chickamauga State Natural Area

0   Kilometer   0.5

N

0   Mile   0.5

Stairway

Boston
Branch
Overlook

N. Chickamauga Creek

Canyon Rim Drive

Hogskin Branch

Lower Hogskin
Branch Trail

Lower Hogskin
Branch Trail

Montlake Road

N. Chickamauga Creek

P
36

To Chattanooga

vide recreational access. With 7,093 acres set aside, this natural area is one of the larger state natural areas. It is managed by Cumberland Trail State Park and is an important link in the planned 300-mile trail system that hopefully someday will cross the state. Your hike covers part of the North Chickamauga Creek Segment, which measures 8.3 miles in total and stretches to Barker Camp Road, but includes some rugged hiking and creek fords.

Miles and Directions

0.0 Start at the parking lot off Montlake Road. Expect lots of cars in the summer.

0.2 You will be on the Lower Hogskin Branch Trail. Almost immediately, you reach the junction with Upper Hogskin Branch Trail. Continue on your trail, paralleling the creek.

0.4 Reach the junction with the Soddy Blue Hole access trail that crosses the creek. Stay on main trail.

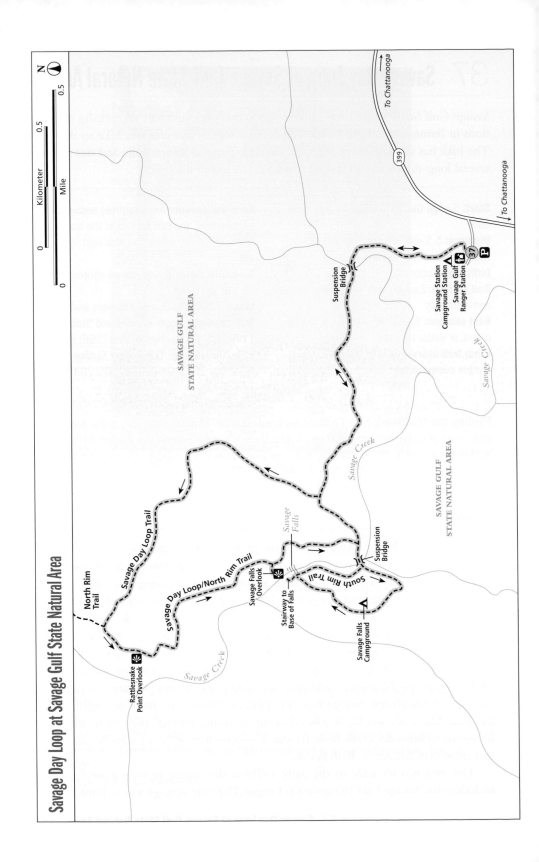

Savage Day Loop at Savage Gulf State Natural Area

Savage Falls is one of the highlights of this scenic area.

time and designated as a natural area to reduce the possibility of development, and to highlight it wilderness qualities. It contains the Werner Big Timber Stand, which is recognized as one of the largest old-growth timber areas left in the Cumberlands. A plaque at Rattlesnake Point recognizes Sam Werner and his family, who protected the area for decades until it was bought by the state. There are no hiking trails down into this large old growth stand, partially to ensure it will remain pristine. You will have to enjoy it from the overlook above it, Rattlesnake Point.

At several points the trail is built atop a rail bed where old small-gauge rail lines were once laid. These "dinky lines" were spread out across the landscape, bringing coal and timber to central collection areas. In several places you will notice coal on the trail that fell off of the rail cars years ago. And coming up from Savage Falls, on the bank of the creek, there are the remains of an old moonshine still that once used the area's isolation and clean water from Savage Creek to cook off a "batch of shine."

A note about the distance: The actual Savage Day Loop is listed as being only a little over 4 miles long. However, the side trail to the base of Savage Falls is very worthwhile. And we also took a side loop through the Savage Falls Campground to look at the thoughtful layout of the area. The described hike winds up being 5.1 miles.

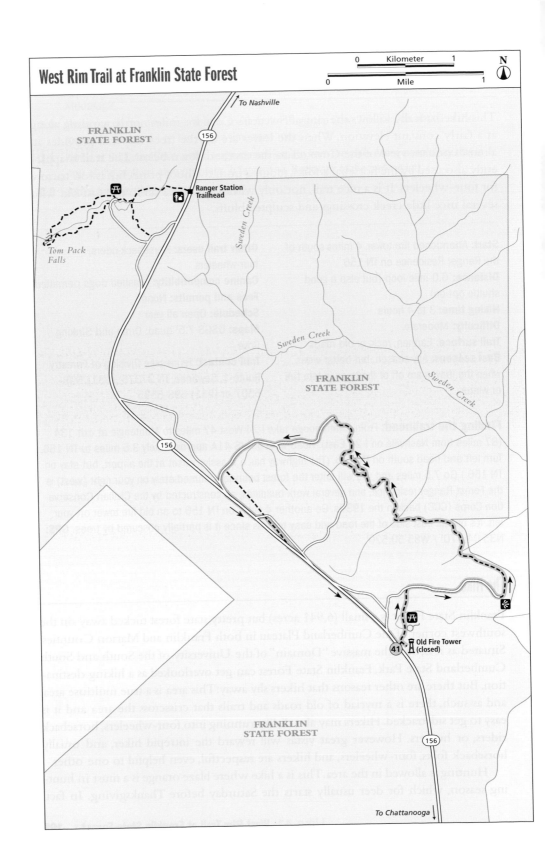

West Rim Trail at Franklin State Forest

To Nashville

FRANKLIN
STATE FOREST

156

Sweden Creek

Ranger Station
Trailhead

Tom Pack
Falls

Sweden Creek

FRANKLIN
STATE FOREST

Sweden Creek

156

41   Old Fire Tower
          (closed)

FRANKLIN
STATE FOREST

156

To Chattanooga

The Sweden's Cove Overlook offers a great panorama of the area.

we recommend staying totally away from areas that allow hunting on the opening week of gun season, and find hiking areas that have either no hunting or safety zones around the trails for that short time period.

This area was set aside in 1936 as a state forest, and the forest headquarters, just inside the north entrance, represents classic CCC structure. A kiosk near the road contains user regulations and a trail map. The trail to Tom Pack Falls begins just behind the large work buildings by the ranger residence (**GPS:** N35 07.102' / W85 51.947'). It is a short hike and the falls and the associated rock overhang are worth the trip. There is also a nice little lake with an associated picnic area, likely also built by the CCC.

The featured West Rim Trail described here, however, begins at an abandoned fire tower. (Most fire towers in Tennessee, if not abandoned, have been torn down, since Forestry has opted to look for fires with airplanes now.) The described hike follows the Rim Trail for several miles, then cuts back to the car via some of the old four-wheeler trails. But these trails can become confusing, so you might want to hike this as a shuttle or an out-and-back trail, coming back along the Rim Trail to be assured of the route and have a better handle on the time.

Miles and Directions

0.0 From the parking area at the fire tower, take the old road to the north for about 320 feet, and turn right into the woods. The trail seems to diverge, and there is a trail sign with mileage for the "West Rim Trail." However, just before this sign is an old road to the left, which leads to an underused picnic area and Cave Spring, which is a small rock overhang, or "cave," that has a spring coming out of it and has been walled in. There is extensive rock work there, probably more CCC handiwork. The trail continues to the north and soon comes out at a gravel road.

0.5 Junction with dirt road. Bear to the right (east) to return to the West Rim Trail.

1.2 There is a great overlook of Sweden's Cove. The trail continues off to the north of that overlook.

1.7 Walk over a small wooden footbridge and cross a road.

2.2 You find nice rock steps across a wet area, followed by a beautiful cascade overlook at 2.3 miles and a new wooden bridge with some nice trail work.

2.7 There is a split in the trail: Horses are directed to the left (west), and hikers to the right (east). We took the horse trail, which stays on the rim; the hiker trail goes down a ravine to a creek. These two trails come back together farther north.

3.3 Arrive at a junction with "F" marking the trail. At this point start navigating the old dirt roads to get back over to TN 156. (If you continue straight, the Rim Trail will return you to TN 156 in a slightly larger arc.)

3.4 Meet a junction with another old road, and bear left.

3.8 Arrive at a big junction, with several dirt lanes, and bear right (west).

4.1 Meet another junction and continue straight ahead.

4.4 At TN 156 you can parallel the highway on dirt lanes for much of the remaining distance, walking for awhile under a power line right-of-way.

4.6 Leave the power line ROW, and walk the highway.

4.7 Bear left on another dirt road toward the fire tower.

6.0 Back at the fire tower and the end of the hike. This would be a great hike to run a shuttle on, so that you can walk the whole rim in peace, and have a ride waiting at the other end. But because a dirt road essentially parallels TN 156 for most of the way, the walk back is not onerous either.

42 Climber's Loop at Foster Falls Small Wild Area

The highlight of the Foster Falls Small Wild Area is the beautiful Foster Falls itself. The main overlook has a very accessible elevated walkway and deck overlooking the 60-foot-high waterfalls and plunge basin below. The Climber's Loop leads you down to the base of the falls, then follows the bluff line before climbing out on top and joining the Fiery Gizzard Trail.

Start: Foster Falls parking lot off US 41
Distance: 1.9-mile loop
Hiking time: About 2 hours
Difficulty: Moderate due to rocky, uneven footing
Trail surface: Rocks, earth in places
Best season: Year-round, something different every season
Other trail users: Just hikers. But you will usually encounter many rock climbers around the climbing routes.

Canine compatibility: Leashed dogs permitted
Fees and permits: If you are going to camp or backpack from here, you must register.
Schedule: Daylight to dark, but be out of the parking area by dark, unless you are going to camp.
Map: USGS 7.5' quad: White City
Trail contact: South Cumberland State Park, 11745 US 41, Monteagle, TN 37356; (931) 924-2980

Finding the trailhead: From Chattanooga take I-24 West for 23 miles, then turn north on TN 28 at exit 155. Head west on US 72 for less than a mile, then right (north) onto Betsy Pack Drive through Jasper, which becomes US 41. Take US 41 7.5 miles, and look for signs for Foster Falls parking area on the left. From Tracy City head south on US 41 for 7.4 miles, and look on your right. Turn in and drive another 0.5 mile to the trailhead parking. **GPS:** N35 10.948' / W85 40.443'

The Hike

There are many things to see, and many places to explore in the Foster Falls Small Wild Area, which is actually owned by Tennessee Valley Authority (TVA) and is cooperatively managed with the South Cumberland State Park. This area has two different camping areas, the Father Adamz walk-in sites and a more developed campground that is open seasonally. The area also is a popular destination for sport climbers on the bluffs just downstream from the waterfalls. Foster Falls is also the terminus for the Fiery Gizzard Trail. But even if you don't want to do a long-distance hike, there are some nice places to explore here, as the Climber's Loop demonstrates.

Miles and Directions

0.0 The trail begins just south of the parking lot. A long boardwalk leads to an impressive overlook of Foster Falls. This overlook itself is worth the stop, even if you don't want to go any farther down the trail! But the trail continues on south of the deck. The trail starts

Climber's Loop at Foster Falls Small Wild Area

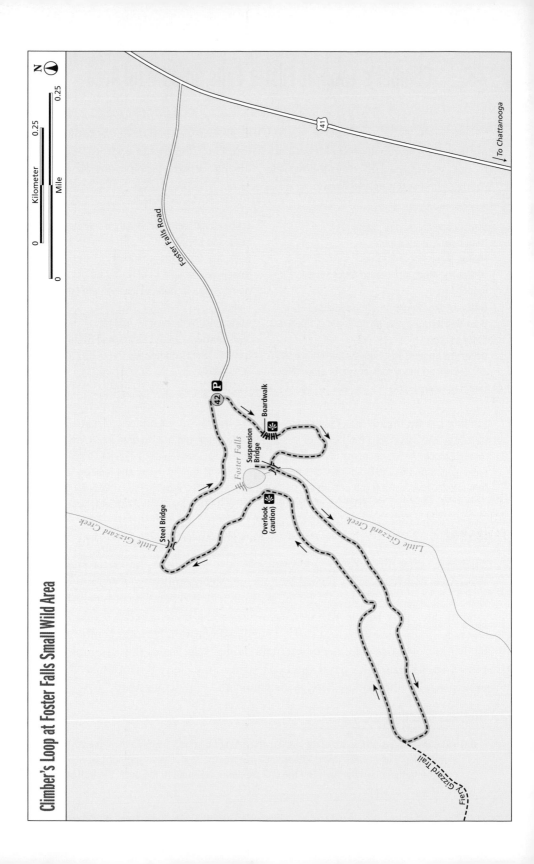

This overlook of Foster Falls is also very steep, with a drop off . . . be very careful.

descending rapidly, along a trail that is very steep in places and is therefore for those that are sure-footed.

0.3 A pleasant suspension bridge spans the creek at the bottom. It is only a short distance over to a great vantage point of Foster Falls from the base. The trail continues on just south of the plunge pool for the waterfalls, and is well marked with white metal blazes. The trail almost immediately climbs to the base of the bluff line and follows the base for a ways. You quickly see why it is called the "Climber's Trail," in that the trail accesses the long, straight bluff lines. With lots of hard sandstone and straight bluff lines, rock climbers find a lot of varied and challenging routes. The area is bustling with climbers, overall.

0.8 A sign points upward for the first "out" from the canyon. The trail quickly ascends up a set of steeply laid steps to the top of the bluff.

0.9 At the top of the bluff, and a short distance down the trail, you come in contact with the longer day loop and with the Fiery Gizzard Trail.

1.2 Reach an overlook that looks back down the canyon.

1.3 Arrive at a junction with a side trail over to Father Adamz Campsites.

1.4 Your grand finale is an incredible overlook to Foster Falls. However, be warned, the rocks are down-sloping toward a tremendous drop off the cliff face. Stay well back from the edge and the down-sloping rocks.

1.7 Cross over the creek on a green steel bridge.

1.9 Return to the parking lot for the end of your hike.

Hike Information

Local organizations

Friends of South Cumberland, PO Box 816, Sewanee, TN 37375; friendsofcsra.org.

43 Trail from Signal Point to Edwards Point at Prentice Cooper State Forest

This is a very diverse hike that starts in the Signal Point Reservation of the Chickamauga Chattanooga National Battlefield and goes over to Edwards Point, a spectacular overlook in Prentice Cooper State Forest. The hike begins in the community of Signal Mountain, a bedroom community of Chattanooga. This is a heavily used hiking area.

Start: Parking area at the Signal Point Reservation of the Chickamauga Chattanooga National Battlefield
Distance: 6.0 miles out and back
Hiking time: About 4 hours
Difficulty: The first part of this trail has lots of steps, with uneven footing. It probably should be considered strenuous.
Trail surface: Rocks, steps
Best season: Year-round
Other trail users: Hikers and runners on the hiking trail. But you will see other users over toward Edwards Point.

Canine compatibility: Leashed dogs permitted
Fees and permits: None required for day use
Schedule: Areas close at dark.
Map: USGS quad Camp Austin
Trail contacts: Prentice Cooper State Forest, 3998 Game Preserve Rd., Chattanooga, TN 37405, or Jim Lane, PO Box 160, Hixson, TN 37343; (423) 658-5551. Chickamauga Chattanooga National Military Park, 110 Point Park Rd., Lookout Mountain, TN 37350.

Finding the trailhead: The trailhead begins in the city limits of Signal Mountain, a small community located on the Walden Ridge, just northwest of Chattanooga. Take US 127 out of Chattanooga, climb the plateau, and just before the first (and only) traffic light in Signal Mountain, turn left on Signal Mountain Boulevard. Follow the NPS signs to the parking area. Notice the street-car rails in the road at one point. **GPS:** N35 07.220' / W85 21.995'

The Hike

This is a diverse hike, and it begins in a diverse area. Even driving over to the parking area, you can see the rails in the street, remnants of the trolley system that used to serve the community of Signal Mountain. The parking area is managed by Chickamauga Chattanooga National Park, the first national battlefield to be set aside in the United States. Signal Point was exactly that: a signal point used by the Union troops to signal information in and out of the besieged town of Chattanooga during the fall of 1863. Even such a small area has the feel of a national park or monument. This hike also represents the southern terminus of the Cumberland Trail.

Most of this hike, however, is located in Prentice Cooper State Forest, one of the larger state forests in Tennessee. Prentice Cooper State Forest was acquired between

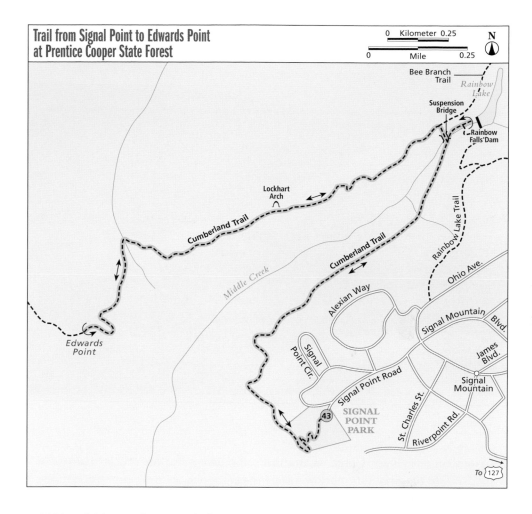

Bee Branch
Trail   *Rainbow*
                      Lake

Suspension
Bridge

Rainbow
Falls'Dam

Lockhart
Arch

Cumberland Trail

Rainbow Lake Trail

Cumberland Trail

Ohio Ave.

Middle Creek

Edwards
Point

Alexian Way

Signal Mountain Blvd.

James
Blvd.

Signal
Point Cir.

Signal
Point Road

Signal
Mountain

43   SIGNAL
      POINT
      PARK

St. Charles St.

Riverpoint Rd.

To 127

1938 and 1944, and is named after Tennessee Governor Prentice Cooper. It is 24,686 acres in size and is divided into several management units, including Hicks Gap State Natural Area, which was established to protect the large flowered skullcap.

Being located in such a heavily populated area, the forest is probably the most heavily used state forest in the system, at least recreationally. Mountain bikers, runners, hikers, birders, and other outdoor enthusiasts head to the area on weekends or on weekday afternoons. There are multiple access points for the forest, and multiple destinations.

As you get nearer to Edwards Point, several other trails appear to join in. And Edwards Point itself appears to be a junction of several trails. On the day we visited, mountain bikers and runners alike were enjoying the views. And the area also appeared to get a fair amount of four-wheeler traffic. But the view down into the Tennessee River Gorge makes it all worthwhile. To the east, you are looking down toward Williams Island and Chattanooga. To the west are the heavily forested flanks

The view from Edwards Point is great, looking eastward toward Williams Island, and Chattanooga.

of the Tennessee River Gorge, an area that some have called the "Grand Canyon of the East." In the river, down below, a large riverboat plies its way upstream, carrying lots of tourists back to dock. After enjoying the scenery, you can start the hike back to Signal Point.

Miles and Directions

0.0 Start in the nice little park maintained by the National Park Service. A beautiful overlook, with interpretive signage, is at the trailhead. To begin the actual trail, look to the west for a gap in the fence. A kiosk there has trail information. Be prepared: You are stepping from a finely groomed and easily accessible overlook to a steep trail where the footing can be slick or unstable.

0.4 A very nice overlook looks west toward Edwards Point. Notice the large chestnut oaks scattered along the hillside. These trees are well adapted for this terrain. Invasive exotic plants have created a little dense area. Most of the bad guys of invasive exotics are located there: burning bush (euonymus), bush honeysuckle, multiflora rose, privet. They are probably escapees from the development above.

1.0 Thank goodness the natives take over again here, with lots of pawpaw shrubs all around.

1.1 You reach a confusing junction. Bear left (south), downhill, beside the boulder.

1.2 Cross a small suspension bridge and continue.

1.3 You reach a larger suspension bridge over a small creek and the junction with Ohio Avenue Trail, with evidence of camping. Explore upstream a bit and you'll come out at a small dam with a spillway, marked "Rainbow Falls." The impoundment is old, and the pond is largely filled in with silt and plants. Was it to supply water for the houses, or reservoir for a water mill? The purpose of the dam and pond remain unknown.

1.6 Back to the suspension bridge on the main trail.

1.7 Pass a huge bluff with a massive collapse feature, with evidence of another campsite.

1.9 The trail turns right, beside a boulder, an easy-to-miss turn, and then turns left on top just before you reach Lockhart Arch, a small but neat arch on the left (east) of the trail. You then pass an overlook back to the east, but the beauty of this overlook is somewhat diminished by a large condominium development on the side of the facing bluff.

2.0 There appears to be another trail coming in from the right (north) side of trail, but no signage, just a post. Bear left (south).

2.1 Once again you reach an overlook facing east toward condos.

2.6 You cross a creek, which should be nice when the water is flowing.

2.9 This is the first overlook in the Edwards Point area. It is shaded and a nice place for a break.

3.0 You arrive at the main Edwards Point Overlook area. It is also the junction for several four-wheeler trails. After taking in the view, retrace your steps along the trail you just traveled.

6.0 Arrive back at the trailhead on Signal Point.

Chattanooga and the Southeast

The southeast corner of Tennessee is steeped in history, like the rest of Tennessee, having been the scene of conflicts between North and South, settler and native tribes, and French and English forces. You can explore each of these conflicts in the hikes in this section. In what was possibly the deciding victory of the Civil War, the North faced the South right on Lookout Mountain in Chattanooga, and you can hike over ground that was covered in gun-smoke 150 years ago. Red Clay State Park was where the Cherokee had their last Great Council with the US government, and they began the 3,000-mile "Trail of Tears" to Oklahoma from this point. And at Fort Loudoun, the British regrouped to fight the French over territorial rights (with the help, ironically, of the Cherokees).

This corner of the state's hiking opportunities are dominated by the southern districts of the Cherokee National Forest (CNF). Within these areas are a wealth of exciting possibilities, all the more enjoyable because they are less frequented than trails to the north. CNF contains 625,000 acres of mostly undeveloped land and stretches along the eastern border of the state of Tennessee, with the Unaka and Watauga Districts north of Great Smoky Mountains National Park (GSMNP), and the Tellico and Ocoee Districts to the south. The districts are named mostly for the river basins within them.

Ocoee is a Cherokee word meaning "apricot vine place," referring to what is now known as the passion flower plant. John Muir, the great conservationist and founder of the Sierra Club, described the area along the Hiwassee River as "vinedraped and flowery as Eden." The Ocoee Ranger District includes the Hiwassee area, Cohutta Wilderness, Rock Creek Gorge Scenic Area, Little Frog Mountain Wilderness, Big Frog Wilderness, and the West Big Frog Primitive Area. The Big Frog and Cohutta tracts combined, in Tennessee and Georgia, create 45,111 acres of wilderness, which is the largest wilderness tract on national forest lands in the eastern United States. All these areas are within the Ocoee Bear Reserve. (Bears were relocated here in the 1970s from GSMNP.) The area also has an abundance of deer, wild turkeys, timber rattlesnakes, and copperheads.

The Tellico Ranger District, with approximately 160,000 acres and 150 miles of trails, is the second-most frequently visited of CNF's four districts. North of the Cherohala Skyway Road (TN 165) is the 16,226-acre Citico Creek Wilderness. This area gets over 70 inches of rain a year, and often trails can get muddy in rainy weather, especially along streambeds. But Citico has some wonderful hikes, some of which are featured in "Additional Great Hikes" at the end of this chapter. The Citico area was logged heavily in the early 1900s, and pictures from surveys during that period show that there were few trees left. However, a portion of the virgin timber was saved by a serious fire around 1925, which burned up the railroad beds before they could bring out the lumber. Since it was too expensive to reconstruct the rails to remove the little timber that was left, the result today is that you can still hike among some 187 acres of virgin cove hardwood forest in the Jeffrey Hell section of the wilderness, which has a very different character than the usual oak–pine forest that now dominates the region. The Falls Branch Trail (see "Additional Great Hikes") wanders through some of this virgin timber.

Stunning views from the Ochs Museum atop Lookout Mountain.

formations along the Bluff Trail are extremely interesting, with many cave-like openings and overhangs. The trail has natural benches along the way for resting, and metal walkways have been created in areas where a passage along the bluff might not be possible.

The Bluff Trailhead is at the Ochs Museum in Point Park, in the middle of a residential neighborhood at the top of Lookout Mountain. Point Park has numerous monuments to the battle, a small museum, and the trailheads or connections for most of the Lookout Mountain trails. The Ochs Museum provides very nice views from an octagon-shaped stone terrace, 1,350 feet above the river. This is where the Kentucky Volunteers climbed the mountain to plant their flag during the Battle Above the Clouds. Right below you here are the Cravens House grounds (free admission), which also can be accessed through the trail system. The photographs in the Ochs Museum are fascinating, really taking you a step back in time.

The view here shows the broad curves of Moccasin Bend, Signal Mountain, and Missionary Ridge. A plaque along the way to the Ochs Museum records an imaginative explanation of local geography provided by the Cherokee Indians: "At first the earth was soft and very wet. The people sent the Great Buzzard to test the land, and the valleys and mountains were formed where his wings hit the ground as he grew weary in his long flight over the earth."

In addition to the Battle of Lookout Mountain, the park and the adjoining Reflection Riding area are also the scenes of other historic events. DeSoto followed the Great Indian Warpath through here in 1540. It was also the site where Chickamauga villages were wiped out by forces under John "Nolichucky Jack" Sevier in 1782 in the last battle of the American Revolution. Landmarks within the historic area include Sunset Rock, Point Park, Craven House, and "Castle in the Sky," a former resort hotel now occupied by Covenant College.

Miles and Directions

0.0 Start from the base of the metal stairs behind the Ochs Museum at the river-view end of Point Park. Make a sharp left to head out on the Bluff Trail. For the first 0.5 mile, the trail gradually descends, following the bed of a narrow-gauge railroad, which was called the Dinky Line.

0.2 You pass the sign for Rock Spring.

0.5 Reach the junction of the Cravens House Trail, where another sign proclaims the distance to Skyuka Spring. You will continue to the left, continuing to follow the contour of the mountain. (You can also begin this hike at the Cravens House, which has free admission.)

1.0 Pass a large crevice in the rock, with a trickle of water coming out of it, and a hint of a cool breeze coming from the crevice.

1.1 Arrive at Sunset Rock. Confederate General James Longstreet stood at Sunset Rock and watched General Joseph Hooker's arrival. A sign directs you here to the top of Sunset Rock, and again contains mileages for Covenant College and Skyuka Spring (which are less than reliable measures).

1.2 The trail passes the junction with the Gum Spring Trail on the right, with more dubiously helpful trail signs.

1.9 Pass the "Giant's Niche," a 100-foot bluff that is popular for climbing.

2.1 The trail crosses a narrow gulch on a metal bridge, over a small stream that tumbles down a series of rock steps in heavy rain.

3.6 Just before you reach the Jackson Gap Trail junction, you will reach an outstanding overlook of the valley below.

3.7 At the Jackson Gap junction, you will veer left (don't follow the Jackson Gap Trail) and make the final climb for 0.6 mile to the Covenant College parking area and the end of the trail on West Brow Road. If you turn right at this junction, you will take the Jackson Gap Trail toward Skyuka Spring. Another option here is to double-back on the Skyuka Trail, giving you a much longer hike.

4.3 You have arrived at Covenant College. You can now return the way you came, or to walk the trail one-way, a car could be parked at Covenant College at Sunset Rock, with the first car parked at the trailhead at Point Park.

8.6 Arrive back at Point Park and the end of your hike.

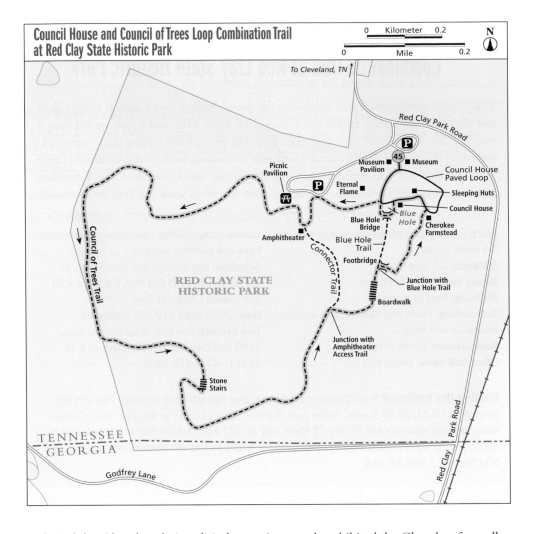

Council House and Council of Trees Loop Combination Trail at Red Clay State Historic Park

0   Kilometer   0.2

0   Mile   0.2

N

To Cleveland, TN

Red Clay Park Road

P

45

Museum

Museum

Council House Paved Loop

Picnic Pavilion

Museum Pavilion

Eternal Flame

Sleeping Huts

P

Council House

Blue Hole Bridge

Blue Hole

Cherokee Farmstead

Amphitheater

Blue Hole Trail

Connector Trail

Footbridge

RED CLAY STATE HISTORIC PARK

Junction with Blue Hole Trail

Council of Trees Trail

Boardwalk

Junction with Amphitheater Access Trail

Stone Stairs

TENNESSEE

GEORGIA

Red Clay Park Road

Godfrey Lane

denied the Cherokee their political sovereignty and prohibited the Cherokee from all political activity in Georgia, including council meetings, for any reason other than to treaty away their land. As a result, the Cherokee moved their headquarters from New Echota, Georgia, first to Alabama in 1831, and then to Red Clay in 1832, where the council met until just before the removal in 1838.

Also located here is the Council Spring and the Eternal Flame of the Cherokee Nation. The Eternal Flame has been burning continuously since the Trail of Tears commenced in 1838. The Cherokee carried hot coals from their council fire at Red Clay on their removal trek to Oklahoma. In the 1950s the flame was transported to Cherokee, North Carolina, and in April 1984, ten Cherokee runners carried the flame with torches to Red Clay, in a symbolic demonstration that the Cherokee spirit is unquenchable. Red Clay is recognized by the Cherokee as sacred ground. It has a quiet reflective atmosphere that you will feel immediately upon entering the grounds.

THE LAST GREAT COUNCIL OF THE CHEROKEE NATION

The October 1835 Council, led by Principal Chief of the Cherokee Nation John Ross, considered a proposed treaty with the United States providing for the removal of the Cherokee to the Indian territory that is now Oklahoma, and was overwhelmingly rejected by the Cherokee. Attending were John Howard Payne, author of *Home Sweet Home* and a champion of Native American rights, a number of prominent US and Cherokee officials, and some observers, such as George Featherstonehaugh, who realized the significance of the event, and whose descriptions of the council meetings are recorded on plaques on the council grounds at Red Clay. His report captures a sense of the event:

> Long after I laid down, the voices of hundreds of the most pious among [the Cherokee] who assembled at the council house to perform their evening worship came pealing in hymns through the now quiet forest, and insensibly and gratefully lulled me to sleep.
>
> The most impressive feature, and that which imparted life to the whole, was an unceasing current of Cherokee Indians, men, women, youth and children, moving about in every direction, and in the greatest order, and all except the younger ones preserving a grave and thoughtful demeanor, imposed upon them by the singular position in which they were placed, and by the trying alternative now presented to them of delivering up their native country to their oppressors or perishing in a vain resistance.

The trail takes you from the pavilion connected to the visitor center to the paved Council House loop trail. You turn right to head to the Council of Trees trail, pass an amphitheater, go over a ridge through a forested area, and loop back to join the paved loop trail, which passes replicas of a Cherokee homestead, a Council House, and sleeping huts, as well as the Blue Hole, a spring that is sacred to the Cherokee people.

Miles and Directions

0.0 Start at the pavilion, which is connected to the visitor center by a covered walkway. Turn right onto the paved loop, heading toward the picnic shelter beyond the trees, passing the Eternal Flame on the right, which is a short distance off the trail.

0.1 Leave the paved loop and turn right to head toward the Council of Trees Trailhead on a connector trail.

Stone formations dating back more than a century mark the Council of Trees loop.

0.2 Another connector trail to the Amphitheater heads off to the left. The trail continues off to the right to reach the Council of Trees trailhead directly behind the picnic shelter and parking lot.

0.3 Reach the Council of Trees Trailhead, and continue on the trail, passing a resting bench at 1 mile. This needle-covered path first takes you through a mixed pine hardwood forest that is strewn with wildflowers in spring and has a pleasant variety of trees, including tulip poplar, black cherry, white oak, and others, in contrast with the surrounding oak-hickory forest.

1.2 At the highest point on the trail, stone steps to the left provide an overlook. While there are no real views to speak of, this is a peaceful place, and the benches are ideal for some afternoon reading. The trail from the overlook makes a sharp right and then curves left.

1.3 Your trail intersects with another and continues straight.

1.6 Cross a service road at a right angle and continue on the trail.

1.7 A boardwalk takes you over the marsh, then T-ends into another trail, and turns right. In a few feet you will cross a footbridge. A small spur trail here heads straight ahead to a meadow. Turn left to continue on the main trail.

1.8 The trail meets the paved Council House loop again. Turning right, you will first come to the replica Cherokee farmstead. After the farmstead the trail passes between replicas of sleeping huts and the Council House where Cherokee leaders met with US negotiators in their desperate last struggle to keep their lands from being treatied away.

1.9 Intersect with the Blue Hole side trail on the left. Take this side trail to see the unique blue waters and cross over the Blue Hole on a bridge. The Blue Hole is a sacred spring to the Cherokee that rises from an underground cave and flows into the Conasauga and Coosa River systems. Over 504,000 gallons of water flow through this 15-foot-deep spring each day. Council Spring provided water to the Cherokee councils. A plaque here explains a Cherokee belief that there is a mirror world under this one, and that the springs, at their heads, serve as the doorways through which we enter this other world.

2.0 Arrive at the end of the paved loop, and walk 350 feet to return to the pavilion.

Hike Information

Local organizations

To see the impressive things the Cherokee Nation is doing today, visit cherokee.org.

46 Big Frog Trail to Low Gap (CNF Trail No. 64) at Cherokee National Forest, Ocoee District

The less visited and less commercialized Big Frog Wilderness contains thirteen trails. They create a web-like, interlocking pattern over the broad face of Big Frog Mountain, and contain some narrow ridge hikes that provide striking views into Tennessee and Georgia, making this a popular backpacking destination. From the Big Frog Trail, there are many outstanding views of the surrounding mountains, including the Cohutta Wilderness to the south and the Tennessee Valley to the west, with lots of possibilities for loop trips and point-to-point trips. The Big Frog Trail makes a gradual climb along the ridgelines and passes the junctions of many of the trails in the network.

Start: The marked trailhead is at a small parking lot about 0.25 mile up FS 221 from the turnoff at Ocoee Powerhouse No. 3.
Distance: 11.2 miles out and back
Hiking time: About 6 to 7 hours
Difficulty: Moderate
Trail surface: Forest earthen trail and rock
Best seasons: Spring and fall (after first frost, to avoid ticks)
Other trail users: None

Canine compatibility: Leashed dogs permitted
Fees and permits: None
Schedule: Unmonitored, but if you are backpacking, check in with the Ocoee Ranger District.
Map: USGS quad: 126SE, Caney Creek
Trail contact: Ocoee Ranger District, 3171 Highway 64, Benton, TN 37307; (423) 338-3300

Finding the trailhead: Follow US 64 along the Ocoee River east from Cleveland to Ocoee Powerhouse No. 3 on the south side of the river, about 18.6 miles east of the intersection of US 64 and US 411. Look for a sign for Thunder Rock Campground. Cross the bridge, turn right, then follow a left fork (FS 45) up to the intersection with FS 221. Turn right on FS 221 and drive about 0.25 mile to the trailhead on the left. There is a small parking area. **GPS:** N34 59.639' / W84.56.744'

The Hike

The long, undulating summit ridge that forms that image of a big frog is also the location of the Big Frog Trail. Big Frog Trail (also known as the Peavine Ridge Trail) begins on an old logging road and climbs fairly steeply at first, then levels out along a ridgeline, until it arrives at Low Gap and the convergence of other trails that provide a plethora of great options. If you continue on from Low Gap to the top of Big Frog Mountain, from this 4,224-foot peak westward, there is no higher mountain until the Rockies or the Big Bend in Texas, though there are higher mountains to the north in the Smokies. A section of the Big Frog Trail is part of the Benton MacKaye

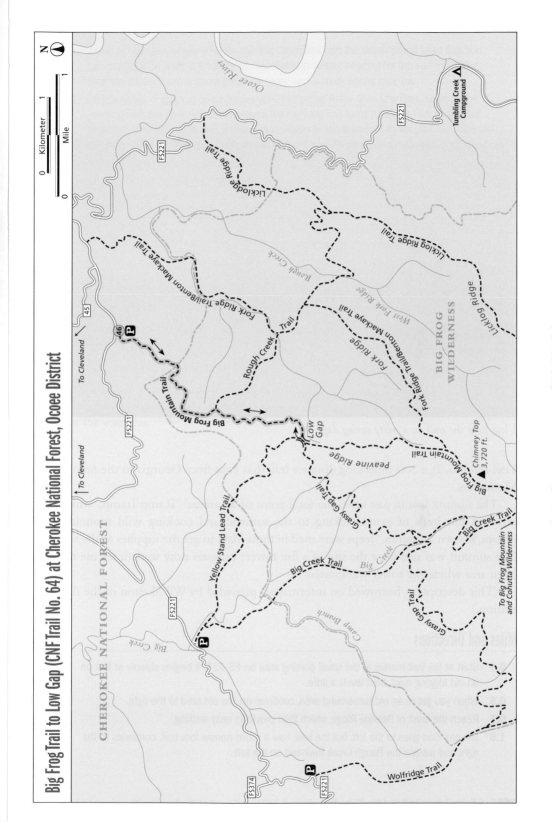

Big Frog Trail to Low Gap (CNF Trail No. 64) at Cherokee National Forest, Ocoee District

47 Benton Falls (CNF Trail No. 131) at Cherokee National Forest, Ocoee District

The Benton Falls Trail starts at Lake McCamy, at the top of Chilhowee Mountain, and provides an easy walk to a large cascade. The spectacular 65-foot, tiered Benton Falls pack a great punch for such a short hike, and the hike makes an ideal option for families with varying hiking abilities.

Start: Lower parking lot at Lake McCamy
Distance: 3.2 miles out and back
Hiking time: About 2 hours round-trip
Difficulty: Easy to moderate
Trail surface: Sand, packed earth, and rock
Best season: Beautiful any season
Other trail users: First portion of trail shared with mountain bikers
Canine compatibility: All pets must be confined to a leash, cage, or in a vehicle. Dogs must remain on a leash not to exceed 6 feet, unless being used for hunting during a designated hunting season where the use of dogs is legal. Pets are allowed in all areas except where posted otherwise (swimming areas, beaches, etc.).
Fees and permits: No entrance fee, but small parking fee to park at Lake McCamy
Schedule: Daily, dawn to dusk
Map: USGS quad: 126NE, Oswald Dome
Trail contact: Ocoee Ranger District, 3171 Highway 64, Benton, TN 37307; (423) 338-3300

Finding the trailhead: From Chattanooga take I-75 north to the US 64 bypass to US 64 at Cleveland, and continue east on US 64 through the town of Ocoee into Cherokee National Forest. Continue on US 64 along the shore of Lake Ocoee, and turn left on FS 77 at the sign for Chilhowee Recreation Area. Head up Chilhowee Mountain for 7.2 miles, turn right near the top toward the campground area, and continue 0.5 mile to the lower parking lot for Lake McCamy. **GPS:** N35 09.002' / W84 36.460'

The Hike

This is one of the most stunning falls in southeast Tennessee, and with the added benefit of the amazingly scenic drive up and the sweet white-sand beach of Lake McCamy, this hike is a real winner. Lake McCamy, where the trail starts, has a small but pretty light-sand beach and provides a relaxed and scenic swimming spot. The smells of earth and plants along the Benton Falls Trail are wonderful, like smoky fires of aromatic wood. Several other trails have their start at Lake McCamy, and two other trails have their start at the Benton Falls Trailhead. The 0.4-mile Forest Walk (#130) loops through the woods behind Lake McCamy, and the McCamy Lake Trail loops around the lakeshore for 0.7 mile.

Although a little difficult to find at the beginning, once you are on the Benton Falls Trail, you will find it very well marked with blue markers. The wide, flat, and

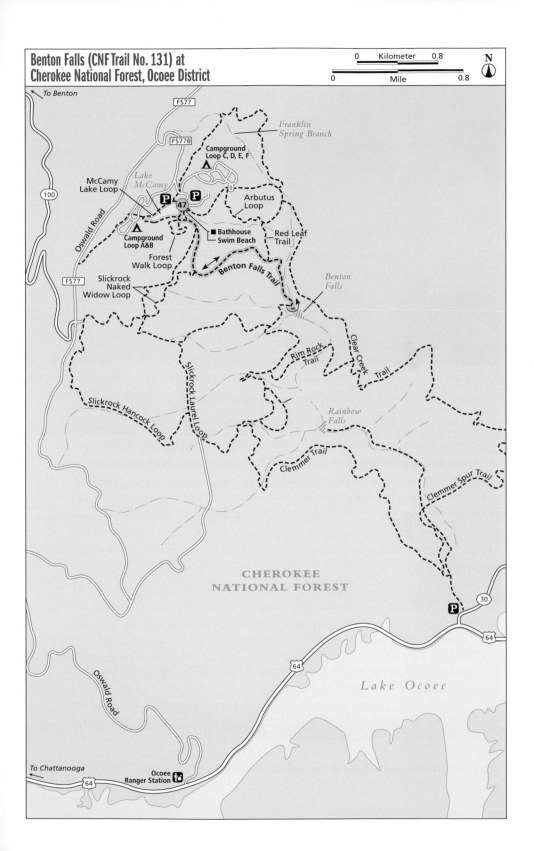

Benton Falls (CNF Trail No. 131) at Cherokee National Forest, Ocoee District

0   Kilometer   0.8

0   Mile   0.8

N

To Benton

FS77

FS77B

Franklin Spring Branch

Campground Loop C, D, E, F

McCamy Lake Loop

Lake McCamy

Arbutus Loop

100

47

Oswald Road

Bathhouse Swim Beach

Red Leaf Trail

Campground Loop A&B

Forest Walk Loop

Benton Falls Trail

Benton Falls

FS77

Slickrock Naked Widow Loop

Rim Rock Trail

Clear Creek Trail

Slickrock Laurel Loop

Rainbow Falls

Slickrock Hancock Loop

Clemmer Trail

Clemmer Spur Trail

CHEROKEE NATIONAL FOREST

30

P

64

Oswald Road

64

Lake Ocoee

To Chattanooga

64

Ocoee Ranger Station

Hikers enjoy the stunning view of Benton Falls.

mostly hard–packed clay or sandy trail is wheelchair accessible almost its whole length (with some maneuvering) until you get to the hard left down to the falls. But even there, the wide stone and rail-road tie steps could almost be managed, and a spur to one side appears to have been created to allow bikes to wheel past the steepest steps, giving access to the top of the falls, though the steps at the bottom are steeper and could not be navigated with a wheelchair. In fact, a good portion of the Benton Falls Trail is used by mountain bikers, who start at Lake McCamy and bike through past the falls on Clemmer Trail to US 64 where it intersects with TN 30 at the bottom of the mountain. Other trails have junctions with the Benton Falls Trail along the way, such as the three Slickrock trails, and give you multiple longer hike options.

After the wide, packed trail surface that is enjoyed through the first part of the hike, the last section of the Benton Falls Trail is steeper and rocky but is also merci-fully short. The trail follows a tiny creek upstream, which you can't imagine will produce much of a fall, but the noise gets louder and louder as you approach, and the 65-foot Benton Falls are a nice surprise, falling over tiered rock ledges, which are not uncommon in this region. Hikers should take care, since some substantial injuries have resulted from hikers scrambling on the rocks around the falls. Return the way you came.

Miles and Directions

0.0 Start from the lower parking lot at Lake McCamy, and follow the embankment to the left to find the trail marker for the Benton Falls Trail and Woodland Trail, straight ahead, at 500 feet from the parking lot. Turn left onto the Benton Falls Trail. (There is an earlier sign and side trail from the lake, but this is the most straightforward route. Within 0.25 mile the side trail joins this trail from the left.)

0.1 At the beginning the trail passes through open forest with little undergrowth, although you will see a thick growth of ferns about 0.5 mile from the start of the trail. At this point the trail meets the 0.5-mile Elderberry Trail (#143).

0.3 Reach junction with Trail 85, the Slickrock Naked Widow Loop (#85, 1.3 miles), which con-nects with the Benton Trail and the Slickrock Hancock Loop (#85, 2.4 miles). (Note that all three Slickrock hikes carry the same number.)

0.5 Meet the other end of the Naked Widow Loop.

1.1 Arrive at junction with Trail 144, the Red Leaf Trail, which connects the Arbutus to the Benton Falls Trail. (The Arbutus Loop [#141] makes a 0.7-mile loop near the campground.)

1.4 The trail is wide and flat until you reach the left turn for the falls, where it narrows, doubling back as it switchbacks down to the base of the falls. Turn left to leave the wide, flat trail and head down to Benton Falls. The Clemmer Trail (#302) starts where the Benton Falls Trail turns off to the falls and continues through the Rock Creek Gorge Scenic Area to reach TN 30 and US 64 in 4.3 miles.

1.5 Arrive at the top of the falls.

1.6 Arrive at the bottom of the falls, and take in the amazing beauty of Benton Falls' tiered water play. Return the way you came.

3.2 Arrive back at the parking lot.

Hike Information

Lodging

Reservations are available for **Indian Boundary Campground, Young Branch Horse Camp, McNabb Group Camp**, and the **Donley Cabin** at recreation.gov or by calling (877) 444-6777.

48 Summer's Point Trail at Cherokee National Forest, Ocoee District

This short, very steep, strenuous hike gives a spectacular result in reaching a point in which you can see far down to the river in two directions, watch the hawks fly by at eye level, and look down at technical climbers who are dangling below you, trying to reach your perch.

Start: An unmarked trailhead across the railroad tracks on Spring Creek Road (a bit difficult to find)
Distance: 0.8 mile out and back
Hiking time: 1 hour minimum (You will need some time to take in the views!)
Difficulty: Strenuous (Note that we hike up the "easy" side, but the back side is popular with technical climbers.)
Trail surface: Rock with some dirt surface
Best season: Year-round
Other trail users: None

Canine compatibility: Dogs on leash permitted, but this trail has vertical sections you will hike using both hands and feet and pulling yourself up, which could be difficult for a dog to navigate.
Fees and permits: None
Schedule: Unmonitored
Map: USGS quad
Trail contact: Ocoee Ranger District, 3171 Highway 64, Benton, TN 37307-5823; (423) 338-3300 (this trail is known but unnamed by the district)

Finding the trailhead: From Knoxville or Chattanooga take I-75 and exit at Cleveland, heading east on US 64 until it intersects with US 441/TN 33. Turn left (north) onto US 441, and follow it to Spring Creek Road, and turn right. Follow Spring Creek Road, with the Hiwassee River on your right, and park in a wide spot on the side of the road at 2.3 miles. You will cross the railroad tracks and see the trail heading up the hill on the other side. You may have to look a little. It starts up the creek ravine for the Watertank Branch. **GPS:** N35 13.495' / W84 31.850'

The Hike

This hike provides a king's view of the wide Hiwassee River valley below you and makes you feel like your head is in the clouds. Though the hike is short, it is not a hike for beginners. The hike follows a streambed for the first part of the trail, after catching the trailhead across the railroad tracks. It then passes along a relatively flat, short stretch on flagstone, and even gives you a pretty little waterfall along the way. It then scrambles over rocks and tree roots in an all-out climb until you reach the first large rock outcropping perch and enjoy the view.

A short and easy 5-minute walk from here, and you will be at the higher perch with a truly magnificent view of the Hiwassee River valley. The hike has a few names, and we were invited to name it by the park service representative, so we named it "Summer's Point Trail," for our youngest hiker, who was turning 6 months old in just

Summer's Point Trail at Cherokee National Forest, Ocoee District

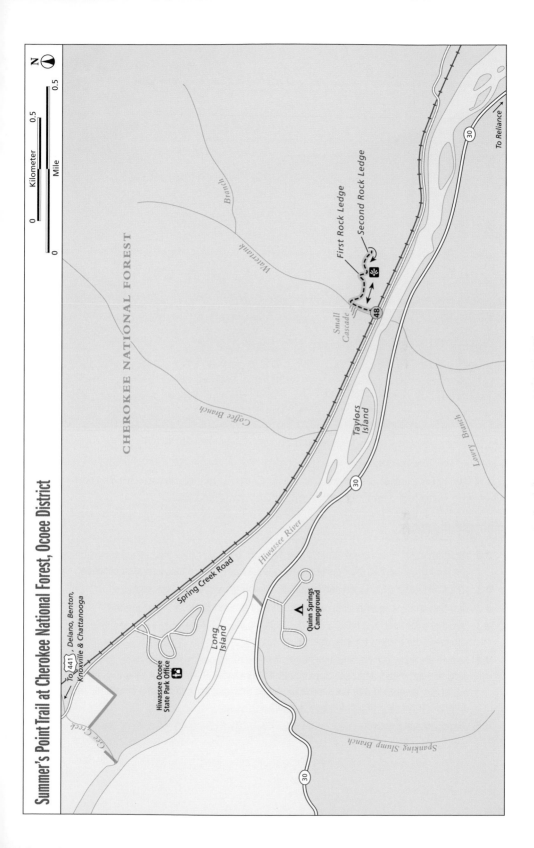

Looking down the Hiwassee River from near the top of Summer's Point Trail.

a few days. Her parents, Jonathan and Kayla Carroll (no relation to Stuart), were the ones who introduced Kelley to this gem of an unmarked trail.

Miles and Directions

0.0 Start from the Spring Creek Road, 2.3 miles from US 441. Cross the railroad track to head up the hill on the trail. After a steep climb the trail crosses a small, secluded cascade.

0.1 The trail makes a hard right and continues climbing, mostly over rock surfaces.

0.2 Turn left and continue to climb along the side of the mountain, heading upward.

0.3 Another hard right, and head out to the rocky viewpoint, where you have a beautiful unobstructed view back at the Hiwassee River Valley.

0.4 Reach the rocky clifftop, and enjoy views in three directions, across the valley to your left, straight ahead, and back to your right, the Hiwassee River Valley. A wide rock ledge at the top combined with the short hike makes this spot an inspirational choice for an impromptu picnic! Return the way you came.

0.8 Arrive back at the road.

Hike Information

Local Events/Attractions

For whitewater rafting, **Ocoee Whitewater Center,** 4400 Highway 64, Copperhill, TN; (423) 496-0100 or (877) 692-6050.

Lodging

More than thirty developed campsite locations are in Cherokee National Park's Southern District. Contact the Ocoee Ranger District, 3171 Highway 64, Benton, TN 37307-5823; (423) 338-3300.

Organizations

Cherokee Hiking Club, 2359 Varnell Rd., Cleveland, TN. See cherokeehikingclub .org or meetup.com/Cherokee-Hiking-Club-of-Southeast-Tennessee.

49 John Muir Trail (CNF Trail No. 152, Benton MacKaye Trail No. 2) at Cherokee National Forest, Ocoee District

This beautiful stretch of the John Muir Trail follows the Hiwassee River and climbs away at times along large and interesting rock formations. Sections of the trail are filled with wildflowers in season, and it is very peaceful. Except for a few climbs up rocks to cross through mini-passes in rock formations, the trail is an easy one, appropriate for all ages.

Start: At the parking lot for Childers Creek, on the right off FS 108

Distance: 12.0 miles out and back (6 miles as a shuttle hike)

Hiking time: About 6 hours out and back

Difficulty: Easy

Trail surface: Earthen, grassy, muddy and rocky surfaces

Best seasons: Spring and summer (more wildflowers, and the trail will be drier)

Other trail users: None

Canine compatibility: All pets must be confined to a leash, cage, or in a vehicle. Dogs must remain on a leash not to exceed 6 feet, unless being used for hunting during a designated hunting season where the use of dogs is legal. Pets are allowed in all areas except where posted otherwise (swimming areas, beaches, etc.).

Fees and permits: No fees, and no camping is permitted along this stretch of the John Muir Trail (though you can if you continue after the Apalachia Powerhouse).

Schedule: Dawn to dusk

Maps: USGS quad 133NW, McFarland; 133NE, Farner

Trail contact: Ocoee Ranger District, 3171 Highway 64, Benton, TN 37307-5823; (423) 338-3300

Finding the trailhead: From the north take US 411 south through Etowah, then cross the Hiwassee River and continue 0.5 mile to take a left onto TN 30. Take TN 30 for 5.7 miles, and turn left again onto TN 315 and cross the Hiwassee River on the Reliance Bridge. Immediately after the bridge, take the first right onto FS 108. Follow FS 108 for 0.5 mile to the sign on the left for "Cherokee National Forest Parking Lot/Childers Creek," and park here. The John Muir Trailhead, marked with a white reflective silhouette of a hiker, is next to a Forest Service bulletin board. **GPS:** N35 11.368' / W84 29.453'

The Hike

This trail is the Hiwassee segment of the John Muir State Scenic Trail, a 18.9-mile trail that runs along part of the route that John Muir, founder of the Sierra Club, used on his Thousand-Mile Walk to the Gulf in 1867. It is also part of the Benton MacKaye Trail system, another long trail system that runs through Tennessee. The Hiwassee area, managed by the Ocoee Ranger District, runs along the Hiwassee River watershed, and includes the Gee Creek Wilderness and the Coker Creek Scenic Area. You

John Muir Trail (CNF Trail No. 152, Benton MacKaye Trail No. 2) at Cherokee National Forest, Ocoee District

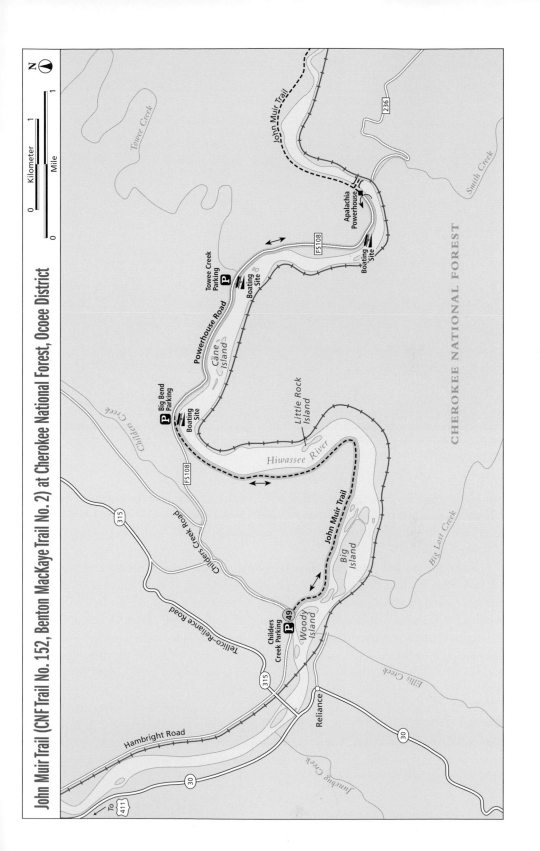

Walking along the John Muir Trail is like a journey through Eden, especially during the wild-flower season.

can learn about its several great trail options at the Ocoee Ranger District office. Unicoi Mountain Trail (4.2 miles) and Coker Creek Falls Trail (2.7 miles) both can be accessed off the John Muir Trail, which continues past the Apalachia Powerhouse at the end of this hike.

Hiwassee is derived from the Cherokee word *ayuwasi*, which means "a meadow at the foot of the hills." This valley was cleared for farming as long ago as 3000 BC, but its original residents preserved the original timber in the mountains. In contrast, within 200 years the white men who followed had eliminated about 75 percent of the virgin forest from these hills, and what you find today is secondary growth forest, with original hardwoods in scarce supply. In a great irony of life, it was these good stewards, the Cherokee, who were driven from their native land in the 1800s, leaving it to be pillaged by the less "enlightened" newcomers.

When this hiker first visited this trail in April a local cautioned, "there may be flowers now," followed by a concerned afterthought, "but now there might be snakes too." While no snakes were found, over twenty-five varieties of wildflowers were passed in the first 0.5 mile. John Muir himself described his walk along the Hiwassee as "vinedraped and flowery as Eden."

THE BENTON MACKAYE TRAIL: PART OF TENNESSEE'S LONG TRAILS SYSTEM

The Benton MacKaye Trail (BMT) is a 288-mile trail that runs from Springer Mountain in Georgia to the northern edge of Great Smoky Mountains National Park. Like the Appalachian Trail, its difficulty level is strenuous. Nearly the entire BMT is over trails, with only 10 miles to be walked on roads. The path passes through some of the most remote backcountry in Georgia, Tennessee, and North Carolina, including eight federally designated wilderness and wilderness study areas. In fact, nearly half the route is on land managed as wilderness. The BMT passes by Rich Mountain in Georgia and through Cohutta and Big Frog in Georgia; Big Frog, Little Frog, Citico Creek in southern Tennessee; Great Smoky Mountains National Park in northern Tennessee; and Joyce Kilmer-Slickrock in North Carolina. Hikers can backcountry camp throughout the route, with all but 10 miles of trail on public lands, and permits are required only for backcountry camping in the Smokies. The BMT has two shelters: One is at mile 50.3 and the other at mile 273.8, northbound. While the BMT is a hiking trail, some segments are routed on local trails that are shared with horses or bicycles. The BMT is generally open year-round, and hikers should be prepared for extreme weather, especially in the higher elevations.

The official blaze of the Benton MacKaye Trail is a white diamond, 5 inches across by 7 inches tall. (Note that no blaze is permitted in wilderness areas.) For further information on the trail and the Benton MacKaye Trail Association (BMTA), go to bmta.org.

The Forest Service does warn hikers to watch for rattlesnakes along rocky bluffs, for copperheads near the water, and for scorpions in holes or under rocks and logs. So this seemingly tranquil scene is not without its hazards!

Miles and Directions

0.0 Start from Childers parking lot off FS 108. There is plenty of parking, and local fishermen throw their lines and wade the river here in an open area.

1.1 The trail begins with a small footbridge across Childers Creek and then passes through a meadow toward the riverbank (full of wildflowers in season), where you can enjoy tremendous reflections when the floodgates at the powerhouse have not been opened. The first 3 miles of the trail is not the most challenging or eventful in terms of views, but it is an excellent location for viewing wildflowers and bird watching in season, and is designed to be accessible for seniors.

1.6 The trail bends hard to the left, and heads north away from the river, passing through large stands of hemlocks, with rhododendron. It then passes through a marshy area and joins an old logging trail.

1.9 In this stretch of the trail, you will do a little climbing, and will pass through some interesting rock formations, with a bluff on your left.

2.5 The trail opens up to the river again and continues to provide some river views.

2.8 A very short spur trail to the river gives you a photo opportunity over the wide, flat river.

3.0 You can see a wooded island in the Hiwassee River from the trail.

3.3 You have reached the Big Bend parking area, located on FS 108, where you could park a car shuttle if you are interested in no more than a relaxed 3-mile stroll along the river. (Note that the sign at Childers Creek says Big Bend is in 3 miles, but this is a bit optimistic.)

4.6 After Big Bend you will hike very close to the road, and reach the Towee Boat Launch at 4.6 miles, where you can sometimes see brave Tennesseans swimming in the river. This takes some bravery because periodically (and without warning) water is released from the dam and causes the Hiwassee River to suddenly swell, converting from a placid mirror to a turbulent stream, which has caused some drownings. (You can leave a car as a shuttle here safely, if desired.)

6.0 You have reached the Apalachia Powerhouse (spelled with only one p for some reason), and it can get muddy in this section, especially between December and March, and when water has been released from the dam. Turn around and retrace your steps back.

12.0 Arrive back at the parking lot.

Options: You can continue on the John Muir Trail if you wish from here for another 16 miles, taking in some delightful river views, and hiking up and down on series of switchbacks, until you reach Coker Creek Campground and on from there to Brushy Creek. This hike is strenuous, in contrast with the Childers Creek to Powerhouse segment. (See John Muir Trail in "Additional Great Hikes.")

Hike Information

Organizations:

Cherokee Hiking Club, 2359 Varnell Rd., Cleveland, TN. See cherokeehikingclub .org.

50 Bald River Falls (CNF Trail No. 88) at Cherokee National Forest, Tellico District

This hike starts at Bald River Falls on FS 210 and follows the river, passing through forest and over numerous rock embankments and cascades, and heading upstream and crossing junctions for other trails along the way, ending on FS 126 by Holly Flats Campground. You will pass through a mixed deciduous and pine forest, with rhododendron and mountain laurel blooming in spring. Like many trails in the Tellico District, this one follows an old logging grade at times, and at other points is narrow and more difficult to hike. The trail is easily accessed and receives considerable traffic, though less on the lower sections of the trail. Several small backpacking campsites are found along the river, and the river is said to be good for trout fishing.

Start: The trailhead, marked Trail No. 88, at the edge of the parking lot for Bald River Falls State Park on FS 210

Distance: 11.2 miles out and back (or 5.6-mile shuttle)

Hiking time: About 6 to 7 hours out and back

Difficulty: Moderate

Trail surface: Forest trail with rocks

Best season: Summer

Other trail users: None

Canine compatibility: Leashed dogs permitted

Fees and permits: None

Schedule: Daily, dawn to dusk

Map: USGS quad: 140SW, Bald River Falls

Trail contact: Tellico Ranger District, 250 Ranger Station Rd., Tellico Plains, TN 37385; (423) 253-8400; fs.usda.gov/main/cherokee/maps-pubs

Finding the trailhead: From Knoxville or Chattanooga take I-75 to TN 68, near Sweetwater. Take TN 68 South to Tellico Plains, then take TN 165 to FS 210, River Road (it follows the Tellico River), and follow it 6.3 miles to the Bald River Falls parking area, located on the right, and look for the trailhead, marked Trail No. 88. **GPS:** N35 17.308' / W84 11.151'. **Options:** Although hiking the trail from Bald River Falls is generally recommended, you can hike it downstream from FS 126, Bald River Road. (This is also where you can park a second car if you prefer to do the described hike as a shuttle hike.) To reach the alternate trailhead, continue past the trailhead on FS 210 (River Road) and turn left at the entrance to the Ranger Station across the bridge onto Wildcat Creek Road (FS 384). Follow Wildcat Creek Road 6.3 miles, turn left onto Bald River Road (FS 126), and follow this road 4.7 miles over Basin Gap and down to the Upper Bald River Trailhead.

The Hike

Bald River Falls is one of those over-the-top, stupendous roaring falls that puts one in an altered state. (Notwithstanding the crowd of other observers around you!) This trail basically begins at the finale, and then goes upstream from there, passing other vistas and cascades along the way, but none as spectacular as the one where you began, so take your time with this one before you move on. The trail follows the Bald River

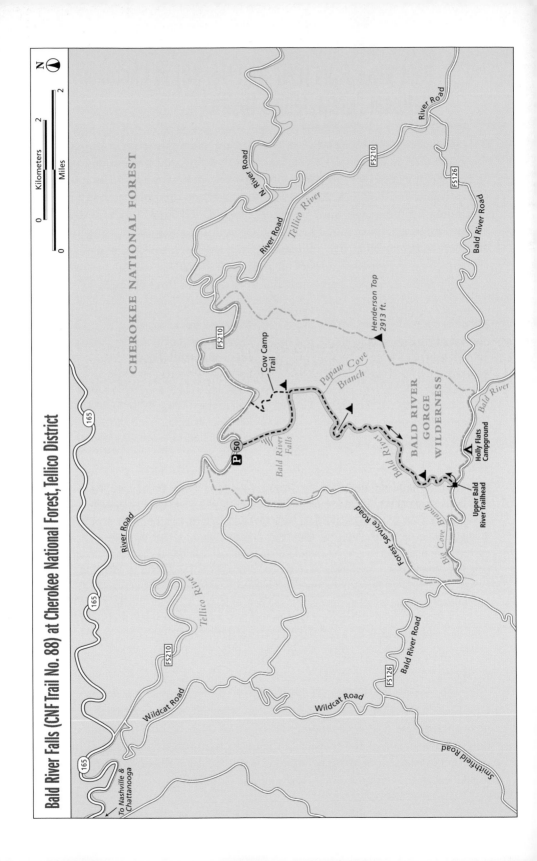

Bald River Falls (CNF Trail No. 88) at Cherokee National Forest, Tellico District

N

Kilometers
Miles

CHEROKEE NATIONAL FOREST

165

To Nashville &
Chattanooga

River Road

N River Road

River Road

Tellico River

FS210

FS210

Cow Camp
Trail

Papaw Cove
Branch

Henderson Top
2913 ft.

BALD RIVER
GORGE
WILDERNESS

Bald River Falls

P 50

Bald River

Bald River

Big Cove Branch

Forest Service Road

Holly Flats
Campground

Upper Bald
River Trailhead

FS126

Bald River Road

Tellico River

FS210

Wildcat Road

Wildcat Road

FS126

Bald River Road

Smithfield Road

165

The one-of-a-kind, photogenic Bald River Falls in autumn.

from the Tellico River Road (FS 210) to Bald River Road (FS 126), passing through deciduous forest and by rock embankments, cascades, and numerous campsites along the Bald River. There are more than nine campsites along this trail, with fire rings and plenty of water. (And also plenty of snakes!) The trail ends with a descent to a large cascade. Holly Flats Campground is on this road 0.5 mile to the east. You can leave a car at Holly Flats to make this a one-way, but the drive from the Tellico River Road Trailhead to the Upper Bald River Falls Trailhead is a slow one.

Miles and Directions

0.0   The trail begins at the parking lot trailhead with an immediate rise up a steep embankment, aided by stairs and a walk ramp built out from the rock face. You will round a corner at the falls to continue along a fairly steep incline past the falls in the first 0.1 mile. (Be careful here, because some have fallen to their death at these falls!) You may see some kayakers at this point, jumping the falls. There is a picnic area here, and some swim in the river, but again, exercise caution, because currents can be stronger than they seem.

0.2   After the falls the trail levels out considerably and continues on an old logging road along the riverbed for 0.5 mile, passing along lesser but nonetheless spectacular cascades. You may find fly fisherman along this stretch of the trail.

0.4   The trail switches back to the left and makes a short climb up to the top of a high rock outcropping. The river bends around the base of the rocks, cascading over several rock ledges. (You can walk along a narrow ridge here over the bend in the river, with steep 100-foot dropoffs on both sides. If you do this, exercise extreme caution.)

0.7   After continuing over the ridge and descending gradually to the river again, you arrive at a beautiful, large cascade.

1.5   You reach the junction with the Cow Camp Trail (CNF No. 173), and a small campsite is found immediately after the junction. (If you follow this well-maintained trail to make a shorter loop hike, you will head over the ridge and back down to come out on Tellico Road 0.9 mile upstream from the Bald River Falls.) Continue to follow the river, passing other campsites along the way, at 2.5 miles and 3 miles.

2.0   The Papaw Cove Branch enters the river to your left.

2.6   Arrive at another campsite.

4.4   Big Cove Branch joins Bald River on the west side, and there is a large campsite.
You are likely to see evidence of beavers, snakes, bears, boars, and other wildlife on the quieter, back section of the trail. Be sure to sterilize the water at these campsites, because the river passes through the Holly Flats Campground, upstream.

5. 6   Arrive at Bald River Road, a short distance from Holly Flats Campground. You can either return the way you came, for an 11.2-mile round-trip, or arrange a shuttle at the Upper Bald River Trailhead here on FS 126. Return the way you came.

11.2   Arrive back at the parking lot.

Hike Information

Restaurants

Krambonz BBQ (9188 New Hwy. 68, Tellico Plains, TN, near the beginning of the Cheruhala Skyway; (423) 253-2019) has amazing barbecue. Open seven days a week. Great prices and quality.

BE A TRAIL MAINTENANCE ANGEL!

Trails in the Tellico Ranger District, as in the rest of the Cherokee National Forest, are maintained by volunteers, and in wilderness areas, maintenance must be done without use of power tools, per regulation. Volunteers use old crosscut saws or axes to remove downed trees and keep trails open. It is not unlikely  to see nine men carrying a heavy log up a trail together, to be used as a joist for one of those wooden bridges that you cross along the trail. Organizations have sprung up to provide this assistance, and many hiking clubs coordinate trail maintenance as part of their club activities. Two such organizations working in the southeast region of Tennessee are the Cherokee Hiking Club and the Southern Appalachian Back Country Horsemen, both based out of Cleveland. These groups often post maintenance events on their websites. Similar organizations maintain trails in the Smokies, and in the north Cherokee National Forest. Most of the state parks have a "Friends of" organization, which you can find either online or through the park headquarters. If you are interested in socializing and helping at the same time, contact these organizations and others throughout the state. Here is a partial list:

Cherokee Hiking Club, 2359 Varnell Rd., Cleveland, TN 37311; cherokeehikingclub.org.

Southern Appalachian Back Country Horsemen, a 501(c)(3) nonprofit organization; (423) 745-8804. Visit sabch.org or email contactsabch@gmail.com.

Tellico Ranger Station, 250 Ranger Station Rd., Tellico Plains, TN 37385; (423) 253-8400.

Friends of the Cumberland Trail, friendsofthecumberlandtrail.org.

Tennessee Eastman Hiking Club, tehcc.org or call Bob Peoples at (423) 725-4409.

Friends of the Smokies, friendsofthesmokies.org.

The now tranquil view to the Tennessee River through the restored Fort Loudoun military compound.

The trail is a combination of the 3.3-mile Meadow Loop and the 1.5-mile Ridgetop Trail, which enables you to walk a good bit of the circumference of the island, and passes through open meadows and along shorelines that give lovely views of both wildlife and the open water. In spring the trail is filled with the scent of wildflowers and has benches placed in locations that are advantageous for relaxing and enjoying the views. Some nice big trees near the end round out the hike and deliver you back to the parking area and the museum.

Miles and Directions

0.0   Start from the far end of the picnic area parking lot in front and to the left of the visitor center, at the connector to the trailhead for the Meadow Loop. (This trail will take you around the perimeter of the island, on the Meadow and the Ridgetop loop trails.)

0.2   Arrive at the first wooden bridge. You will cross another in another 0.2 mile.

0.5   The trail takes a hard turn to the left and continues along the Little Tennessee River shore.

0.9   You arrive at the junction of the uniquely named Lost Shoe Loop. You will reach the other end of this 0.5-mile loop at 1.1 mile on this trail.

IN ADDITION: A REMARKABLE STATESMAN: SEQUOYAH AND THE CHEROKEE WRITTEN LANGUAGE

Sequoyah was born in the late 1770s, near the museum that honors him. He was born of an English father and Cherokee mother, and fought for the Americans against the British in the War of 1812. While away from his Cherokee family, he began to toy with the idea of creating a written language, so that the Cherokee could write letters home and record events. When he returned home, while working as a silversmith, he developed a written language employing eighty-five symbols, devoting twelve years to the project.

Amazingly, within a few months of his completing the language in 1821, thousands of Cherokee were literate, within four years much of the Bible had been translated to Cherokee, and by 1828, seven years later, the Cherokee had their own newspaper. Sequoyah was honored by his people and served them as a statesman and diplomat until his death.

1.3 You enter into an open glen, followed by an open meadow. The area is very tranquil. You will cross straight across the meadow, before you turn left toward the other shore.

1.7 Arrive at the other side of the meadow.

1.8 Cross Fort Loudoun Road, very close to the entrance, and continue down to the shore, to meet the water for the first time on the hike. The next 0.4 mile, you will be following the Tellico River shore, enjoying views across the water.

2.0 You pass an excellent fishing spot, and a 0.1 mile later, you pass a spot where the water is on your left and the meadow is on your right.

2.3 You walk around a point, with good views of heron in the water, and from this point you begin to head inland again, climbing up on the Ridgetop Trail. Over the next 0.2 mile, in the spring the air is rich with the scent of flowering bushes along the sides of the trail.

2.5 The trail crosses a jeep road and continues to climb, curving right, until it reaches the top of the ridge.

2.7 You arrive at a bench and a trail sign for the Ridgetop Trail. You will head to the left to continue on the Ridgetop Trail. You are now following along the top of the ridge, and midway across, you are afforded some nice views from a bench that has been provided.

2.9 At the end of the ridgetop, you begin to descend, and are welcomed by a big, old tree that embraces you with its wide branches. The trail turns sharply to the left here, and curves down the other side of the ridge, toward the water.

3.2 You arrive near the water's edge and make a hard right, this time at an information kiosk and another delightfully large tree. From here the trail remains fairly level until you finish.

3.5 The trail delivers you to the other end of the parking lot, near the visitor center entrance. You will now need to walk on the pavement for the final tenth of a mile, to return to the trailhead.

3.6 You pass the boat dock and picnic area and shelter to your left, as you head back to your starting point.

Hike Information

Local Events/Attractions

You should really try to visit the **Delano Community Farm Market,** 351 Needle Eye Ln., Delano, TN. This Amish farmers' market, produced by a community of approximately 200 who operate without electricity or motorized equipment, sells delicious organic produce and bottled sauces. Open Mon through Sat from 9 a.m. to 5 p.m. from Apr through Oct.

18th-Century Trade Faire, held every Sept, has a colonial marketplace with entertainers, merchants, and artisans.

Sequoya Birthplace Museum (576 Highway 360, Vonore, TN 37885; 423-884-6246), across the street from Fort Loudoun, is open Mon through Sat, 9 a.m. to 5 p.m., and Sun from noon to 5 p.m. The museum presents information about the history and culture of the Cherokee people in eastern Tennessee, and has a variety of educational programs.

Additional Great Hikes

G   Flats Mountain Trail at Cherokee National Forest, Tellico District (CNF Trail No. 102)

This 6.2-mile moderate hike starts at the top of Flats Mountain and follows its ridge downhill to Beehouse Gap, providing spectacular views of the Tellico Ranger District and Citico Creek Wilderness, including Indian Boundary Lake. The trail starts out on a grassy jeep road that hosts wildflowers in spring, and passes through lichen-covered hardwoods, then through grassy meadows and on through an oak forest. It then opens you up in less than 1 mile to a rock outcropping where you can see the river and the whole Tellico District to the northwest. (You need to watch for the red blaze markings.) This varied trail then goes over the mountain and descends through pine forests in switchbacks, then basically continues to descend for the rest of the hike, mostly along a ridgeline, following the wilderness boundary, until you arrive at Citico Creek Road at Beehouse Gap, with a parking area across the road from the trailhead.

Finding the trailhead: From Tellico Plains take TN 165 (the Cherohala Skyway) to Eagle's Gap just past a steep curve 4.8 miles east of the junction of TN 165 and FS 345. The trailhead is marked with a USFS sign "No. 102" on the left side of the road, at a small paved road that leads off to the left up a steep embankment. To the top of the embankment, you will find a wide parking area. The trailhead is at the end of the wide parking area, and begins as a fairly well-worn jeep trail.
Maps: 140SE, Big Junction; 140NE, Whiteoak Flats

H   Falls Branch Trail at Cherokee National Forest, Tellico District (CNF Trail No. 87)

This 1.3-mile trail has a concentration of beauty in a short, easy distance, passing through virgin forest and concluding at a magical and private 80-foot cascade. The trail follows old forest road beds for 0.9 mile through old-growth virgin forest, never logged, and passes beautiful sections of rhododendron and other wildflowers in season. This is one of the few areas of virgin timber remaining in the Tellico District, in this area called Jeffrey Hell. Near the trail at 0.5 mile is a large birch tree with arched roots that form a crawl space with a convenient rock seat underneath. You cross a couple of streambeds, and come out at 1.1 miles just below the 80-foot falls. The trail levels off near the falls, and the sound of the falls increases as you walk. This trail is one that can put a person in a timeless state of mind, with the worries of life far distant and the presence of nature filling the senses.

Finding the trailhead: From Tellico Plains continue on TN 165 (the Cherohala Skyway) east, bearing right and continuing on TN 165 from the junction with the Indian Boundary Lake turnoff. Continue 8.4 miles to the trailhead. The parking area is in a clear area on the left side near Rattlesnake Rock, a half mile past Post 22. Trailhead signs, marked "87" and "196," are at the western end of the parking lot. Hike down 100 feet to where the Falls Branch Trail continues to the left, and the Jeffrey Hell Trail (CNF No. "196") goes to the right.

I   Whigg Meadow at Cherokee National Forest

This is the shorter of the two Whigg Meadow access trails. (The other departs from Mud Gap and takes about 1.6 miles to get to Whigg Meadow.) This 0.5-mile short, easy hike yields a big reward, making its way on a grassy jeep road to Whigg Meadow, with 360-degree views into the Tellico District to the west and north, and North Carolina to the east, though partially obscured by brush and low trees in full foliage. The trail begins at the north end of the parking area at Big Junction, and follows an old jeep road up a gradual incline along the ridgeline, passing through low brush and trees, to a clearing at the top of the mountain, which has a fire ring. The grassy trail is carpeted with purple wildflowers in the spring and is quiet, except for the sounds of birds. The trail opens up into Whigg Meadow, a large grassy clearing at the high point of the ridge. There is a lone tall pine tree that really marks the end of this trail, which can be seen from the fire ring. If you are a tree climber, the view from those upper branches should be unparalleled! This a good trail for early spring or winter hiking, though it can get windy on the ridge. Dogs should be leashed, though this outpost can be very quiet and secluded, depending upon the time of year. Part of the pleasure of this short hike is the drive up, along the ridge that marks the North Carolina–Tennessee boundary. On the North Carolina side is Stratton's Bald, a long trail that leads down through Joyce Kilmer Wilderness to some old-growth virgin forest that is some of the last of its kind in the region. (Joyce Kilmer, who was killed in World War I, was the author of the poem "I think that I shall never see / A poem as lovely as a tree.")

Finding the trailhead: Take Cleveland exit 20 from I-75 North. Follow US 64 East along the Ocoee River and the Ocoee Scenic Byway to Copperhill. Take TN 68 South to Cherohala Skyway. Turn Left at Cherohala Skyway. Follow it to Big Junction, a gap with a parking area alongside the road that provides a view into both states. (After Big Junction the road curves a hard left to head into North Carolina, so you will know if you have gone too far.) This unmarked trailhead starts about 10 feet from the end of the metal guard rail at the parking turnout.

J   Big Fodderstack Trail at Cherokee National Forest, Tellico District (CNF Trail No. 95)

This 10.6-mile trail runs along the crests of Little Fodderstack, Big Fodderstack, and Rockstack Mountains, has camping along the trail, and includes one of the best vistas in Citico from Bob Stratton Bald, off a short spur trail along the way. It is rich with experiences! This trail is part of the Benton MacKaye Trail. The trail begins by mounting a forested ridge and following it, then turns through some clearings that afford views of the district, followed by a steep climb that skirts Little Fodderstack along its west side (with a spur to the top), and continues to a sister knob with some great views of the peak, and a campsite. The trail continues along the ridgeline, reaching another knob at 3 miles. It passes near the excellent campsite at Crowder Place, passes trail junctions along the way, and climbs a ridge again, descending to Big Stack Gap and then beginning the climb up Big Fodderstack Mountain (4,200 feet) at around 4.5 miles. After reaching the summit (you may have to bushwhack a bit to get to the real top), you will descend and ascend through a series of gaps and knobs, until you reach the junction for Bob Stratton Bald, which in 0.4 mile will deliver you to a bald that is 5,261 feet high and gives one of the best views in this area. From here, it is basically downhill to Cold Spring Gap and the end of the hike. (If you decide to hike the jeep road back to its intersection with TN 165, your total hike will be 12.1 miles, ending at the point where TN 165 reaches the North Carolina border.)

Finding the trailhead: From Tellico Plains take TN 165 approximately 16 miles to Indian Boundary Lake. Turn right onto FDR 35 and continue 6 miles to Doublecamp Road. Turn right, and continue another 6.7 miles to the parking area. The trailhead is a short distance up the road, at the high point of Farr Gap.

K   John Muir Trail–Apalachia Powerhouse to Brushy Creek at Cherokee National Forest, Ocoee District

This 13-mile extension of the Childers Creek segment of the John Muir Trail starts at the Apalachia Powerhouse, and connects with the Coker Creek Trail at 11.7 miles, crossing TN 68 before coming to an end on FS 311. From the powerhouse, the trail passes down under a suspension bridge, continuing along the north side of the river, which is the side opposite the Powerhouse. The hike begins with nine steep switchbacks, then returns to the river, and leads back into the trees to begin another series of switchbacks, giving some glimpses of river views. You reach the top of the bluffs at 5.2 miles, and are rewarded for your efforts by a spectacular view of the river. Another series of switchbacks returns you to the river again to join the Coker Creek Trail, following it to the Hiwassee River. After a brief road stint, the trail heads up Coker Creek again, diverges and crosses the Unicoi Mountain Trail, and after more ascending and then descending switchbacks, crosses a footbridge and reaches a waterfall at

The Smokies and the Northeast

Northeast Tennessee's hiking opportunities are dominated by two great federally owned tracts of land, the Great Smoky Mountains National Park (GSMNP), with over 816 square miles (and over 244 million acres located in Tennessee), and Cherokee National Forest, with 1,024 square miles in four districts (and 170,000 acres each in the northern Unaka and Watauga Districts). These large tracts of forested, largely untouched land dominate the landscape of northeast Tennessee, and to some degree shape the lives of its people. Tennesseans in this part of the state are not just nature lovers, they seem to be connected to the beautiful mountains around or near them, and embrace that beauty with frequent visits on those mountains' hundreds of trails, together with visitors from all over the world.

Great Smoky Mountains National Park

GSMNP has become the most visited national park in the United States, with over 9 million visitors per year. The Smokies are considered by many to contain the most spectacular mountains in eastern Tennessee, with sixteen peaks over 6,000 feet high within the park. While many of the trails are heavily traveled, there are many others among its more than 800 miles of trails where you can hike all day and hardly see another face. The park straddles the state line of Tennessee and North Carolina, and a section of the Appalachian Trail runs north–south through the park's center, generally along the state line.

No hunting is permitted in GSMNP, which makes it not only a safe alternative during hunting seasons, but also a great place to view wildlife. Of course, the Smokies are a native habitat of the black bear, and it is not unlikely that you will encounter bears or evidence of them during your visit. (See the sidebar in the introductory chapter to this book on how to handle bear encounters.) If you enter via Pigeon Forge and Gatlinburg, you will follow US 441 into the park.

The beautiful and serene Cades Cove has been a haven for farmers for generations, and now annually hosts millions of hikers seeking to anchor themselves in the mystical beauty of the Smokies.

You can take a bypass to the right as you approach Gatlinburg to avoid its business district and go directly to the park. The Sugarlands Visitor Center, which has a wealth of information, is worth a stop. Road access to the park's many hikes is provided on Laurel Creek Road, which leads to Cades Cove, a large loop road that circles a mountain park, with camping and hiking along the way; Cherokee Orchard Road and Roaring Fork Loop Road (closed in winter), just out of Gatlinburg; Little River Road; and Newfound Gap Road (US 441), which leads to the North Carolina state line. Greenbrier Road and US 321 complete the access points from the Tennessee part of the park. It goes past several of the park's most popular hikes, such as the Alum Cave Trail (a hike not for the faint of heart, which arrives at the summit of Mount LeConte), and the Appalachian Trail (accessed from Clingmans Dome), which is heavily trafficked in either direction and gives some of the very best unfettered mountain views in the eastern United States. Newfound Gap Road can be very heavily traveled in the spring, summer, and fall, and is open year-round (except for during heavy snows), though the side road to Clingmans Dome is closed with the first heavy snow and reopens in the spring.

Grotto Falls Trail at Great Smoky Mountains National Park

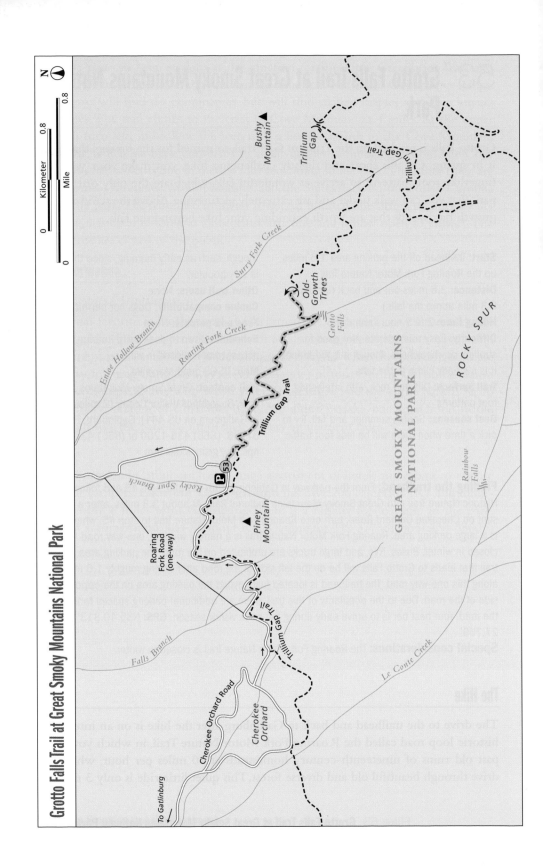

Hikers enjoy passing under the cascade, an opportunity unique to Grotto Falls within Great Smoky Mountains National Park.

from downtown Gatlinburg, so it takes no time to get there and immediately begin to enjoy the natural beauty and the history offered.

You will actually reach the falls on the Trillium Gap Trail, so named for the profusion in the spring of beautiful white and yellow trillium along the trail, along with other wildflowers such as white violets and Dutchman's breeches. For most of the hike, the trail hugs the side of the mountain on the right, and the left has a fairly steep drop-off. You can walk under these falls easily, and even without getting wet, and then continue on the well-traveled Trillium Gap Trail to the summit of Brushy Mountain in approximately 2 miles, or up to Mount LeConte in another 5.6 miles. Mount LeConte, 6,593 feet in elevation, is a popular destination and can be reached via several trails within the park. If you continue above the falls, you will see some old stands of trees, some with diameters as large as 6 feet across. These tall, extremely straight trunks reach far up into the sky, and offer a comforting presence.

Miles and Directions

0.0 Start from the access trail to the Trillium Gap Trailhead, 1.6 miles after you turn on the Roaring Fork Motor Nature Trail, at the end of the parking lot and across the street. (If

Abrams Falls Trail at Great Smoky Mountains National Park

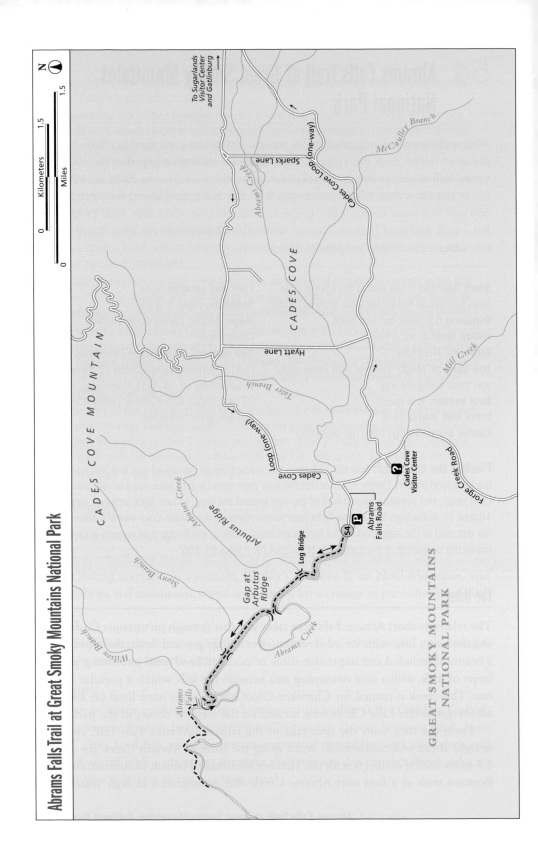

A hiker enjoys a winter view of Abrams Falls, a favorite for hikers who like a moderate challenge.
PHOTO COURTESY OF MARK FRADELLA

its junction with the Abrams Falls Trail, the Little Bottoms Trail leads in another 2.3 miles to the Abrams Creek Campground, off the Foothills Parkway and US 129 at the extreme west end of GSMNP.

The interesting rock formations that you see on this hike and others in the Smokies and Cherokee National Forest are caused by the creation of the mountain system called Unaka, which began over a billion years ago. The sedimentary rocks were compressed and broken, and molten rock extruded from the interior of the earth and cooled. The area uplifted and then eroded, depositing rocks in formations that became the Ocoee Series. More folding and faulting took place about 450 million years ago, repeated again 375 million years ago, and again 250 million years ago, when the range was pushed up above sea level. Some believe that at one time, the Smokies were higher than the younger Rocky Mountains, but have been eroded and worn down over the years. Another theory is that the Smokies eroded as they were raised, and thus never reached the height of the Rockies. Erosion is credited with the creation of the formations that exist today. A glacial period from 50,000 to 20,000 years ago caused freezing and thawing, which caused rocks to crack and huge boulders to fall to the valley floors. They can be found in the beds of streams, which could not possibly have carried them to their present locations.

VIEWING ELK IN GSMNP

In this area elk were all but eliminated by overhunting and loss of habitat at one time. In Tennessee the last elk was killed in the mid-1800s, and by 1900 they were in danger of extinction. In 2001 twenty-five elk were brought from the Land Between the Lakes, located mid-state along the Tennessee-Kentucky border, to Great Smoky Mountains National Park, with twenty-seven more brought in the following year. Ten years later GSMNP was home to 140 elk, with the population growing. In the early years many calves born here were eaten by black bears, because these elk had not faced these predators before. But in time they learned to defend and hide their newborns, and survival rates have improved. Elk can be seen most easily in the Cataloochee area in the southeastern section of the park. They are best seen in early morning and late evening, and they like to be out before and after storms. A rule of thumb when viewing elk and other wild animals, from the park: If you approach an animal so closely that it stops feeding, changes direction of travel, or otherwise alters its behavior, you are too close!

To reach Cataloochee, take I-40, exit 20, and go 0.2 mile, then turn right onto Cove Creek Road and continue 11 miles into Cataloochee Valley (allow 45 minutes from I-40).

Miles and Directions

0.0 Start by crossing over a large footbridge over Abrams Creek. (The stream here is a popular foot-cooler.) To the right after the footbridge is a side trail to the Elijah Oliver house. Elijah Oliver was the son of the first white settler in Cades Cove in 1818, John Oliver. Elijah died in 1905. Another family dwelling known as the John Oliver House is the first house you will see as you start the loop road.

0.5 The trail begins to climb gradually to reach a height above the stream, then turns a corner at 0.5 mile to the right and descends again to follow the river.

0.6 The trail reaches the river bottom again, and then stays level for a considerable distance, crossing a log bridge. In this stretch of the trail, children frequently depart the trail to enjoy the water while their parents wait patiently along the trail.

1.1 After another steep climb, you arrive at a rocky gap of Cades sandstone at the top of Arbutus Ridge; the trail switches back to the right and descends again to Abrams Creek.

1.7 You switch back again to the left over a side creek on a log bridge, and curve right to follow the creek again for a flat stretch.

2.2 The trail then makes a final climb, again to a ridgetop high above Abrams Creek. It curves right at a point where you can hear the falls below you.

2.4 After descending steeply arrive at another log bridge over Wilson Branch. After crossing this bridge, the trail curves left to follow the creek on the other side.

2.5 In a very short distance, another bridge appears to the left. Cross this bridge to follow the short spur trail to the 20-foot Abrams Falls. The pool at its base is 100 feet across and is a popular playground for children visiting the falls. Be careful in the water at Abrams Falls, because the rocks are extremely slippery, and it is easy enough to catch the edge of a rock in a fall. Parents should probably escort small children across the faster part of the stream (and the slicker rocks) to the shallow sand bar at the center of the pool at the base of the falls. Return the way you came.

5.0 Arrive back at the trailhead.

55 Alum Cave Trail at Great Smoky Mountains National Park

This 5.9–mile (11.8 miles out and back) trail in the heart of Great Smoky Mountains National Park is deceptively challenging, but provides a variety in trail experiences as you make your way from the river at the bottom, past caves and massive overhangs, and along steep inclines, to reach the LeConte Lodge at the top.

Start: Trailhead marker for the Alum Cave Trail, next to the parking lot on Newfound Gap Road
Distance: 11.8 miles out and back
Hiking time: About 4 hours
Difficulty: Strenuous
Trail surface: Mostly rock, with some dirt and sandy surfaces
Best seasons: Spring and fall
Other trail users: None

Canine compatibility: Dogs not permitted
Fees and permits: None
Schedule: Dawn to dusk
Map: USGS quad
Trail contact: Great Smoky Mountains National Park, Sugarlands Visitor Center (2 miles south of Gatlinburg on US 441), Gatlinburg, TN 37738; (865) 436-1200 or (865) 436-7318; nps.gov/grsm/index.htm

Finding the trailhead: From Knoxville, take I-40 east, and exit onto TN 66 at the signs for the park. Continue south on TN 66 through Sevierville, then join US 441, and pass through Pigeon Forge and Gatlinburg. A Gatlinburg bypass will take you straight to the Sugarlands Visitor Center without passing through Gatlinburg. From the Sugarlands Visitor Center, drive 8.7 miles south along Newfound Gap Road. The trailhead parking lot will be on your left. There are two parking areas for this hike, and you may want to arrive early during peak season, or on any weekend with nice weather throughout the year, because these lots fill up quickly. **GPS: N35.63014' / W83.44936'**

The Hike

The Alum Cave Trail is not for the faint of heart, especially if you have determined to take it on in less than ideal conditions, such as during any type of rainy or cold weather. The way can become muddy and/or slippery, and it gets cold at the higher elevations. When snow is melting, giant, sharp icicles from the cave ceiling can fall and impale a person, and the hike is almost as challenging going down as it is going up, because of steep inclines.

But this is one hike that is worth the effort. The rock formations found on this trail are fascinating, the views are beautiful, and if you go all the way to the top, you can reward yourself with a hot chocolate, or even a bunk, at the lodge, if you plan ahead. The lodge itself is a complex of buildings that has a rustic "mess hall"–style restaurant and a warm and welcoming office/reception lodge. There you can read about the history of the area, learn more about the park, or simply listen to someone play the guitar that is on hand for anyone interested. There is just something nice about

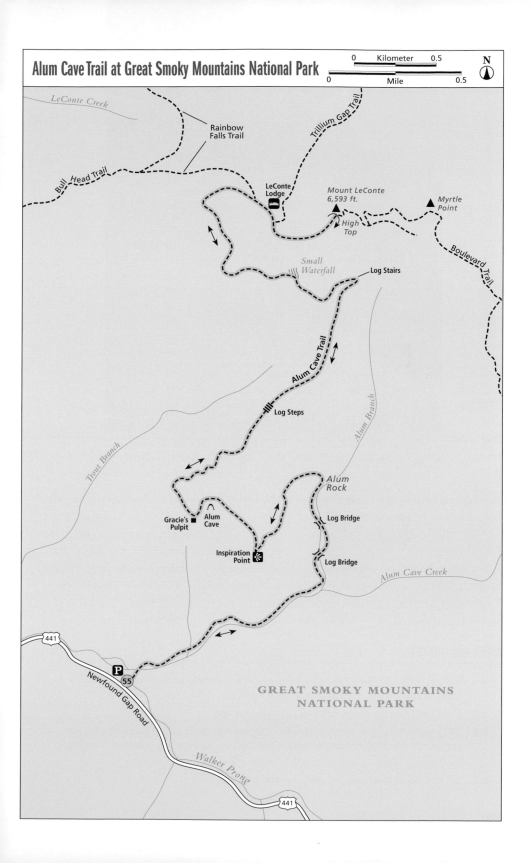

Alum Cave Trail at Great Smoky Mountains National Park

Kilometer 0 — 0.5
Mile 0 — 0.5

N

LeConte Creek

Rainbow Falls Trail

Trillium Gap Trail

Bull Head Trail

LeConte Lodge

Mount LeConte 6,593 ft.

Myrtle Point

High Top

Boulevard Trail

Small Waterfall

Log Stairs

Alum Cave Trail

Log Steps

Alum Branch

Trout Branch

Alum Rock

Gracie's Pulpit

Alum Cave

Log Bridge

Inspiration Point

Log Bridge

Alum Cave Creek

441

P 55

Newfound Gap Road

GREAT SMOKY MOUNTAINS NATIONAL PARK

Walker Prong

441

A group of Ohio hikers enjoys a brief rest under the cave overhang before continuing on to the lodge at the top of the Alum Cave Trail.

having a comfortable indoor rest stop at the top of a mountain, especially when the hike was somewhat strenuous.

Alas, they mean it when they say you must book far in advance for the LeConte Lodge. (Information on the lodge is at the end of this hike.) From there it is only a short half mile to the top of "High Top," as Mount LeConte is known, because from its base near Gatlinburg to its summit, it is the tallest mountain in the eastern United States. From Myrtle Point, approximately a half mile past the summit of Mount LeConte, you can enjoy commanding 360-degree views of the majesty of the Smokies around you.

Miles and Directions

0.0 Start from the trailhead marker at the Alum Cave Trail parking lot. You begin by following a creek for over a mile, crossing back and forth over it.

1.1 Cross creek on pipe bridge, followed by two log bridges.

1.5 Arrive at the Arch Rock, which is more like a tunnel with stone steps leading up into the unknown. It is a delightful natural feature. The arch was formed by a process of freezing and thawing, which caused softer rock to erode from under harder rock.

1.7 The trail moves away from the creek and starts to climb.

2.0 You reach "Inspiration Point," which has beautiful views of the valley. Myrtle Point, near the top of Mount LeConte, can be seen to northeast, and Little Duck Hawk Ridge to the west. You can even see the perfect hole in the rock at the top of Little Duck Hawk Ridge, called "the Eye of the Needle." (By the way, "duck hawk" is a nickname for peregrine falcons, which frequent this area.) Take a sharp right to continue. The next stretch is challenging, with climbing over rock and steep sections of trail.

2.3 You reach Alum Cave, which is really a bluff of rock, with a concave opening, about 80 feet high by 500 feet long. In winter, water dripping from the top of the bluff turns to icicles, and as they thaw, they become dangerous missiles, shooting down on the unsuspecting hikers below. So use caution if you are visiting under those conditions. The views from under the cave bluff are astounding.

2.6 After a couple of hard switchbacks, the trail curves gradually to the right around an edge of the mountain. This point is called "Gracie's Pulpit," named for Gracie McNichol, who hiked to Mount LeConte on her ninety-second birthday. This marks the halfway point to Mount LeConte. Over the next 2 miles, you will be hiking over rock ledges, and using cable to pull yourself up in several cases. These ledges get slippery in icy winter weather! Some of these ledges look out over steep drop-offs.

3.2 Make your way up some log steps as you continue to climb.

3.9 The trail makes a hard left switchback, and then within 0.1 mile goes around a sharp bend, where you need to rely upon cables for sure footing.

4.2 Pass a small waterfall, and enjoy some nice views from the side of the mountain, as you continue to climb.

4.7 After one final left and wider right bend, the trail levels out again, and you enter a spruce forest.

5.1 The Alum Cave Trail ends and you turn right onto the Rainbow Falls Trail. Shortly after this, you will see LeConte Lodge on your left. You may be tempted to end your hike at the lodge, but if you continue only another half mile, you will be at the true summit of Mount LeConte, at 6,593 feet, which is called "High Top."

5.3 Just before you reach the top, you will hit the junction of the Trillium Gap Trail (which is used to arrive at Grotto Falls).

5.5 Arrive at the summit of Mount LeConte, which unfortunately has no views. To get a good view, you will have to go past Mount LeConte's summit to Myrtle Point, another 0.2 mile on the main summit trail, which is called Boulevard Trail at this point, and then another 0.2 mile on a spur trail on the right. (There are also two side trails leading to Cliff Top, on your right, as you hike to High Top. Cliff Top is the best location for sunset views.) When you're done, turn around and retrace your steps back.

11.8 Arrive back at the parking lot.

Hike Information

Lodging
LeConte Lodge, 250 Apple Valley Rd., Sevierville, TN; (865) 429-5704; lecontelodge.com.

Organizations
The **Smoky Mountains Hiking Club.** For more information, go to smhclub.org.

56 Appalachian Trail: Newfound Gap to Icewater Shelter

This heavily traveled trail runs from the easily accessible Newfound Gap, in the middle of the park, to Charlie's Bunion, through a section of unique, jagged Anakeesta formation that contrasts sharply with the geology of the surrounding area and provides spectacular views throughout the hike.

Start: Across the street from the parking lot at Newfound Gap

Distance: 6.2 miles in and out

Hiking time: 4.5 to 5 hours

Difficulty: Moderate

Trail surface: Forested pine path, earthen with rock, and rock surfaces

Best season: Winter (less traffic and better unobstructed views)

Other trail users: None

Canine compatibility: Dogs not permitted

Fees and permits: None

Schedule: Dawn to dusk

Map: USGS quad: 165NE, Mount Guyot

Trail contact: Great Smoky Mountains National Park, Sugarlands Visitor Center (2 miles south of Gatlinburg on US 441), Gatlinburg, TN 37738; (865) 436-1200 or (865) 436-7318; nps.gov/grsm/index.htm

Finding the trailhead: From Knoxville, take I-40 east, and exit onto TN 66 at the signs for the park. Continue south on TN 66 through Sevierville, then join US 441, and pass through Pigeon Forge and Gatlinburg. A Gatlinburg bypass will take you straight to the Sugarlands Visitor Center without passing through Gatlinburg. From the Sugarlands Visitor Center, take Newfound Gap Road (US 441) for 13.2 miles to the parking area at Newfound Gap. The trailhead is near the restrooms at the east (left) side of the overlook. **GPS:** N35 36.656' / W83 25.480'

Special considerations: Conditions can get wet and muddy on this trail so exercise caution, especially if walking on wet rock.

The Hike

The AT crosses at Newfound Gap on US 441. This section of the AT was built with picks and shovels in 1932, in one month's time. The trail passes first through a mixed pine and hardwood forest, and is wide and hard-packed from heavy travel. As you make your way, you can see Mount LeConte through the trees before you reach the first ridgetop and the junction with the Sweat Heifer Trail, which connects with the Kephart Prong Trail. The AT ascends steeply, providing some spectacular views into North Carolina before it reaches its highest point and descends to the junction with the Boulevard Trail on the left at 2.7 miles, which leads to the summit of Mount LeConte, and the Icewater Spring and Shelter in 3.1 miles. If you continue on after the Icewater Shelter, you will then descend through a rutted section, and at 3.7 miles you will pass out of the red spruce and Fraser fir forest, curve around the shoulder of Mount Kephart, and be rewarded by a dramatic view of Charlie's Bunion.

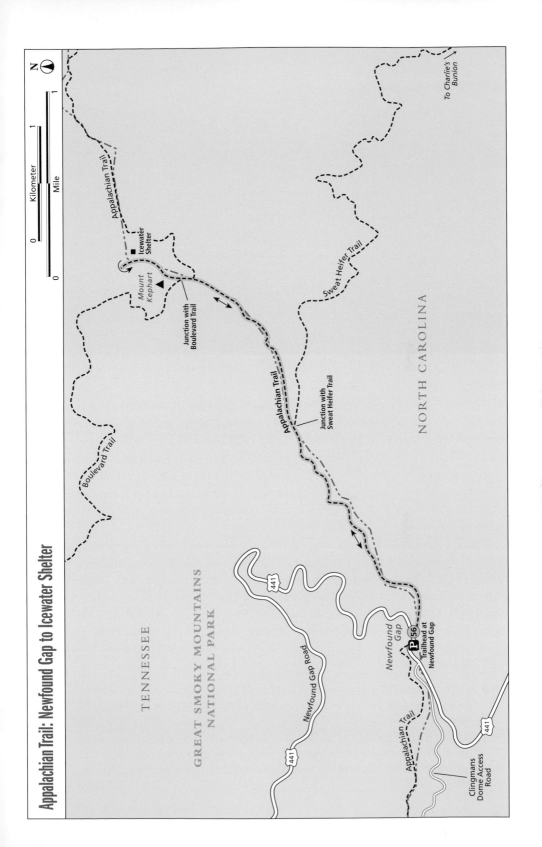

Appalachian Trail: Newfound Gap to Icewater Shelter

N

0   Kilometer   1
0   Mile   1

Boulevard Trail

Appalachian Trail

Icewater Shelter

Mount Kephart

Junction with Boulevard Trail

Appalachian Trail

Junction with Sweat Heifer Trail

Sweat Heifer Trail

To Charlie's Bunion

TENNESSEE

NORTH CAROLINA

GREAT SMOKY MOUNTAINS NATIONAL PARK

Newfound Gap Road

441

441

Newfound Gap

P 56

Trailhead at Newfound Gap

Appalachian Trail

441

Clingmans Dome Access Road

Winter views from the Newfound Gap to the Charlie's Bunion section of the Appalachian Trail.

The exposed rock of Charlie's Bunion was created by a combination of events. First, this area was clear-cut for timber, and unwanted brush and limbs were left on the slopes. These exposed slopes caught fire in 1925, and 400 acres of the forest were destroyed by a fire that burned for a week. After this fire a heavy rain in 1929 washed away what was left on the surface, exposing the rocky crag of Charlie's Bunion. Horace Kephart, who was on the naming committee for the park, chose to name the peak after a bunion on the foot of a friend of his, Charlie Conner, who climbed the peak to survey the damage with him after the 1929 rain.

Because it is easily accessed from Newfound Gap Road, and the rock walls and crags are so unusual for the Smokies, Charlie's Bunion gets heavy traffic on summer weekends. Around the rocks there are 1,000-foot drop-offs, so you should use extreme caution if you attempt to scramble them. The AT continues across the top of Charlie's Bunion, providing dramatic views into the Tennessee side of the park. The jagged peaks here were named "the Sawteeth" by Arnold Guyot in the 1850s.

Miles and Directions

0.0   Start from the parking lot at Newfound Gap (US 441), approximately 13.2 miles from the entrance to the park on Newfound Gap Road. Cross the street and climb to find the trailhead.

0.3   The trail bends to the left and then swings to the north side of the ridge. From here you can easily see through the trees (especially in winter) the southern slopes of Mount LeConte, the 6,593-foot peak that is accessible off the Boulevard Trail, the junction for which is up ahead.

1.1 Arrive at the top of a rise, after a steady climb through the trees, turn right, and continue with a slight descent. A spur trail to an overlook to the north is here, with average visibility.

1.7 The trail levels out, rejoins the ridgeline, and you meet the junction with the Sweat Heifer Trail. The Sweat Heifer Trail descends along the creek by the same name on the North Carolina side of the divides, to connect with the Kephart Prong Trail at the Kephart Shelter in 3.7 miles. A sign here also shows junction with the Boulevard Trail in 1 mile, and the Icewater Spring Shelter in 1.3 miles.

2.7 After passing through an open area with some fabulous views into North Carolina and climbing to the summit of this ridgeline, you descend and arrive at the junction with the Boulevard Trail, your access to Mount LeConte. Continue straight, to curve around Mount Kephart.

3.1 Arrive at the Icewater Shelter. It is now closed, except to through-hikers on the AT. If you continue a short distance past the Icewater Shelter, you will pass a couple of grassy areas and find a piped spring to the left, which was the original "icewater" that gave the name to this area. (The water is very cold but should be treated before drinking, especially in light of the illegal camping that takes place right above the spring.) If you continue another 0.6 mile, you can enjoy some beautiful views of Charlie's Bunion, a unique formation for this area. Otherwise turn around and head back to the trailhead.

6.2 Arrive back at the parking lot.

Hike Information

Local Events/Attractions

Around Apr 26 through May 1, the annual **Wildflower Pilgrimage** offers hikes, indoor and outdoor programs, lectures, and other events focusing on the landscape of the Smoky Mountains region. Contact the GSMNP for more information.

Organizations

Appalachian Trail Conservancy Headquarters and Visitor Center, 799 Washington St., PO Box 807, Harpers Ferry, WV; (304) 535-6331. E-mail: info@appalachiantrail.org.

GREENEVILLE AND THE CIVIL WAR: UNION OR CONFEDERATE?

On the way to Margarette Falls, you will pass through the town of Greeneville, which was the home of Andrew Johnson, the seventeenth president of the United States. Johnson succeeded Abraham Lincoln after his assassination and took the Union out of the wreckage left by the Civil War. A plaque at the courthouse also commemorates another famous figure, General John H. Morgan, the "thunderbolt of the Confederacy," demonstrating the schizophrenia of Tennessean loyalties regarding the Civil War.

The town has several historic sites that relate to the Civil War. At the Greene County Courthouse on Main Street, local leaders met to vote on whether East Tennessee should secede from the rest of the state after Tennessee joined the Confederacy. They voted unanimously to stay aligned with the Union, but their plans were thwarted when East Tennessee was occupied by troops from the rest of the state and essentially endured a military occupation. To add insult to injury, the Confederates instituted a draft for young men into the Confederate Army. Many young men loyal to the Union escaped over the mountains to Kentucky to avoid the draft, some going on to join Union ranks instead. Perhaps 30,000 Tennesseans fought for the Union in the Civil War—a substantial number in light of the small population of the area at the time.

A visitor center and museum complement the Andrew Johnson Home, which is the main attraction. At the nearby courthouse you will learn about General John H. Morgan, a Confederate Brigadier General in Tennessee. According to the plaque, his command "was renowned for boldness and celerity on raid, carrying terror into the region north of the Ohio." The plaque concludes, "His heroism is the heritage of the South." Apparently there is little concern with the inconsistency of honoring, on the same city block, a great hero of the Confederacy and a president whose major struggle had been to squash its rebellion. A similar balancing act must have been necessary for President Johnson personally, since he served as President Lincoln's right-hand man, yet kept slaves himself here in Greeneville until the Civil War.

At the Johnson home a local "reenactment club" encamps at times in the back garden. Women cook a big beef stew over a fire while soldiers practice their formations on the wide lawn nearby, with actual Civil War rifles over their shoulders, reenacting an encampment to protect the president's residence during reconstruction. Johnson's generous stance toward reconstruction of the South (following the directives of the now deceased President Lincoln) were very unpopular among many angry Unionists, who wanted to punish the South for its treasonous behavior.

A conversation with one of these participants will immediately impress you with the depth of knowledge acquired by local residents of this relatively brief period of time in history, and will also give an almost eerie feeling of being thrown back in time. For these Tennesseans, this reenactment scenario is very serious business. Great local pride is taken in the area's military history and its role in the War Between the States, whichever side one was on.

57 Margarette Falls (CNF Trail No. 189), Nolichucky District at Cherokee National Forest

Margarette Falls may be the most spectacular short hike in Tennessee. Within this 1.4-mile span, you will walk along a creek bed past small cascades, crossing the stream at times, and pass under the shadow of the imposing Cathedral Rock formation, finally arriving at a surprisingly tall and delicate waterfall, which will make you feel that you don't want to leave.

Start: Parking lot and gate on Shelton Mission Road

Distance: 2.8 miles in and out (including access road)

Hiking time: 1.5 to 2 hours

Difficulty: Moderate

Trail surface: Gravel road, earthen trail with rocks and boulders, some stream crossing

Best season: Springtime, for the flowers

Other trail users: None

Canine compatibility: Leashed dogs permitted

Fees and permits: None

Schedule: Unmonitored

Map: USGS quad 190SW, Greystone

Trail contact: Unaka Ranger District, 4900 Asheville Hwy., Greeneville, TN 37743; (423) 638-4109

Finding the trailhead: This trailhead is a little bit difficult to find. From Knoxville take I-81 north to the Greeneville/US 11E exit, and follow US 11E to Greeneville. Although there are several ways to get to the trailhead, one option is to take TN 107 east to the intersection with Horse Creek Road on the right, just after passing Chuckey Road (TN 351) on the left. Take Horse Creek Road south, and turn at the third left, in approximately 1.3 miles, onto Greystone Road. After 4 miles turn right onto Shelton Mission Road at its first intersection with Greystone Road. Go 2.2 miles on Shelton Mission Road, past farms, past a stone foundation of a nineteenth-century building on the right, and past the Shelton Mission Church on the left and a graveyard on the right, and continue until you reach a small stretch of woods without residences. A very rough road of dirt, gravel, and rock will lead off to the left, just before a big curve in the road, which is lined by more residences. Turn left here into a small clearing, and park. **GPS:** N36 10.38' / W106 41.03'

The Hike

This short, manageable trail follows West Fork Dry Creek past the impressive Cathedral Rock, to end at the picturesque and protected Margarette Falls. The falls are quite a good size and are tucked in between steep cliffs, giving a secluded feeling, although they are well frequented by locals. Keep in mind that this area was damaged by flooding and was slow to recover.

At one point in time, a lumber shoot ran all the way down this streambed from the falls, but when it was destroyed by storm, it was never replaced. You can still find remnants of the structure along the creek. You can also find salamanders under the small

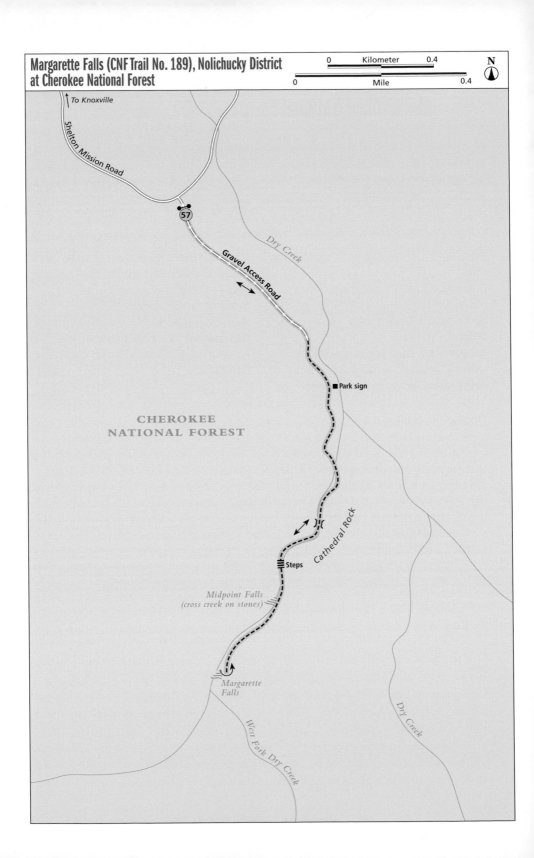

0   Kilometer   0.4

0   Mile   0.4

N

↑ *To Knoxville*

Shelton Mission Road

57

Dry Creek

Gravel Access Road

■ Park sign

CHEROKEE
NATIONAL FOREST

Cathedral Rock

Steps

Midpoint Falls
(cross creek on stones)

Margarette
Falls

West Fork Dry Creek

Dry Creek

rocks at the base of the falls. You'll notice their movement as they scurry off. Locals test their reflexes by catching these little rascals between their fingers before they slip away. In springtime this path abounds with the wildflowers that are common all through East Tennessee.

Miles and Directions

0.0 Start from the parking lot and gate, just off the dirt road off of Shelton Mission Road. You will start on a dirt access road that leads both left and right, but the right road merely dead-ends after a short distance. A left fork also should be disregarded as you head to the trailhead for Margarette Falls.

0.4 Arrive at an open area next to a stream. To your right, following the stream, you will see blue blaze markers painted on the trees marking the Margarette Falls Trail.

The mysterious and easily accessible Margarette Falls on a misty, rainy day.

0.5 You will see a forest board, and the trail forks, with one trail branching up the hill steeply to the right. This is a cutoff to the Bullen Hollow (pronounced "Bullin Holler") Trail (CNF Trail No. 2), a 3.9-mile trail that climbs steeply to follow the top of Reynolds Ridge and on to Rocky Ridge, then passes into Bullen Hollow. You will go left, and continue following the creek bed. The Margarette Falls Trail leads up a medium grade following the West Fork Dry Creek, crossing it several times as it climbs.

0.8 You will get a good view of Cathedral Rock, a large formation along the steep bluffs, made of Cambrian-period sandstone, as the trail rises above the river.

0.9 Cross a bridge, followed by a steep section of the trail.

1.0 You will walk up some steps to a pretty little cascade, we call it Midpoint Falls, because they are at the midpoint between the marked trailhead and the falls. At this point you will have to cross the creek, hopping stones, just above the falls.

1.3 At this point the creek widens, and you find some small pools large enough to take a dip in (And on warm days, it is tempting to do this!). The trail continues to climb but not strenuously.

1.4 You arrive at the lovely Margarette Falls, a beautiful 60-foot, fan-shaped cascade, which falls over interestingly stratified layers of rock, which have almost certainly been here for eons.

2.8 Arrive back at the trailhead.

THE APPALACHIAN TRAIL: CONSERVATION IN ACTION

The Appalachian Trail (AT) is perhaps the most recognized hiking trail in the United States, and the longest. Its approximately 2,168 miles pass through federal, state, and private lands in Tennessee and twelve other states, from Springer Mountain, Georgia, to Mount Katahdin, Maine. Its creation is a prime example of private sector and government cooperation, which continues today. The Appalachian Trail Conservancy (ATC) now serves as the primary organization to coordinate efforts between the volunteer clubs and government agencies in cooperatively managing the trail. (See appalachian trail.org for more information.)

The Appalachian Trail heading north out of Great Smoky Mountains National Park, across bare and windy balds common in this region.

The AT was completed in August of 1937. With the passage of the National Trails System Act in 1968, a major program began to acquire an 800- to 1,000-foot-wide protective corridor and reroute the AT off the many roads where it had been pushed when private landowners would no longer permit it on their property. The ATC has continued this acquisition work, in cooperation with federal, state, and local agencies and clubs. Since its inception in 1925, the ATC has helped acquire over 200,000 acres of land for the AT. As of this writing, the ATC is pursuing acquisition projects in Tennessee in the Risphin Wetlands, Rocky Fork, Rich Mountain, and Shook Branch areas.

The AT in Tennessee is currently 225 miles long and is maintained primarily by the GSMNP, CNF, the Smoky Mountains Hiking Club, and the Tennessee Eastman Hiking and Canoeing Club. Tennessee Eastman currently maintains 135 miles of the trail, on a purely volunteer basis. To join in, contact them at tehc.org.

58 Appalachian Trail: Dennis Cove to Laurel Fork Creek Trailhead (CNF Trail No. 1) at Cherokee National Forest, Watauga Ranger District

This Dennis Cove section of the Appalachian Trail (AT) provides great variety in its spectacular river views, picturesque Laurel Fork Falls, massive rock faces, and gorge views from ridges, before it diverts to US 321 and the Laurel Fork Creek Trailhead. This area offers flame azalea, mountain laurel, and rhododendron blooms in season, and some of its trees date back to the Civil War!

Start: Dennis Cove AT Trailhead parking lot on Dennis Cove Road in Hampton
Distance: 3.9-mile shuttle hike
Hiking time: About 2.5 hours without stops
Difficulty: Strenuous
Trail surface: Earthen, stone steps, some boulders and roots
Best seasons: Spring or fall
Other trail users: None
Canine compatibility: Leashed dogs permitted

Fees and permits: None
Schedule: Unmonitored
Maps: USGS quad 207SW, Elizabethton; 207SE, Watauga Dam
Trail contacts: Appalachian Trail Conservancy, Regional Office, 160A Zillicoa St., Asheville, NC 28801; (828) 254-3708. Watauga Ranger District, 4400 Unicoi Dr., Unicoi, TN 37692; (423) 735-1500.

Finding the trailhead and endpoint: To Dennis Cove Trailhead: From Knoxville take I-81 North to the exit for Johnson City. Take US 321 to Elizabethton, then US 19E south for 5 miles, and turn left onto US 321/TN 67 at Hampton, and drive through Hampton for 0.8 mile to Dennis Cove Road (County 50). Turn right and continue 3.7 miles on a winding road to the parking lot on the left.

To Laurel Fork Creek Trailhead (park a second car here to do this as a shuttle hike): Stay on US 321 east through Hampton, rather than turning onto Dennis Cove Road. In another 0.75 mile the trailhead is on the right, after the river.

To Shook Branch Trailhead: Drive through Hampton on US 321 east, past the Laurel Fork Trailhead, for 3.2 miles, and turn left into the Shook Branch Recreation Area and park. Walk up to US 321 from the parking area and look for trail blazes on the other side of the highway.

Dennis Cove Trailhead **GPS:** N36 15.862' / W82 07.389'

The Hike

Found within the Pond Mountain Wilderness, now managed by the Watauga Ranger District, this section of the AT stretches from Dennis Cove past the Laurel Fork Falls on the AT, and out at the Laurel Fork Trailhead, leaving the AT as you exit. It is a truly spectacular short hike, though the trail signage is not the easiest to follow. Even hiking this in wintertime, with the mist and the subtle colors of the rock faces along the trail, the hike was breathtaking, as was Laurel Fork Falls itself.

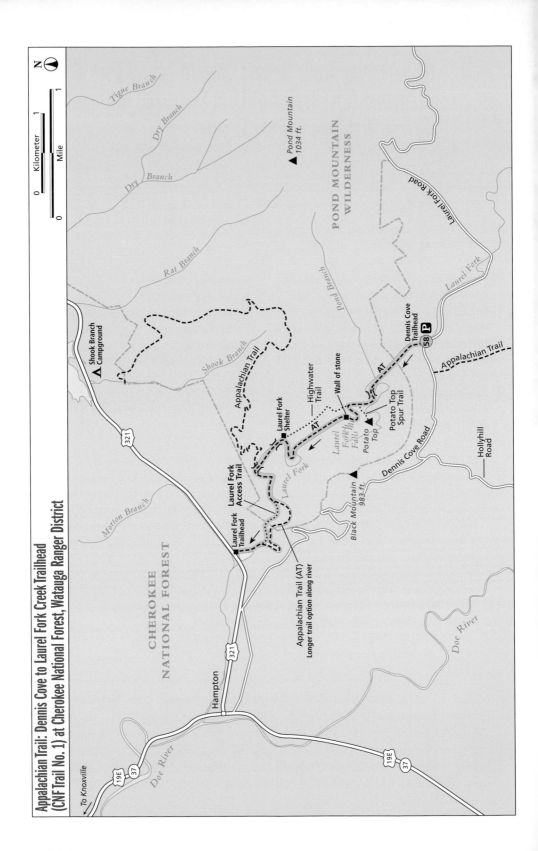

Appalachian Trail: Dennis Cove to Laurel Fork Creek Trailhead (CNF Trail No. 1) at Cherokee National Forest, Watauga Ranger District

View down the river on the Dennis Cove section of the Appalachian Trail.

At this writing, parts of the Laurel Fork Access Trail had been washed out and were being repaired by volunteer workers with the Tennessee Eastman Hiking and Canoeing Club, which has taken responsibility for 135 miles of the AT in this area. Some volunteers have logged over 10,000 hours in maintaining the AT, in good weather and bad. On the day we hiked, there were approximately ten working in the rain, hauling heavy rocks with slings and prying them into position with "rock bars" (which is difficult work even when one's hands aren't red and numb), and they did it all in good spirits, and even gave this hiker a ride back to her car at Dennis Cove. The National Forest Service does not permit the use of power tools on the trails, so when bridges are rebuilt, like the first one on this hike, the logs weighing up to 800 pounds each are carried in by hand. Stones are pulled out from the mountain to create the steps under you with the use of mattocks. (We might think of them as pickaxes, which is apparently the less precise way to refer to them.) Information on how you can join Tennessee Eastman and enjoy winter rock-hauling is found at the end of this hike description.

Miles and Directions

0.0   Start from the Dennis Cove parking lot. The hike begins by joining the AT as it passes through a fence, and follows an old railroad grade along Laurel Creek.

0.5 The hardwood forest here includes hemlocks, beech, and maple, with Carolina hemlocks. Turn to the right and descend to Laurel Creek, with views of rock cliffs on the way down.

0.6 You hike through a passageway between two rock faces, and pass a spur trail to the left that will take you to Potato Top, for nice views of the valley.

0.7 Cross a creek on a small footbridge built by the Tennessee Eastman Hiking Club, with CNF help. Climb back to an old railroad grade again, and continue along the rim of the gorge.

1.0 From this junction, if you take the fork that doubles back sharply to the left, you will stay on the AT and descend steeply into the gorge to Laurel Fork Falls. If you continue here straight ahead on the blue-blazed Highwater Trail, you will follow a railroad grade another 0.5 mile to meet the AT again at the Laurel Fork Shelter. (The blue-blazed trail is an alternate route used when high water below the falls makes the AT impassable.) Continue on the AT (the left-hand trail) you immediately begin descending steeply on stone steps, which are arranged out of stones found in the area in a natural staircase that leads nearly the entire way to the falls. These stairs were created by a crew made up entirely by women, under the leadership of a local female landscape designer. These stairs are unique in that the height of the steps contemplates a smaller frame, and thus they are more comfortable for everyone.

1.3 You arrive at the base of Laurel Fork Falls, a large, beautiful cascade approximately 50 feet high and 60 feet wide, falling over uneven tiers of rock. To loop back up to the Laurel Fork Shelter, retrace your steps a few feet on the stone stairs you have left, and you will find the loop trail on the left. It will wind down to a large rock abutment next to the river (or just follow the river to the rock abutment).

1.5 Where the wall meets the water, you will note a narrow ledge, which is made of rock and cement. Head for that, and take it around the corner, and you will find yourself on another well-worn trail, which bears right and up to the top of the ridge.

2.0 Arrive at the top of the ridge, with the Laurel Fork Shelter, which sleeps six, on your right approximately 200 feet away. (Water can be found 150 feet north.) There is a sign, but it is easy to miss, so look carefully if your plan is to turn right here and head back to the Dennis Cove Trailhead on the blue-blazed Highwater Trail.

2.1 Continuing on, follow the ridge, then descend and join the wide trail again near the creek.

2.2 A trail comes in to join you from the left.

2.4 Cross the river to the left side on a wooden bridge, and then back to the right side on yet another, at 2.7 miles.

2.9 A marker here shows the way to continue on the AT to Shook Branch, and the way on the Laurel Fork Falls Access Trail (321), which is straight ahead here.

3.2 You will continue to hug the shore of the river for quite some time, before the trail narrows and nearly disappears along a rock and mud face that runs directly into the river. (This is the point where the cheerful Tennessee Eastman volunteers were happily hauling rocks in near-freezing weather.)

3.6 Pass a junction where a shortcut trail heads off to follow the river from a higher elevation than the river trail you are on.

3.9 Arrive at the Laurel Fork Trailhead. If you chose this option, you will have hiked downhill the entire way (except a brief climb up the ridge to the Laurel Fork Shelter).

Options: If you choose to continue on the AT at the trail marker for Shook Branch, you will climb steeply high above the creek and follow an old railroad road, providing nice ridgetop views of White Rock Mountain and the Highlands of Roan, and arriving at the Pond Flats campsite at 5 miles. Head down Pond Mountain, catching some views of Watauga Lake and Iron Mountain on the way down, past the Pond Mountain Wilderness boundary at 8.1 miles, and reaching the Shook Branch Road Trailhead in 8.6 miles. Turn to the right on the paved road and go 200 yards to reach US 321 and Shook Branch picnic area by Watauga Lake. This is a good place to leave a shuttle vehicle if you start this trail from Dennis Cove, and have opted for the longer Shook Branch hike, rather than the Laurel Fork hike.

Hike Information

Lodging

Kincora Hostel is right at the Dennis Cove Trailhead, at 1275 Dennis Cove Rd., Hampton, TN 37658; (423) 725-4409. Inexpensive lodging.

Organizations

Visit the **Tennessee Eastman Hiking and Canoeing Club** at tehcc.org, or call club member Bob Peoples at (423) 725-4409.

59 Appalachian Trail: Section from Carvers Gap to Roan High Bluff, Highlands of Roan at Cherokee National Forest

This truly unique section of the Appalachian Trail along Roan Mountain is known for the famous rhododendron gardens, just steps away from the trail. This hike winds up from Carvers Gap, giving you a superlative view with little effort from Roan High Knob, and then continuing past the ruins of the historic Cloudland Hotel to the rhododendron gardens and out to Roan High Bluff, for unparalleled views into North Carolina, virtually all along a ridgetop or knob. Does it get any better?

Start: Trailhead at the parking lot at Carvers Gap on the Tennessee–North Carolina line
Distance: 6.7 miles out and back (including the round-trip spur trail to Roan High Knob on the way)
Hiking time: 4 hours (with stops for gardens and views)
Difficulty: Moderate
Trail surface: Packed earthen, rock, pavement
Best season: June, for the famous display of flowers

Other trail users: None
Canine compatibility: Leashed dogs permitted
Fees and permits: None
Schedule: Unmonitored
Map: USGS quad
Trail contact: Roan Mountain State Park, 1015 Highway 143, Roan Mountain, TN 37687; (423) 772-0190. (**Note:** The state park is 8 miles from the trailhead.)

Finding the trailhead: From Elizabethton follow US 19E south through Hampton, and continue to the town of Roan Mountain. Turn right onto TN 143 and follow it for 12.7 miles to Carvers Gap and the parking area. You will note a road just to the right of the road leading up to the rhododendron gardens. A fence post contains the white blaze marking of the Appalachian Trail, which either continues right toward the gardens or east (left) across the road toward 19E. **GPS:** N36 06.372' / W82 06.631'

The Hike

The mountaintop trails on Roan Mountain are known for being carpeted with a sea of colorful rhododendron in the spring. The peak comes at a little different time each year, usually during June at the upper elevations and in May at the lower ones. You can call the state park to time your visit right, and to find out about guided wildflower tours. This is quite a production, with seas of visitors every year, but there is a reason for their enthusiasm. Tennessee has few views so breathtaking as the blue mountains of North Carolina in the distance, framed by a carpet of startlingly bright

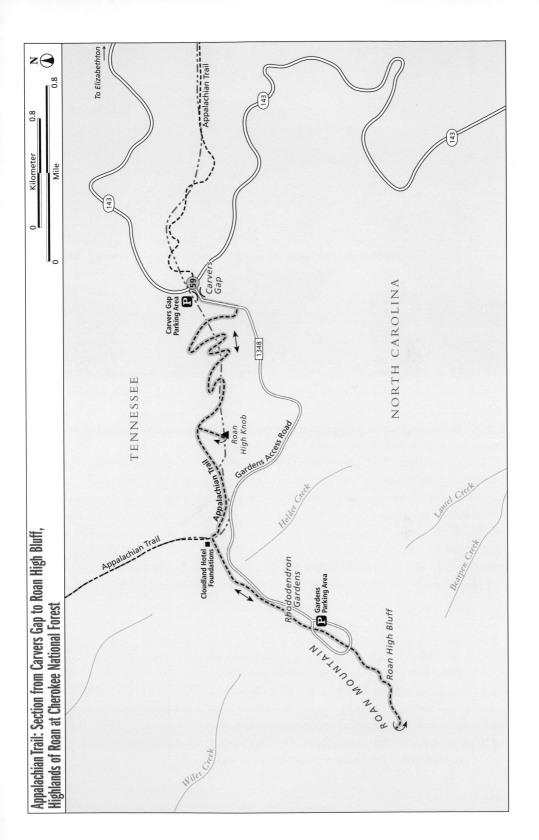

Appalachian Trail: Section from Carvers Gap to Roan High Bluff, Highlands of Roan at Cherokee National Forest

Dramatic and colorful view along Roan Mountain when the rhododendron bloom in June.

rhododendron. Vegetation is somewhat of a specialty in this area. You can find more species of native plants in East Tennessee than in all of Europe.

The Appalachian Trail passes over the top of Roan Mountain for 18.2 miles through the Highlands of Roan Scenic Area, and provides the most spectacular hiking in this area. Two trailheads are located at Carvers Gap, located at the right turnoff to the Roan Mountain Gardens. The mountains here are frequently in the clouds, but if you can catch them during clear weather, you won't be disappointed by the view. Roan Mountain State Park, which manages the gardens, is located down the mountain, and you will pass it on the way in. Roan Mountain is also the only state park in the South that offers cross-country skiing, with lessons and equipment rental.

Miles and Directions

0.0 Start from the Carvers Gap parking lot at the North Carolina line. Head toward the right (signs for Rhododendron Gardens). If you go to the left and cross the street, you will be heading north on the AT toward Grassy Ridge and 19E.

1.3 Arrive at the spur trail to the Roan High Knob, after a series of switchbacks at a fairly gradual grade. The spur is less than 0.2 mile each way and is well worth the diversion.

1.6 Return to the AT, and continue on to where the trail forks.

2.2 Near this junction are the foundations of the old Cloudland Hotel, which used to host celebrities back in the day. Head left and follow the road.

2.4 Arrive at the left turn for the Rhododendron Gardens, right off the trail. These are really stunning in the summer, and in June Roan Mountain has a flower festival featuring hand-made crafts, traditional music, and folkway demonstrations.

3.5 Continue on the well-used trail to Roan High Bluff, where on a clear day you can see stunning views into North Carolina. Return the way you came.

6.7 Arrive back at the parking lot (assuming you do not make the side trip to Roan High Knob a second time.)

Hike Information

Local Events/Attractions

Rhododendron Festival is held the third weekend of June, usually in Roan Mountain State Park.

Lodging

Roan Mountain State Park has two campgrounds and twenty furnished cabins.

Restaurants

Fred's Whiteway Grill, 7317 Highway 19E, Roan Mountain, TN; (423) 772-3026. Cheap eats, and you get the mountain hospitality for free. Fred's mother gave us two free pieces of cake. ("I'm just gonna have to throw it away anyway, honey, why don't you take it?")

Organizations

Friends of Roan Mountain, friendsofroanmtn.org.

60 Appalachian Trail: Section from Carvers Gap to US 19E (CNF Trail No.1)

The combination of magnificent vistas, open grassy balds, unusual vegetation, and marvelous campsites makes this traverse of the spine of the Appalachians along the AT from Carvers Gap to US 19E a classic. However, the steep ascents and descents, combined with sometimes difficult footing and exposed campsites, make this trip a real challenge for the novice backpacker.

Start: Trailhead across the street from the parking lot at Carvers Gap on TN 143
Distance: 13.1-mile shuttle hike
Hiking time: 6 to 8 hours, depending upon stops for views and breaks
Difficulty: Strenuous
Trail surface: Forested pine path, earthen with rocky areas, rock surfaces
Best seasons: Spring for flowers, summer for warmth

Other trail users: None
Canine compatibility: Leashed dogs permitted
Fees and permits: None
Schedule: Unmonitored
Maps: USGS quad: 208SE, Carvers Gap; 208NE, White Rocks Mountain
Trail contact: Appalachian Trail Conservancy, Regional Office, 160A Zillicoa St., Asheville, NC 28801; (828) 254-3708

Finding the trailhead: From Elizabethton follow US 19E south through Hampton, and continue to the town of Roan Mountain. Turn right onto TN 143 and follow it for 12.7 miles to Carvers Gap. A fence post to the left of a forest board contains the white blaze marking of the Appalachian Trail. Cross the road to begin the hike on the AT toward 19E. **GPS:** N36 06.397' / W82 06.637'

The Hike

This one way shuttle trip is described from south to north, the easier direction, and is often done as a two-day backpack. On this hike you will have a variety of experiences, passing fresh springs, feeling you are alone in the world on windswept balds, staying comfortable in shelters that are interspersed along the AT, passing by flowers and through wooded sections, and finally descending to 19E to finish.

Special consideration: The word is that there are problems with vandalism to the cars left at either Carvers Gap or on 19E overnight. For this reason, a cottage industry of shuttle services has sprung up in the town of Roan Mountain. Check with the park office. Alternatively, you can do your own shuttle, leaving one car at a small package store just over the North Carolina State Line on the way to Elk Park, NC, and the other at Carvers Gap, where there is less of a vandalism problem.

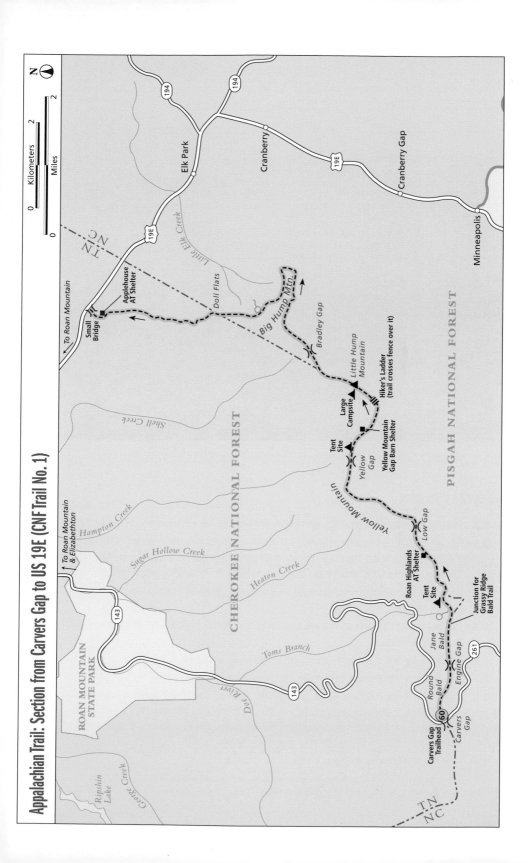

Appalachian Trail: Section from Carvers Gap to US 19E (CNF Trail No. 1)

Views west off of Round Bald, on the Carvers Gap section of the Appalachian Trail.

Miles and Directions

0.0 The trail begins by crossing through a wooden fence at the western base of Round Bald.

0.3 You will pass a small patch of lovely high-altitude fir trees near the summit of Round Bald (5,826 feet), opening into superb views of Grassy Ridge Bald and Big Hump Mountain. For the next 1.3 miles, the vistas may "blow you away" if the frequent breezes do not.

0.6 Begin a moderate descent and notice the interesting moss and lichen, and huckleberry bushes nearby.

0.8 The trail flattens out through Engine Gap, amidst carpets of wildflowers in season, including flame azaleas.

1.0 Begin the ascent of Jane Bald, reaching a large rock formation at 1.1 miles.

1.2 Now descend, reaching a low saddle, and beginning to climb again.

1.6 The Grassy Ridge Bald Trail, which is a 0.8-mile side trip, each way, rambles from here across some of the finest high country in the southern United States, and is well worth the short climb. From this junction, the AT forks left and traverses the north side of Grassy Ridge Bald.

1.7 Pass the first of many springs.

1.8 The trail tunnels through dense rhododendrons, ferns, and beech trees, and begins to descend steeply a spur of Grassy Ridge Bald through deep woods.

2.0 A small, sheltered tent site without water is in a grassy opening, and the descent moderates after a half mile.

2.8 Roan Highlands AT Trail Shelter (5,050 feet) can accommodate up to six hikers and has a spring down a side trail to the south.

2.9 Wild strawberries are at your feet in season (mid-June-ish), and a great view of the east face of Grassy Ridge.

3.0 The trail tops out at a small campsite, then enters woods for a gradual descent.

3.5 Over most of the next mile, the trail undulates, mostly level.

4.7 A small knoll provides space for three tents. Water is 0.2 mile away off Yellow Gap. The cow parsnip here can be taller than head-high!

5.0 The Overmountain Victory National Historical Trail crosses the AT at Yellow Mountain Gap. A small campsite is here, with water 0.1 mile south on a side trail to the right. South and west is the barn-like Overmountain Shelter, which accommodates twenty but it is not visible from the trail unless you get out into the field to the south.

5.4 After leaving the woods, and a steep climb, join an old roadbed and enter woods again.

6.0 The trail turns left and crosses a fence line on a "hiker's ladder," reaches an open area, and continues to climb.

6.6 You arrive at the summit of Little Hump Mountain, and one of the most spectacular campsites on the Tennessee–North Carolina state line. The 360-degree views will take your breath away. But the views come with a price: You are exposed to whatever Mother Nature wants to throw at you. If winds pick up, rain or snow can be really unpleasant. More sheltered, sloped sites are on the south side of the bald near a beech forest. Water is near the AT, farther ahead.

6.8 Leaving the bald at the northeast corner, descend and enter woods. A small, hardpacked dirt campsite is here, with water on an old road about 250 yards south.

7.1 The trail breaks out into the open again.

7.4 Bradley Gap starts the 600-foot ascent of Big Hump Mountain. This steep climb will force you to rest frequently, which should be fine, since the views continue to improve. Watch for white AT blazes.

8.0 Just below the summit, turn a sharp right and stop for a few moments to drink in the views. They don't get much better than this, at 5,587 feet!

8.8 Follow vertical AT blaze markers to the left. In June you will be treated to carpets of yellow wildflowers.

9.2 Leave the ridge now and enter woods, jogging right and left, and start to cross the northeast face of Big Hump Mountain, with some rocky, slow going.

10.1 A spring here has a nice water flow.

10.7 After a small meadow, arrive at Doll Flats, a great place to camp or have lunch, with its shade trees and a nearby spring. (Left off the AT 50 yards, then right on an old roadbed 200 yards, and listen for a spring to the right in the woods.) The AT bears to the right from here and begins a steep and slippery descent. Watch your footing, and for a short detour to the left to a rock outcropping and a great view of the valley.

11.2 Nearly a half mile of steep switchbacks lead to a level area, a fence line, and a small waterless campsite.

This 12-mile round-trip, strenuous hike with an elevation change of 2,600 feet is well worth the reward of the view from the GSMNP's only public-accessible fire tower on Mount Cammerer, off the AT. You will be on the Low Gap Trail for a steep 3 miles until it intersects with the AT, where you will go left toward Mount Cammerer. The trail levels a bit but continues to climb, until you reach the steep spur trail to the octagonal fire tower, which was built using hand-cut stone by local laborers and the Civilian Conservation Corps in the late 1930s. Some say the views from the tower are the best in the park, and this trail is the shortest and most popular way to access Mount Cammerer. Mount Cammerer is a place to bring a topographic map, since from the peak and the tower, you can see many highlights of the park in a 360-degree view. To the north is Stone Mountain, with white quartzite on its slopes. To the east is Snowbird Mountain, at 4,263 feet, Max Patch, a grassy dome, and Naked Place, a sharp peak, and Mary's Knob, a peak that is bald on one side. To the south are Mount Sterling, Balsam Mountain, and Mount Guyot. To the west are Webb Mountain, Bays Mountain, and Clinch Mountain.

Finding the trailhead: From Gatlinburg take US 321 east 18.2 miles to Cosby, then take TN 32 southeast for 1.2 miles, and when the road forks, turn right into the park entrance at Cosby Cove. Continue another 2 miles to the Cosby Picnic Area, where you can park for day hiking. The Low Gap Trailhead, which connects with the Lower Cammerer Trail in 0.4 mile, is behind Camping Area B.

P   Squibb Creek Trail, Sampson Mountain Wilderness, Unaka Ranger District at Cherokee National Forest

This 2.2-mile charmer of a trail follows the stream up, passing by numerous small waterfalls and cascades, and crossing back and forth over the stream approximately fifteen times before you arrive at Squibb Creek Falls, a beautiful 25-foot cascade, at 2.2 miles. You pass connections with Turkey Pen Cove Trail and Middle Spring Ridge Trail along the way. (**Note:** At 0.4 mile the trail crosses behind an A-frame house and crosses the creek over rock stepping stones at this point, so don't let this confuse you.)

Finding the trailhead: From Greeneville, Tennessee, take TN 107 north for 6 miles. Follow signs to Horse Creek Recreation Area and park at the Horse Creek Picnic Area (where the pavement ends). A dirt road continues a short distance up Horse Creek to a wooden footbridge on the left, which marks the beginning of the trail.

About the Authors

KELLEY ROARK is a veteran traveler and outdoors lover, with an interest in all things historic. Her long-standing interest in the outdoors was cultivated during her childhood in Colorado, where she grew up on a farm and she and her family were active hikers and campers. She has since hiked in places as far-flung as Iceland, Austria, Brazil, and Costa Rica, but her favor-

ite highlands for hiking are still those of Tennessee, because of its rich history, parks, and untouched wilderness. She wrote the first edition of *Hiking Tennessee*, with the collaboration of many Tennessee hiking enthusiasts, including Stuart Carroll, who now co-authors this edition. Kelley has authored titles on a variety of topics, and current projects include a travel memoir on living in Costa Rica.

Roark's interest in Tennessee stems from the state's unique history, geology, and natural beauty, and the fact that her family hailed from the Appalachian highlands of East Tennessee more than one hundred years ago. Roark is a graduate of Georgetown University's law school and currently splits her residence between Miami, Florida, and Costa Rica.

STUART CARROLL works for Tennessee State Parks up on the Cumberlands, at Fall Creek Falls State Park. His current duties entail managing two beautiful natural areas, Lost Creek and Virgin Falls, and working as resource manager at Fall Creek. For most of his thirty-plus-year career with state parks, he has organized and led hikes and other

interpretive programs, sharing the area's rich cultural and natural history with visitors. He has also assisted conservation groups and state agencies in better protecting Fall Creek, which is a "New Deal" park, and the park has grown by 10,000 acres during his stay there. He was also instrumental in organizing a residential environmental education center, which has brought thousands of schoolkids to the park to learn and explore. He also fills additional roles in these areas as a law enforcement officer and EMT.

Stuart grew up in West Tennessee, his family basically involved in farming, logging, and sawmilling. His father Frank was also a park ranger at Chickasaw State Park for a time. Overall, he gained his love of the woods and history from his father, and the family pastimes included roaming the countryside, hunting the old swamps and sloughs of the Obion or Forked Deer Rivers, or studying the local Civil War battlefields. He was raised on a farm that has been in the family since the 1830s.

Stuart's bachelor's degree is in Resources Management from the University of Tennessee, and his master's degree is from Tennessee Technological University. This is his first book project, although he has had numerous publications in magazines and newspapers.